WORKING WOMEN AND FAMILIES

Volume 4
Sage Yearbooks in WOMEN'S POLICY STUDIES

WORKING WOMEN AND FAMILIES

Edited by

KAREN WOLK FEINSTEIN

 SAGE Publications   Beverly Hills / London

For information address:

SAGE PUBLICATIONS, INC.
275 South Beverly Drive
Beverly Hills, California 90212

SAGE PUBLICATIONS LTD
28 Banner Street
London EC1Y 8QE

Printed in the United States of America

Library of Congress Cataloging in Publication Data

Main entry under title:

Working women and families.

   (Sage yearbooks in women's policy studies ; v.4)
   Includes bibliographical references.
    1. Wives—Employment—United States—Addresses, essays, lectures.   2. Mothers—Employment—United States—Addresses, essays, lectures.   I. Feinstein, Karen Wolk
HD6055.W67   331.4'0973   79-639
ISBN 0-8039-1158-0
ISBN 0-8039-1159-9 pbk.

FIRST PRINTING

The following chapters were reprinted by permission from Volume 11, Numbers 1 and 2 of *The Urban & Social Change Review's* "Special Issue on Women and Work," a publication of Boston College:

Chapter 1   Alan Pifer
Chapter 3   Mary Lindenstein Walshok
Chapter 4   Frank L. Mott
Chapter 5   Diana Pearce
Chapter 9   Denise F. Polit
Chapter 10   Ralph E. Smith

CONTENTS

To the memory of my grandfathers
NATHAN SANDLER and CHARLES KRUM
and to STEVEN, JEREMY, and TIMOTHY
for whom I work.

PREFACE

KAREN WOLK FEINSTEIN

Working Women and Families is the fourth volume of the *Sage Yearbooks in Women's Policy Studies.* Its objective is consistent with that of the preceding three volumes in the series; that is, to present the work of persons who are in the forefront of efforts to understand and develop various policy positions related to the status of women in America. Like the other volumes, the approach is pragmatic and articles are selected on the basis of their ability to contribute to constructive social change. The authors represent a variety of disciplines; they are outstanding in their ability to combine scholarship with activism.

In this regard, the introduction by Alan Pifer establishes the theme of the book. Pifer notes the increasing number of women participating in the labor force and examines the new pressures on women workers and their families as a result of this trend. The clash of traditional mores and attitudes, which assign homemaking and childrearing responsibilities to wives, with increased labor force participation by women has placed an enormous physical and emotional burden on women workers with families. The absence of wives and mothers from the home during all

AUTHOR'S NOTE: This volume was edited by Karen Wolk Feinstein with the assistance of the staff of *The Urban & Social Change Review:* Mary-Catherine Deibel, Rosemary Mahoney, and Robert Moroney. It was conceived as an expanded version of *The Urban & Social Change Review*'s "Special Issue on Women and Work" which was published in April 1978. We are grateful to the authors (both those whose work was originally published in the *Review* and those who joined us for book publication) for their cooperation and assistance with this project.

or part of the day has also created new demands on husbands, new needs related to the care of children, and new attitudes toward work on the part of both husbands and wives.

Families with working wives experience external pressures which exacerbate the effects of internal disruptions in conventional family roles. Although the "second income" which women earn is essential to the economic well-being of many families, discrimination in the workplace results in lower wages for many women workers. Employer rigidity in work schedules and personnel policies compounds the problems involved in combining employment, childrearing, and homemaking. As more and more women become wage earners, however, the family with only one wage earner is at a relative disadvantage; women often cannot afford to stay home. For the female who is a household head, all of the problems discussed above are further compounded. Full-time work combined with sole responsibility for childrearing is tremendously demanding; however, welfare policies offer such low benefits that, for many, they are not a viable option.

Pifer notes the pressures on families as a result of the fact that "social policies have not yet caught up with changing social practice." He also offers some policy and programmatic adaptations to reduce these pressures and "to remedy the defects of the present situation . . . to work toward the creation of a new type of society." Most promising is his suggestion that the present problems and disparities are temporary and that, if the necessary changes in services and procedures are effected, a new type of society might be created which offers a broader range of options for all family members and, hence, a more satisfying life.

The focus of this book is on working women and family life. Contributors to this volume respond to and elaborate on issues raised in the introduction. Like Pifer, they outline the problems and pressures created by the movement of women into the labor force; like Pifer, they also offer concrete proposals for alleviating these difficulties, and they foresee a future which includes an improved quality of work and family life. Sharlene

Hesse in "Women Working: Historical Trends" examines the external economic influences which have shaped the work experiences of women in American history. In the past, law, custom, national events, and necessities of survival have determined women's work roles and, hence, the nature of family life. Even now, women do not enjoy as broad a range of choice as to work role as do men because of a host of societal and labor force constraints.

The response of employers to the problems of women workers and their families has not been adequate. Nijole Benokraitis discusses the employment problems of women, using the federal government experience as an example. Because of the low wages and limitations to career advancement in most jobs which are currently available part-time (see Ralph E. Smith, "Hours Rigidity: Effects on the Labor-Market Status of Women"), many women are forced to seek full-time work. In her chapter on "Nontraditional Work Schedules for Women," Denise Polit reviews some work options which might alleviate the pressures on all workers who wish to balance work with family life. Employers also have been lax in providing adequate retirement income for women workers. Pension benefits for women workers and their survivors are very low because of the patterns of labor force attachment common to many women and because of pension plan policies (see William Spector, "Women's Retirement Income").

The response of government to the increased labor force participation of wives and mothers also has been disappointing. Frank Mott, in studying racial differences in work patterns, has discovered that black women have the same attitude toward work as white women, but that many cannot or do not participate in the work force because the only jobs available to them are so low paying that existing on welfare or husband's earnings is preferable. Mott blames the present high unemployment rates for discouraging low-skilled and less-educated black women from labor force participation. Diana Pearce suggests, in her chapter on "Women, Work, and Welfare: The Feminization of Poverty," that welfare is no longer a viable alternative to work.

Instead, because of low benefit levels and policy pressures, welfare mothers must exist on a combination of work *and* welfare, which further strains family life and yet offers no real career advancement or economic self-sufficiency.

Women workers with families find themselves in a difficult position. Paid employment is necessary for economic or other reasons. (see Walshok, "Occupational Values and Family Roles: Women in Blue-Collar and Service Occupations"). Yet employment policies exacerbate the difficulties involved in balancing family and work responsibilities. Other societal institutions, such as the public school, also have been slow in responding to new needs of children and families (see Karen Wolk Feinstein, "Directions for Day Care"). And, within families, husbands have not assumed substantial household and child-care responsibilities to alleviate the pressure on employed wives, as Sarah Fenstermaker Berk points out in her chapter on "Husbands at Home: The Organization of the Husband's Household Day."

Ideally, many of the pressures and problems now facing working women with families will be resolved in ways which redistribute the responsibilities for home, children, and work among husbands and wives and other community resources. Employment policies would be changed to permit flexible work hours, adequate compensation, and career advancement in part-time jobs, and sufficient time off for husbands and wives to make childbearing and rearing more satisfying. Government policies would provide adequate benefits for mothers or fathers who wish to remain home and care for their children. This would enable all families to experience a higher quality of life, and all persons to have more options of when and how to participate in the labor force. As Elise Boulding postulates in the conclusion, new flexibility in life cycle patterns for men and women is both desirable and possible. Experimental life styles and work arrangements, such as job sharing (see Arkin and Dobrofsky), will enable persons to achieve a more balanced mix of work, study, child care, leisure, and creative achievement over an entire lifetime.

1

Introduction

WOMEN WORKING:
TOWARD A NEW SOCIETY

ALAN PIFER

Recent times have seen dramatic changes in American family life, in male-female relationships, in expectations about sex roles, and in our social attitudes and behavior. While the fresh currents of thought and emerging new social conventions are by no means acceptable to everyone, their existence is undeniable, and their impact on American society can be easily observed. Despite this, important governmental and private-sector policies that intimately affect the family, not to mention our individual lives, are still in the main geared to earlier value systems and beliefs. Social policies have not yet caught up with changing social practice.

Nowhere in this disparity between reality and myth as the foundation for social policy more evident than in regard to the large-scale movement of somen in the labor force—a phenome-

AUTHOR'S NOTE: 1976 Annual Statement of the President, Carnegie Corporation of New York.

non that could have consequences of immense magnitude for the nation. Its effects on the economy, on the labor market, on family welfare, and on community life are already apparent. It has become both an aspect of change and a prime mover for further change. Yet, in our failure to take account of this occurrence may lie the cause of hardship and inequity for increasing numbers of people, and the potential for considerable social unrest.

Women have always contributed to the nation's economy. In addition to meeting their domestic responsibilities, they have, especially in earlier times, earned income for their families by producing goods at home for sale in the market. What is new in the twentieth century, however, is the increasing proportion of women working away from their homes. In 1920, 20 percent of all women 16 years and over were in the work force. Their labor force participation has risen steadily since then, accelerating during the 1960s and reaching 43 percent in 1970. By the end of 1976, nearly half of all women were working or looking for work, making up approximately 41 percent of the labor force. This shows a cumulative change in degree sufficient to constitute a change in kind.

Although the pace may slow somewhat, there are no signs that the trend will be reversed. On the contrary, since women outnumber men in the population by seven million, and since the labor force participation rate of males has been slowly declining with the trend toward earlier retirement, it may not be too long before one out of every two American workers is a woman. Certainly, projections to the year 1990 indicate a situation in which adults born during the post-World War II "baby boom" will have been fully absorbed into the labor force, and there will be 1.3 million fewer young workers than there are today. Assuming the jobs will be there, labor demand for women should intensify.

The fact is, women are being drawn into the labor force today not, as in World War II, by a temporary crisis but by powerful economic, demographic, and social forces and far-reaching attitudinal changes. It is pointless, therefore, to try to judge, on moral social, economic or any other grounds, whether women working is harmful to the nation or not. Women must work, they want to work, and their labor is needed. Recognition of these realities should help us to institute new policies that not only make appropriate accommodations but spur wide-ranging reforms in many areas of life. Indeed, the large-scale movement of women into the work force opens up the exciting possibility of creating a much improved society for all Americans.

CHARACTERISTICS OF THE WORKING WOMAN

Who are these working women? Most of them, in contrast to earlier times, are married and living with their husbands and are likely to have school-age children. By last year, in approximately 46 million intact marriages in the nation, over 21 million of the wives were working full or part-time.

As may be expected, the second largest category of female workers, now totalling more than 15 million, is composed of individuals who are single, separated, widowed, or divorced, with divorced women showing the highest participation rates. A large proportion of this group, furthermore, has young children, reflecting the startling fact that over the past decade families headed by women on their own have grown ten times as fast as two-parent families. In the short period from 1970 to 1973, the number of female-headed families with children rose by over a million. As of March 1975, they totaled 7.2 million—one out of every eight families in the country.

Although the presence of children is thought to inhibit women's labor force participation, in 1975 nearly 28 million children under the age of 18 had working mothers; of these, six and a half million were under the age of six. Mothers of almost half the children in the nation, therefore, were at work earning, or helping to earn, the family's living.

Some of the forces encouraging women into the labor force are clear enough. Among economic factors are the need to be self-supporting, unemployment of husbands, the effects of inflation on family budgets, changing notions of what constitutes a decent standard of living, and accelerated demand for female labor through the growth of service and technical jobs where women have been traditionally employed. Strongly associated with women's rising labor force participation are drastically lowered fertility rates. With a longer life span and two children increasingly the norm, many women are spending a shorter period of their lives raising children and thus have time available for other endeavors. More opportunities for post-secondary education have raised women's expectations and their qualifications for employment. Other factors are advances in household technologies, improved family health, and new legislation promoting equality of opportunity in education and in employment.

One cannot discount the impact of diminishing social prejudice against the idea of women moving out of the home into areas of public life. Credit must go to the women's movement for helping to generate a more positive climate for these changes, for giving moral support to women who do work, and for inspiring them to fight for more equal treatment in the workplace.

There has undoubtedly been a marked change of attitude about work on the part of younger women. Many still go through adolescence and their early twenties thinking that their future economic security will be largely dependent on the marriages they make. Increasingly, however, women of this new generation are growing up believing that whatever their fate, be it a stable marriage, divorce, or remaining single, they must expect to be all or partly self-supporting, and to provide for any children they may have. This very anticipation of working is impelling more women into the labor force.

Finally, women work not only for income but, like men, because of their desire for achievement and the satisfaction that comes from using their skills and being recognized for it. This tends to be overlooked in the emphasis on economic motivation.

CONSEQUENCES

The accelerated movement of women into the work force is allied to changes of major consequence for the nation as well as for the family and for individual lives. First, while some strong rearguard actions are being fought, more and more Americans are beginning to see the full employment of women's abilities as a social and political imperative. Not only is it a national moral obligation stemming from our country's basic principles, but, more pragmatically, we are beginning to realize that the safety and prosperity of the nation will increasingly depend on the maximum use of our entire stock of human talent.

In the national economy we are seeing, with the emergence of the two-worker family, a fundamental change in the manner in which families provide for their economic welfare. The median income of a two-worker family in 1975 was $17,237, compared with $12,750 for a family with only one member employed. With their extra income, families in which both the husband and wife work have been better able to keep pace with inflation and in some cases to increase their consumer buying power substantially. Double incomes in addition have provided some families with their only hope of meeting the cost of educating children. Interestingly, wives are more likely to work if their husband's income is already in the middle range than if it is either very high or very low. This pattern has served to narrow the disparity between the wealthy and the average American family.

To discover the full effects of the shift to the two-worker family, however, one needs to look beyond the economic indicators. We can assume, for example, that once they are employed, many women achieve new dimensions of self-confidence and a sense of pride in their ability to support themselves or contribute to the support of a family. For some, the environment of work makes their lives more interesting and broadens their horizons. For others, the work itself provides a sense of accomplishment or fulfillment that care of the home alone has left unsatisfied. Although outside employment may in some instances lead to role conflicts and add strains in a woman's relationship with her husband and children, in others, it may actually serve to strengthen these ties by establishing the relationship on a more equalitarian basis. For the single woman, work can become the most important element in her existence, giving her not only the means of support but human companionship and the security of a recognized position in the community.

With more women working, age-old mores about the distinctive roles of the sexes and appropriate relationships between them are being questioned, notably by younger couples but also by others. There is now an assumption by such people that women will work and, hence, acknowledgment of the fact that household maintenance and child care must be shared by both marriage partners. Other effects on social norms and lifestyles are just beginning to be studied, and while they may not yet extend throughout the society, they are nonetheless profound.

In the workplace, many employers, increasingly concerned about job satisfaction and productivity, and also responding to pressures to recognize the dual responsibilities of women workers for home and job, have begun to experiment with more part-time work or with arrangements that provide flexibility in the hours of the work day or the work week. Some firms have shortened the work week by lengthening the work day, or they have instituted flexible starting and finishing times and staggered work schedules for individual employees. The result is, at the very least, no decline in work performance. Employees of both sexes report a better balance between work and private life, and improved morale and loyalty to employers.

Businesses, in addition, are facing changing outlooks toward work in male employees who have working wives. Men in this position are less willing to transfer from one location to another, and their unemployment rates have been higher during the recession than those of male heads of households generally. There are some indications also that men are showing a preference for shorter or more flexible work hours. We may one day see a time when considerable numbers of men and women, whether by choice or necessity, will be nearly alike in their attitudes toward work.

Working women's organizations and other women's interest groups have been exerting more pressure on employers and government to implement equal employment opportunity and equal pay laws and to remedy the effects of past inequities through affirmative action. Awareness of the role of education in preparing women for the world of work has led to extensive legislation promoting equal educational opportunity. In 1977, to mention only one change, education institutions will be required to initiate programs to overcome sex discrimination and sex stereotyping in vocational education programs and to make all courses accessible to everyone. The entry barriers to many traditionally sex-related jobs have been crumbling, allowing a certain number of women to enter male-dominated occupations. Some employers are making sincere efforts to recruit and promote women into positions men have held in the past. Evidence shows the impact of the changes. Since 1960, the rate of increase of women in the skilled crafts has exceeded that of men. The greatest advances, however, have been made in the professions by highly educated women. Graduate and professional schools are reporting rapid rises in enrollments among women; the employment of women lawyers, physicians, and dentists more than doubled between 1960 and 1970 and is still rising. Clearly some improvement has already occurred in women's employment status in the last decade or so, not all of it reflected in existing statistics.

While maternity leaves, pension and other benefit programs, and social security policies are a burning issue for women's organizations, progress has been made in these areas to reduce discrimination against women. Such progress is based on recognition of the existence of the working wife and elimination of the presumption of female dependency. Part-time workers, however, the majority of whom are women, are still denied major benefits because they are not considered a permanent part of the work force. The recent decision of the U.S. Supreme Court permitting the exclusion of pregnancy disabilities from an employer's disability compensation plan, and the New York State Supreme Court ruling that such exclusion is unconstitutional point up, if nothing else, the need for the country to establish a coherent set of policies that reflect emerging realities and recognize the interdependence of work and family life.

Despite some favorable omens associated with women working, problems, already existing but hidden, or resulting from failure of social policy to make accommodations, have become evident. In the first place, while the addition of a wife's earnings has helped middle-income families fight inflation, and even improve their living standard, those intact families which have only one income earner, or single men or women with children, are comparatively worse off. Particularly disadvantaged is the family headed by a woman on her own. Women's earnings in the aggregate are three-fifths those of men for full-time year-round work; overall, their median earned income in 1975 was only two-fifths that of men, partly because of their predominance in part-time work. The earning capacity of a female head of family is further limited because her educational attainment tends to be low. Relatively poor skills and the presence of children often make it impossible for such women to work at all. One in three female-headed families, in fact, has an income below the poverty level. Indeed, the hardship faced by these families, whether the mother is working or is on welfare, is one of the greatest social problems the nation has today.

Second, research shows that the greatest increase recently of mental depression in the American populace has been among young, poor women who are single parents and young married mothers who work in low-level jobs. Stress and a sense that they lack the power to improve their circumstances seem to be the chief causes of low morale.

Third is the immense physical and emotional burden that dual responsibilities for home and job place on both married women and single women heading families. One survey suggests that the average employed woman puts at least 26 hours per week into household duties in addition to her job, making a 66-hour working week, plus travel time. Obviously such a schedule leaves little time or energy for organized recreation or even for simple relaxation. Role conflicts in addition can leave working women feeling guilty. While husbands are beginning to help with housework and child care, sharing of these responsibilities is still not general because of the persistence on the part of both men and women of traditional ideas about appropriate sex roles, because of force of habit, and because the demands of some kinds of jobs held by men bring them home exhausted, too.

A fourth and crucial problem associated with women working in increased numbers is that of what happens to their children. Families today get by with various child-care arrangements—hiring baby-sitters, placing their preschool youngsters in publicly supported or private daycare facilities, or leaving them with relatives, friends, or women who look after small groups of children in their homes. Older children are in school part of the day, but the availability of after-school care is extremely limited. Working parents often have no alternative but to give their children the house key and hope for the best. Taken together, these measures, all of which, except possibly the last, are adequate for some families in some circumstances, fall short of constituting a national solution to the problem. For too many, the unavailability of good, affordable care remains a chronic problem, causing anguish to parents and in some cases having a direct bearing on whether women can work at all.

We have not yet learned the full effects of all these pressures on the family, but we do know that they are most severe for lower-income wives and mothers, who are also the women with the least access to services and opportunities that might ameliorate their condition.

Finally, there are the economic consequences arising from the changing size and composition of the work force. The question is whether the large-scale entry of women—coming just at a time when the pool of potential new workers among the nation's youth is swollen as a result of the post-war baby boom and, further, when minority-group unemployment continues at about 13 percent—has greatly diminished any prospect that the country will ever achieve full employment. An apparent paradox of the past two years has been the expanding number of jobs filled at a time when unemployment has also been at its highest level since the Great Depression. At present, more than 88 Americans actually hold jobs and about 7.9 million are officially unemployed, making a civilian labor force of about 96 million. If one adds to this a considerable number of "discouraged job seekers," we have a national labor force at the present time approaching 100 million, not counting the category of potential workers who are, at present, essentially unemployable because they lack the necessary skills.

Manpower economists on the whole agree that young people and adult women trying to enter the labor market do not compete with each other directly for the same jobs—aside from the obvious competition between younger and older women for certain kinds of positions, especially for part-time work. Nevertheless, the only hope that considerable numbers of young people, minority-group members, and women have of working is in those relatively unskilled jobs that permit substitution of one type of worker for another. There is therefore at least theoretical competition among them, in which it would seem that the addition of ever-greater numbers of women to the labor force—some 1.5 million just in the past year—cannot but be a complicating factor. This could become an important question for the future as we move toward greater occupational integration.

The long and the short of it is that more Americans than ever before want to work, but we have not developed the means to provide them with jobs. Whether the problem is regarded as structural or economic or both, any solution we devise will unquestionably have to reckon with the reality that women in large numbers are in the labor force to stay. The answer will not come about by inducing women to leave their jobs and stay at home "where they belong"—as if this could just be mandated or as if the majority of women and their families really had a choice under present conditions.

Laws prohibiting discrimination, promoting equal opportunity, and requiring employers to take "affirmative action" where inequalities are found are on the books, but there has been a mounting outcry among women's and civil rights organizations about the slow progress being made to give these laws full effect. A major hindrance, even when employers make sincere efforts to comply with the law, seems to be the long-standing problem of occupational segregation of men and women. Many employers traditionally limit hiring for certain job categories to one sex. Such sex-typing discourages male entry into such challenging fields as nursing or teaching, but the preponderant effect is to deny women training, job opportunities, and wages commensurate with those of men. A high proportion of the jobs that are open to women are in the marginal, low-paid, low-status areas generally lacking in opportunities for advancement. And while more women are entering male-dominated occupations, their numbers remain relatively small, and limitations on their upward mobility are still prevalent.

The areas of greatest job expansion for women continue to be in certain kinds of technical and professional occupations and in clerical and service jobs. This employment is mainly in government at all levels, particularly in educational, health, and welfare services, and in banking and insurance. Most women go into white-collar jobs, more than one-third of them in book-keeping, secretarial, typing, and clerical work. The rest are in blue-collar factory and farm jobs (18 percent) and in service work (21 percent).

A high proportion of the women holding jobs in these areas do not receive wages commensurate with the level of responsibility or skill demanded of them. This widespread undervaluation of their work goes far to explain why women earn only three-fifths as much as men.

Other reasons for women's lower earnings may have to do with employers' complaints that women are less skilled than men or are less motivated to try for those jobs that lead to advancement. This is a question more of public attitudes and the educational system, they say, than of anything that goes on in the workplace. There is also the prevailing belief among employers that women's work attachment is intermittent, making it a poor investment to train them for greater responsibility. Many women do drop out of the labor force temporarily to have children, or they find that their home responsibilities allow them to work only part-time. Nevertheless, their total time in the labor force has risen dramatically—from an average of six years in 1900 to 22.9 years today (compared with 40.1 years for men). In spite of this, the myth of women's work instability has helped to keep them in those low-earning, dead-end jobs that seem structured to fulfill the very prophecy that provides employers the excuse not to train them for better positions.

Incredible as it may seem, the average wage differential between men and women is wider today than it was 20 years ago, even though the educational attainment of working women has reached that of men, women's work-life expectancy has risen greatly, and more women are securing higher-level and better-paying positions. Beyond the continuation of some out-right discrimination, one can only speculate on the causes. One reason may be that a larger proportion of female than male workers are working at, or near, entry levels of pay. Another may be that, as more women work or look for work in the traditional "female" fields, the more they come into direct competition with one another, allowing employers to pay them less. It must be remembered, that, despite women's rush into the labor force, their unemployment rate is still higher than that of men.

All of these factors serve to restrict severely women's chances of upward mobility in employment and hence increased earnings—a situation that is particularly unfair to the substantial, and growing, proportion of women who do remain in the labor force full-time from entry until retirement.

Another consequence of the increasing labor force participation of women is a decline in the number of women available for traditional community voluntary activities—in schools, health care facilities, churches, and welfare organizations. Women and men who have reached retirement age, are still in good health, and want to remain contributing members of society will possibly make up the difference. Some successful experiments with retirees suggest this will not be too hard to do, but it will take time.

To sum up, on the favorable side there are signs that American society is accepting the philosophical, legal, and pragmatic rationales for the full employment of women's talents in the work place. The rights of women are specifically protected by legislation and by Presidential executive orders, and will be further reinforced by passage of the Equal Rights Amendment. Women have made some advances in their employment status, and the benefits to the nation are evident—in added family income, in a stronger national economy, and in improved service to the public. There is also evidence that greater equality at home and in the workplace is giving women increased confidence and a greater sense of efficacy. Finally, there are indications that institutions are beginning to recognize the special problems of the working woman and to make some needed adjustments.

There are other aspects of women working, however, attributable mainly to society's failure to accommodate rapidly enough to their needs, that are cause for concern. Women frequently are the victims at work of occupational segregation the law seems powerless to affect, suffer from low earnings, and have limited opportunity for advancement. A large proportion of women heading families live in poverty, with virtually no chance to improve their circumstances. The heavy burden implicit in women's dual responsibility for home and job has not been sufficiently eased by a sharing of housework and child care on the part of men. The unavailability of child care during working hours of parents remains a major problem.

In a more speculative vein, new stresses in the lives of women with children, caused by divided loyalties to family and career, may be giving rise to physical and emotional problems and adding strains to family life. The kinds of studies necessary to understand these problems fully have not yet been done and should be given high priority in the future.

Finally, although the ultimate consequence of women working in such large numbers should be beneficial both to the economy and the nature of American society, there are likely, in the shorter run, to be disturbances and special problems in the labor market before employment generally adjusts to the new phenomenon.

TWO POSSIBLE FUTURES

If, as it seems, the conclusion is valid that the working woman is now a fixture in American life, two possible futures can be envisioned. The most realistic suggests that the present situation will simply be allowed to drift on. In time, after decades have elapsed, a new generation has reached maturity, much additional hardship has been suffered, and a good deal of militant social action by women has taken place, the nation, in both its public and private sectors, will perhaps yield to the pressures and make fundamental changes.

An alternative future, designed to avoid the hardship and social unrest the first course would cause, envisages the nation setting out now to remedy the defects of the present situation and, in the process, to work toward the creation of a new type of society. This would entail looking at the reality of the working woman as the opening wedge for broad social reform. It would require study of the entire structure of work and family life as it affects women, men, and children, and then active planning for change. Such a future is unquestionably optimistic and idealistic, but it is not beyond the realm of the possible if we have the national will to press for it.

What would be the chief characteristics of such a new society? It would be informed by four basic principles: the right to a job for anyone who needs to or wants to work; equal opportunity and fair rewards for everyone in all sectors of employment; development and utilization of the abilities of every citizen; and maximum flexibility for each person in the organization of his or her own pattern of life.

The new society would have the aim of greater occupational equality and freedom of choice for men and women in the workplace. It would assume cooperation between men and women in the sharing of family responsibilities. It would entail better articulation than now exists between work and home life and between work and education. It would permit flexibilities in the amount of time an individual might allocate to education, work, family life, and leisure at any age during the course of a lifetime.

Interrelated and interdependent, these goals, if they were achieved, would lead to a fundamental reordering of the values underlying American life—in which the objectives of greater choice for the individual and improved quality of life would for the first time be equated with our traditional concern for productivity.

To meet these goals, broad changes will be needed in six major areas: in employment, in family life and child care, in welfare and tax policy, in education, in sex roles, and in the phasing of stages of the life cycle. Some of the required steps would be quite new and speculative; others have been tried on a small scale and would now have to be given wider application; and still others would constitute an intensification of major trends already under way. All would require cooperation among educational institutions, employers, government, and the community.

In the area of employment, the first and most obvious need is for vigorous new measures to reduce unemployment. Not only must additional job opportunities and training be created, but flexibility must be introduced into the work structure to permit more people to be absorbed into the labor force. This could include the encouragement of "flexitime," work sharing, shorter work days or weeks, part-time jobs, and work-study arrangements in which employees would interrupt work to pursue further education. Work exchanges—that is, shifting jobs within firms—would also broaden horizons, extend skills, and introduce flexibility into employees' career patterns.

Second, employers, policy-makers, and organizations representing the interests of women must continue to press for compliance with laws that prohibit discrimination against women in the work force and mandate affirmative action to remedy the effects of past discrimination. Recognition of the child-rearing responsibilities of men and women should be built into employment policies. For too long women have been penalized for their reproductive role, with no choice but to adapt to a rigid work structure or drop out. Any weakening of present provisions guaranteeing women's right to equal treatment in employment must be resisted.

There is much that management within a large firm or organization can do to assist both the advancement of women and their entry into occupations traditionally considered appropriate only for men. It is true, of course, that if unemployment is high in the jobs in which men predominate, and if the seniority system is well entrenched, the chances of women moving into these areas may be virtually nonexistent. Nevertheless, a chief executive officer personally committed to equal opportunity can bring about considerable progress.

Most of the measures that can be taken to advance women are well known and include the appointment of women to boards of directors, vigorous recruitment of women into an organization, with concomitant training and promotional opportunity, the advancement of existing female employees into management positions, and programs to build a supportive environment for women in new kinds of jobs.

The opening up of opportunities for women in large organizations, whether governmental or private enterprise, will help but will not alone solve the issue of occupational segregation, since our social, legal, educational, and economic systems all interact to perpetuate this employment pattern. A full answer will be found only in basic changes in the labor market demand for women and in new societal values. Such changes will not come painlessly, but they must come. Useful here would be a broad educational effort aimed at altering public attitudes as to what are "proper" kinds of employment for the respective sexes, both in the home and in the market. The broadcast media, especially television, could be particularly helpful in presenting men and women in nontraditional roles and in publicizing the entry of men and women into fields conventionally associated with the opposite sex.

Whatever progress is made in giving women's work a higher value and in promoting greater occupational integration will necessarily depend on the individual initiative and determination of women themselves, and on their willingness to work together to press for recognition and reward for what they do and to achieve power over decisions that affect their lives. The responsibility that women must take upon themselves to accomplish these objectives cannot be overstated.

Another priority must be the provision—for all families which need them—of adequate day care and after-school care arrangements for children. Related to the provision of child care is the creation of an income support system for families. A number of proposals, including the negative income tax, a system of family allowances, or a combination of the two, have been made that would achieve this purpose. All of them contemplate elimination of the present program of aid to families with dependent children, which appears to drive potential male contributors to child support out of the home and to lock women who might well become self-sufficient workers into being permanent welfare recipients.

The point is to achieve a condition in which those with incomes well below the national median can be assured a decent standard of living without the indignities of the present welfare system. Whatever policy is adopted, it must be so designed that it expressly meets the needs of the single parent with dependent children, most of whom will be women. This means that it must enable those who prefer to stay at home caring for their children to do so while not penalizing those who want to work.

What is really needed is a comprehensive family support system which provides direct financial assistance to those families that need it and makes available to all families a wide range of services. American society expects a great deal of its families, but it does not provide sufficient help to enable them to give their children the best possible start in life.

Naturally, a combination of measures to provide jobs for more people, to ensure a decent guaranteed income for all, and to make possible the provision and funding of an adequate family support system will cost a great deal of money. It should be possible, however, to offset these costs by elimination of public expenditure for families with dependent children (AFDC), a reduction of other types of welfare costs, and a lessening of the very heavy burden of unemployment compensation. Growth in the economy resulting from expanded employment could also be expected to produce higher tax revenues to government.

It seems doubtful that public opinion in this country is yet ready to accept something like the Swedish experiment in "parental insurance." Under this program, supported jointly by government and employers, husbands whose wives have just given birth are allowed up to seven months leave at 95 percent of salary to stay at home helping with care of the baby and housework. If both parents work, they can divide the leave between them. Sweden, however, is a nation that puts a far higher value on the family and children in its scale of national priorities than does the United States.

In the educational realm a large number of changes can be made that will have an influence on equal opportunity for women in the world of work. These measures would affect every level of education, from preschool to graduate training. They include a continuing attack on sex-stereotyping in curricula and in educational materials, new efforts to interest girls in mathematics and science during their high school years, attention in counseling at both the high school and college level to the relationship between course selection and later occupational choice, new programs at community colleges to encourage women to enter male-dominated occupations where the prospects for advancement and high pay are good, particular efforts by college placement officers to help women find jobs in areas where they are not well represented, and, finally, the expansion of opportunities at colleges and universities for adults to earn degrees or otherwise add to their qualifications through part-time or external study.

The educational world must also move vigorously to put its own house in order on the employment front by making every effort to overcome the effects of past discrimination against women. In public education all over the country, there are still very few female principals, at least at the high-school level, and female superintendents are all but unknown. In higher education, relatively few women have been appointed to senior administrative positions, and the same is true in regard to tenured faculty positions. The fact that little growth is taking place at any level of the educational system today of course makes the advancement of women exceptionally difficult. Nonetheless, the problem is not totally intractable, if effort and good will are applied to it.

Higher educational institutions must of course maintain equality of opportunity for women in both undergraduate and graduate enrollments and equal treatment of women on the campus. Of particular importance is the granting of undergraduate financial aid and the award of fellowships for graduate or professional study on a nondiscriminatory basis.

In the area of relationships between the sexes there will have to be substantial changes as we move toward a new society. Most importantly, the traditional assumption of female dependency, on which so much of our social and economic structure rests, will have to disappear. New women's rights laws have already made illegal many types of discrimination that assumed women's inferior status and dependency on men, but public opinion still predominantly holds to the traditional position. One can, nevertheless, envisage a gradual erosion of old beliefs and practices and the coming of a time when the governing relationship between the sexes will be one of mutual respect based on the full autonomy, independence, and freedom of choice for both men and women. Establishment of this new relationship will be fundamental to true equality for women—as much so for those who choose the responsibilities of home or of home and volunteer work as their mode of life as for those who opt for outside paid employment.

Finally, there is the intriguing possibility of major alterations in the traditional stages of life cycle. At present, for most people, the pattern is inflexible. The educational phase of their lives usually ends somewhere between the ages of 16 and 22. This is followed by an unbroken stretch of from 40 to 50 years of work, which in turn is followed by retirement.

In practice, this normal progression is modified for some people through involuntary periods of unemployment. Others modify it deliberately by interrupting the work phase of their lives with a period of full-time study aimed at gaining higher qualifications. Many women leave the labor force for several years to have children, sometimes taking the time to engage in volunteer work and further education or training before reentering paid employment. They can, however, pay heavily for this "irregularity" by having to start all over again at beginning entry levels, forfeiting seniority and hence opportunity for advancement both in position and in earnings, and losing the chance to compete for more interesting jobs.

One could imagine a new, flexible arrangement, however, in which it would be normal for most people—women and men—to alternate periods of study, employment, and work in the home and to plan their lives accordingly. While this would require major changes in present administrative structures and financial arrangements, the idea of making new life patterns possible for those who want them should not be out of the question in a nation as rich as the United States. Proposals such as two free years of study "in the bank" for everyone, available at any time one chooses, have indeed already received wide discussion.

The gains to be expected from greater flexibility in life patterns are many. If, for example, it were to become normal practice for both men and women to withdraw temporarily from the labor force, for periods of study, to retrain for new careers, to care for children, or just to pursue special interests, intermittent employment would have to be accorded society's official sanction, and the special onus now placed on women would be removed. For both men and women, periodic interruptions in the long grind of employment would certainly refresh their spirits, increase personal satisfaction, enhance loyalty to employers, and possibly increase productivity. It might, furthermore, enable more people to be absorbed into the labor force.

Most importantly, in making these changes, the nation would be confirming a belief in individual development and self-fulfillment and in the need to give higher priority to the quality of human life. It would not for a moment be to suggest that work is not important. Rather, it would be a declaration that other things are also important and that the major portion of a lifetime given to work should have many compensations to it beyond simply economic reward.

Finally, it would permit the growth of a new societal attitude in which education would be seen not just as preparation for life but as part of life itself, to be enjoyed simply as recreation or for its ability to enhance human understanding and capability over the entire life cycle.

IN CONCLUSION

It is possible therefore to regard the new phenomenon of women's large-scale entry into the labor force as an unprecedented opportunity for building a better nation. The new society would be moral, pragmatic, and humane. It would be moral because it would be founded on a belief that the worth and dignity of the individual and his or her right to be respected are more important than the claims of corporate structures or of the state. It would be pragmatic because it would release presently suppressed human abilities to the nations' creative and productive processes. It would be humane because it would have the flexibility to allow for the free expression of individual differences and would recognize that when these differences become disadvantages in the quest for job equality, as in the case of the female capacity for bearing children, society must make adjustments.

Realistically, of course, implementation of these ideas faces some severe constraints. We have to recognize that tradiational beliefs about the respective roles of the sexes, though changing, are deep-rooted and persistent. We must also recognize that without a strong and growing economy, new public policies of the kind envisaged will be difficult to achieve. Nevertheless, even with these constraints, much progress toward the new society can be achieved if we but have the will to press for it. The alternative is to incur the immeasurable cost of doing nothing—of allowing the drift in our national policy to continue.

2

WOMEN WORKING: HISTORICAL TRENDS

SHARLENE J. HESSE

Women workers play a necessary and important role in the economic structure of this country and have done so throughout its history. However, little attention has been given to what kinds of work have been performed by women in different periods; thus, their efforts and accomplishments have not been recognized. Women have been "invisible workers," whose labor and skills have been considered insignificant in relation to those of men. Traditionally, American social scientists have discussed and researched men's participation in the labor force while giving little recognition to women workers. Many studies of the work force use the term "heads of household" to refer to men, identifying women workers by such terms as "secondary earners." Such definitions tend to emphasize women's economic dependence and insignificance in contributing to national economic expansion.

> The Census imposed definition of husband-wife families as male-headed is a convention that offers little gain in simplicity for what it costs in observing household differences of possible interest. It is a convention which assumes the social and economic dependency of wives without inquiring into the facts and as such is not only

AUTHOR'S NOTE: I wish to acknowledge the research assistance of Mimi Huber.

demeaning to many women, but is also likely to become an increasingly obsolete description of reality over time [Ross and Sawhill, 1975:10].

The census definition of work as paid labor has become the national standard for categorizing an activity as "work"; such activities as housework and volunteer work and child care, which are unpaid, seem less important. Women have performed and do perform economically and socially useful work which is not measured by the Department of Labor.

American attitudes, especially in the 1960s and even as late as the 1970s, indicate that most people (including many women) disapprove of women working outside the home, particularly when they are also mothers (Axelson, 1963; Morgan et al., 1966; Oppenheimer, 1970). Historical research on women and work, by taking a similarly narrow definition of work, has also underestimated the female contribution to the economy; historical writers have tended to limit the scope of women's history. It has been pointed out that most historical studies of women fall into three broad categories: (1) institutional histories of women's organizations and movements; (2) biographies of important suffragists and "token women"—first ladies, isolated nineteenth-century professional women; and (3) "prescriptive history"—discussions of class or societal ideals rather than actual cultural practices—for example, content analyses of child-rearing practices (Gordon et al., 1971). In general, there is a paucity of research studies on what women have done as workers in and outside the home throughout history. Only recently has this been the subject of wider historical interest (Baker, 1964; Smuts, 1971; Baxandall et al., 1976; Wertheimer, 1977).

Employment statistics confirm women's growing participation in the national labor force over time. Table 1 shows the historical increase of women in the labor force since 1890, especially between the years 1940 and 1978. Twenty-nine percent of the entire female population 16 years of age and over in 1940 were employed, while in 1974 this figure rose to almost 46 percent and by 1978 this rate had risen to almost 50 percent.

TABLE 1: Women in the Civilian Labor Force, 1890–1978

Year	Number (Millions)	Percentage of All Workers	Percentage of Female Population
1890	4	17	18
1900	5	18	20
1920	8	20	23
1930	10	22	24
1940	14	25	29
1945	19	36	38
1947	17	28	31
1950	18	30	34
1955	21	32	36
1960	23	33	38
1965	26	35	39
1970	32	38	43
1974	36	39	46
1977	39	**	48
1978	41	**	49

*Figures are rounded to nearest whole number
**Not available

Note: Pre-1940 figures include women 14 years of age and over, other years include women 16 and over.

Sources: U.S. Department of Labor, Women's Bureau, *1969 Handbook on Women Workers*, Bulletin no. 294 (Washington, D.C.: Government Printing Office, 1969), p. 10; U.S. Department of Labor, Manpower Administration, *Manpower Report of the President*, April 1975 (Washington, D.C.: Government Printing Office, 1975), p. 203; U.S. Department of Labor, Bureau of Labor Statistics, "Employment in Perspective: Working Women," report no. 531 (Washington D.C.: Government Printing Office, 1978), p. 2.

In 1940, women workers constituted a quarter of employed persons; by 1974, women were nearly two-fifths of the working population.

This chapter will focus on the economic, demographic, and social forces which have defined women's work experiences throughout history. Attention will also be given to the characteristics (class, marital status) which influence the work roles and work conditions of American women in different periods. Hopefully, this examination will clarify the accomplishments of women throughout our nation's history and provide broader recognition of the roles of women and women's work.

WOMEN WORKERS: PREINDUSTRIAL AMERICA

In the preindustrial economy of the American colonial period, the family was the economic unit and family members were dependent on one another for their basic subsistence. Men performed the agricultural work while women worked chiefly in the home, manufacturing nearly all the necessities of life. The American colonial woman's home was a true center of industry; in addition to cooking, cleaning, and caring for offspring, she spun and wove and made lace, soap, candles, and shoes (Flexner, 1959).

While colonial women worked primarily in the home, they also worked outside the home as innkeepers, shopkeepers (many owned general stores), craftspersons, nurses, printers, teachers, and land holders (Dexter, 1924). Women acted as physicians and midwives in all of the early settlements, producing medicines, salves, and ointments. The list of known occupations colonial women engaged in continues to grow as old documents are discovered and new histories of women's work are written. It appears that, at one time or another, women engaged in all the occupations available to men (Leonard et al., 1962). Many of the women who worked outside their homes were widows with children to care for who had stepped into their late husbands' work roles. Even if a widow remarried, she was not debarred from continuing this type of employment. It appears that there was no objection to a married woman supplementing the family income by any means she found convenient.

In general, the rights and privileges granted women in colonial America varied, some granting approximate equality with men and some negating equal rights. The law, in most cases, protected women's property rights and their rights of inheritance, but rights in marriage were limited. Women could inherit and own property, both personal and real, but not convey or transfer property to another.

Single self-supporting women, however, were afforded fewer rights than married or widowed women to discourage spinsterhood. Single women in the New England colonies in contrast to married women, were not often granted their share of tillable land. Presumably, this avoided "all precedents and evil events of granting lots unto single maidens not disposed of" (Abbot, 1910: 11-12). An explanation for this practice is that single women with property rights tended to remain single. They posed a threat to the economic stability of colonial communities, whose men needed women to marry, produce children, and provide for all household needs (Wertheimer, 1977).[1] This attests to the importance placed on the role of women and women's household work during this era.

Slave women in the southern colonies were the source of much labor critical to the operation of southern households. In Virginia in the year 1640, the slavery system was legalized; the word "slave" was written into the Virginia laws by 1662. Women and men, along with their children, were subjected to a lifetime of bondage.[2] These women worked primarily in the fields, but they were also expected to weave, spin, sew, knit, and produce household items. Many of these women were domestic servants who also took charge of the cooking, laundry, and children of their masters. The extended family was of vital importance under the slave system. Black mothers worked most of the day, while their own children were left to be cared for by grandmothers and old or disabled slaves.

In comparison with later periods, women (with the exception of slaves) were given relatively high status in colonial America for a number of reasons. First, women's labor was in great demand because of the shortage of women; second, women's roles as home managers and producers earned them respect; third, because of the acute shortage of labor, many women performed work outside the home (Wertheimer, 1977).

INDUSTRIALIZATION AND WOMEN'S WORK

With the advent of industrialization, many of the products women produced at home—cloth, shoes, candles—were produced in the factory, drawing women into the formal labor market. At first women produced goods for the domestic market, but still performed the work at home. Merchants would contract for work to be done, supplying women with the raw materials that were made into finished articles. This "putting out" system was a precursor to the factory work of the early nineteenth century. Factories were more efficient in meeting the increasing demand for goods. As textile manufacturing moved into factories outside the home, a large number of women became wage earners for the first time. The demand for women workers in the new mills was great, and families—now spared the necessity of producing their own cloth—could spare their daughters for such work.

In 1790, the first factory designed for the spinning of cotton was introduced to Americans by an English immigrant, Sammuel Slater. This factory, in Pawtucket, Rhode Island, incorporated machinery powered by nearby waterways (Wertheimer, 1977). The establishment of such factories had a tremendous effect on the economic growth of America. Within 10 years, 15 mills could be found in the New England area alone. By the year 1814, which marks the introduction of the power loom, most of the cloth previously produced in the home was manufactured industrially (Baker, 1964).

The New England textile mills provided the first opportunity for large numbers of women to work outside their immediate families in nondomestic employment. These first women factory workers were typically young, usually single, and relatively well-educated (Wertheimer, 1977). They viewed their work as an interlude before marriage and family life. Many were recruited from miles away and housed in "respectable" boarding houses. The boarding house soon became a community for the mill women:

> They spent thirteen or more hours a day together at work, their evening together in the boarding house sewing, talking, reading and singing, and their Sundays together at church and walking by the river [Wertheimer, 1977].

American industry depended on the labor of these women, since there was a shortage of male labor. Men performed essential agricultural tasks and either were unavailable or unwilling to enter the factories. In part, this accounted for the higher wages, the respectability of the jobs, and the relatively high status of the mill girl (Lerner, 1969). The following account by Lucy Larcom (1824-1893) is from her book, *A New England Girlhood,* in which she documents her ten years of work experience as one of the young girls in the mills of Lowell, Massachusetts:

> I went to my first day's work in the mill with a light heart. The novelty of it made it seem easy, and it really was not hard, just to change the bobbins on the spinning-frames every three quarters of an hour or so, with half a dozen other little girls who were doing the same thing. When I came back at night, the family began to pity me for my long tiresome day's work, but I laughed and said,—"Why, it is nothing but fun, It is just like play." And for a little while it was only a new amusement. I liked it better than going to school and 'making believe' I was learning when I was not. . . . I never cared much for machinery. The buzzing and hissing and whizzing of pulleys and rollers and spindles and flyers around me often grew tiresome. I could not see into their complications, or feel interested in them. But in a room below us we were sometimes allowed to peer in through a sort of blind door at the great waterwheel that carried the works of the whole mill. It was so huge that we could only watch a few of its spokes at a time, and part of its dripping rim, moving with a slow measured strength through the darkness that shut it in [Brownlee and Brownlee, 1976:155].

The entry of women into paid employment was regarded favorably by many people. Women and children were viewed as an "untapped reservoir of labor," and they soon constituted the bulk of the new industrial work force. Alexander Hamilton, then Secretary of the Treasury, hailed women's place in the factory by stating:

> Beside this advantage of occasional employment to classes having different occupations . . . [is] the employment of persons who would otherwise be idle, (and in many cases a burthen on the body, or some other cause, indisposing or disqualifying them for the toils of the country). It is worthy of particular remark, that, in general, women and children are rendered more useful, and the latter more early useful, by manufacturing establishments, than they would otherwise be [Baker, 1964:6].

The continued technological and scientific advancement of industry brought more and more women's work outside the home. The changes in women's work, in part, were determined by the directions in which the new economy was growing and therefore by the kinds of work that became available. While women played a crucial role in the development of the first important manufacturing industry—textiles—there were numerous other occupations in which they found employment during the early period of industrialization. As railroads and business enterprises expanded and consolidated, women's work began to encompass these occupations as well. In fact, the U.S. Labor Commissioner, Wright, reported that by 1890 only nine out of 360 general groups to which the country's industries had been assigned did not employ women (Baker:1964).

An examination of Table 2 reveals the range of employment for women during this period (Baker, 1964). We note that more than five million, or about one in every five of the female population 10 years old and over had become a paid employee by 1900. While a large proportion remained close to home in domestic and personal service (40 in every 100), women's participation in this occupational group was declining at the turn of the century. More than one-fourth of all women were employed in the manufacturing industries (1,300,000), working in cotton mills, in the manufacture of woolen and worsted goods, silk goods, hosiery, and knit wear. The third largest group of employed women were working on farms—over 18 percent of all employed females. Women in the professions, primarily elementary and secondary teaching, constituted close to nine percent of the total number of employed women. Finally, women were also in the trade and transportation industries as saleswomen, telegraph and telephone operators, stenographers, clerks, copyists, accountants, and bookkeepers (Baker, 1964). The fastest growing of these occupational groups were manufacturing and trade and transportation. For instance, in the last 30 years of the century, the number of women working in trade and transportation rose from 19,000 to over half a million—more than a 25-fold increase.

TABLE 2: Gainfully Employed Women in 1900

| | 10 Years of Age and Over | 16 Years of Age and Over | Percent of All Employed Women | | Women as a Percent of All Employees 16 Years and Over |
			10 Yrs. and Over	15 yrs. and Over	
Total	5,319,397	4,833,630	100.00	100.00	17.7
Agriculture	977,336	770,055	18.4	16.2	8.3
Professional service (teachers and professors in colleges, etc.)	430,597	429,497	8.1	8.6	34.2
Domestic and personal service		(327,206)		(6.5)	(73.4)
Trade and	2,095,449	1,953,467	39.4	40.2	36.8
transportation	503,347	481,159	9.4	9.9	10.4
Manufacturing and mechanical pursuits	1,312,668	1,199,452	24.7	25.1	17.6*

Female population 10 years and over: 28,246,384 – 18.8% employed
Female population 16 years and over: 23,485,559 – 20.6% employed
Male population 16 years and over: 24,851,013 – 90.5% employed

*An alternate source gives 19%

Source: Adapted from Baker, 1964.

The kinds of women employed in different occupational groups varied. The typical factory worker, especially after 1830 to 1840, was young, single, an immigrant, or a daughter of an immigrant. By the late 1830s, immigrants were a competitive permanent work force, willing to be employed in the factories at subsistence wages and under highly pressured conditions. By the late 1850s most of the better-educated, single, native Americans had left the mills to marry, to become teachers or to obtain employment in white-collar occupations (Wertheimer, 1977). Few factories employed married women, and many black women were denied entrance (Smuts, 1971).

Half the women in domestic service were of foreign-born parentage and another fourth were black. The majority were young, single girls, usually working until they married. In subsequent years, black women were an increasing proportion of those in domestic service occupations because they faced discriminatory hiring practices in the alternative, newly expanding office and sales jobs. The following account is a representative picture of the work of the black domestic servant:

> I frequently work from fourteen to sixteen hours a day. I am compelled by my contract, which is oral only, to sleep in the house. I am allowed to go home to my own children, the eldest of whom is a girl of 18 years, only once in two weeks, every other Sunday afternoon—even then I'm not permitted to stay all night. I not only have to nurse a little white child, now eleven months old, but I have to act as playmate or 'handy-andy,' not say governess, to three other children in the home, the oldest of whom is only nine years of age. I wash and dress the baby two or three times each day; I give it its meals, mainly from a bottle; I have to put it to bed each night . . . and I see my own children only when they happen to see me on the streets when I am out with the children, or when my children come to the 'yard' to see me, which isn't often. . . . You might as well say that I'm on duty all the time—from sunrise to sunrise, every day in the week. I am the slave, body and soul, of this family. And what do I get for this work—this lifetime bondage? The pitiful sum of ten dollars a month [Brownlee and Brownlee, 1976: 245-246]!

The typical professional woman was young, educated, and single, of native-born parentage. Teaching at the primary and secondary level attracted the majority of educated working women. Other professions—law, medicine, business, college teaching—tended to exclude women and did not employ large numbers of people. Women in trade and transportation were young and single native-born Americans, but immigrants and minority women were excluded from these white-collar positions.

Few wives worked away from their homes during this time. It is estimated that among the four million working girls and women counted by the 1890 census, only a half-million were married women. Among black and immigrant populations, a larger minority of wives were employed outside the home. Married women, however, continued to contribute to their families' economic security:

> Most of the clothing of women and children was still made at home. In addition there were curtains and sheets to be hemmed, caps and sweaters and stockings to be knitted and darned. Every prospective mother was expected to knit and sew a complete wardrobe for her first child, and to replenish it thereafter as needed [Smuts, 1971:13].

American wives entered the twentieth century with the traditional obligations and responsibilities—the majority continued to be the managers of home and family. Yet, in the late nineteenth and early twentiety centuries, an ever-increasing number of young single women moved into industrial employment. Such factory jobs, however, were demanding. The work was long and working conditions were poor; women were limited to low-paying and unskilled jobs which carried little, if any, promise of advancement. A typical response to women who complained of low wages was: "But haven't you a male friend that helps support you?" (Baker, 1964).

Sexual harrassment was also an "occupational hazard" which affected women in almost every occupation (Bularzik, 1978). In 1908, Harpers Bazaar printed a series of letters in which working women wrote of their experiences of city life. The following is a letter from a stenographer and is not atypical of these times:

I purchased several papers, and plodded faithfully through their multitude of 'ads.' I took the addresses of some I intended to call upon . . . The first 'ad' I answered the second day was that of a doctor who desired a stenographer at once, good wages paid. It sounded rather well, I thought, and I felt that this time I would meet a gentleman. The doctor was very kind and seemed to like my appearance and references; as to salary, he offered me $15 a week, with a speedy prospect of more. As I was leaving his office, feeling that at last I was launched safely upon the road to a good living, he said casually, "I have an auto; and as my wife doesn't care for that sort of thing, I shall expect you to accompany me frequently on pleasure trips." That settled the doctor; I never appeared. After that experience I was ill for two weeks; a result of my hard work, suffering and discouragement [Bularzik, 1978:25].

Women's working conditions were further aggravated by the lack of attention they received from the organized labor movements of the day. Some women workers in a number of industries formed their own unions, but these affected only a small minority of women:

Despite the efforts of groups like the Working Girl's Societies and the Women's Trade Union League to show otherwise, the traditional belief that women were invariably temporary workers and the notion that a woman must only be working for "pin money" or out of selfish disregard for her familial responsibilities remained strong for many years in the Twentieth Century [Gordon et al., 1971:43].

By the turn of the century, the labor market was clearly divided according to gender. Fewer manufacturing jobs were being defined as women's work, especially with the rising importance of heavy industry—in which employment was considered indelicate for female workers. Instead, more women were drawn to the rapidly growing office and sales work. Such jobs were often seen as "more appropriate to the supposed unique attributes of women as defined by the "Cult of Womanhood" (Brownlee and Brownlee, 1976).

CLASS DISTINCTIONS AND THE CULT OF WOMANHOOD

During the last quarter of the nineteenth century, a sharp break occurred between middle- to upper- and working-class women. During this time, social class lines were becoming more prominent in American society:

> Middle and upper class prejudice against paid employment for women was reinforced by the scarcity of jobs suitable for the daughters of families that had begun to climb the social and economic ladder. When the father had advanced to the pay and status of craftsman or white-collar worker, when the family had moved into a comfortable flat or into its own home in a pleasant neighborhood, a daughter could not be permitted to suffer the drudgery, dirt, noise, and even danger of unskilled factory work. Nor could she be allowed to associate with the uncouth immigrants who worked in factories [Smuts, 1971:4].

This new prosperity of the early nineteenth century made it possible for more and more middle-class women to aspire to a position formally reserved for the upper classes—that of "lady":

> The nineteenth century replacement for woman's earlier role in the family was in fact idleness, expressed positively as gentility. The cultural manifestation of this ideal has been aptly called 'The Cult of True Womanhood,' for the rigid standards held by society amounted to religious-like rites. The True Woman symbolized and actualized fragility—expressed in her own virtues of piety, purity, submissiveness and domesticity ... thus woman was in a sense transformed from a human being into a living object of art, existing for the pleasure and pride of her husband. She was a creature of solely decorative worth, possessing a beauty which rested on her fragility, delicacy, purity and even asexuality [Gordon et al., 1971:28].

Some of these middle-class women became part of a feminist movement and were often involved in social reform, volunteer activities, and employment outside the home in professions such as teaching or nursing.

Working-class women, on the other hand, were increasingly devalued by their continued participation in activities men had taken over, for example, factory work. Such activities were seen as lacking in the Victorian virtue and purity intrinsic to the "Cult of Womanhood." Male working-class immigrants whose wages rose sufficiently encouraged their wives to withdraw from the market place "to pursue the goal, often illusive, of equipping their children to join the middle class" (Brownlee and Brownlee, 1976:31).

WOMEN'S WORK IN THE TWENTIETH CENTURY

WOMEN AT WORK: THE WAR YEARS

World War I accelerated the entry of women into new fields of industry, although men were once again given priority in job hiring after they returned from the war. Historical research studies of trends in the women's labor force have noted that during times of social upheaval, such as wars, women are drawn into the labor force to act as a reserve army—pulled in during times of shortage and pushed out when their services are no longer needed. Historically, we can note this during the American Revolution and the Civil War, as well as with more recent world wars. At such times, women take up jobs that are otherwise male-dominated. During the Revolutionary War, many women took full charge of economic and agricultural enterprises. Women were also visible alongside men in war zones as cooks, nurses, laundresses, and water carriers. Less prominent, but real, were the women who passed as male recruits and entered the army as soldiers (Wertheimer, 1977). During the Civil War, women also became clerks in government offices and farm laborers.

American women's roles in World War I, after the turn of the century, was no exception to this rule. The pressure of war production and the shortage of male industrial workers necessitated the introduction of women into male dominated occupations:

> Thousands, ultimately millions, of women emerged from "forgotten woman" status and began to assume a new range of responsibilities. In large measure they kept the wheels of industry turning, the business offices manned, the population at home fed and clothed [Havener, 1972:40].

After World War I, many women left the labor force voluntarily or were forced out by layoffs. Many state and local governments revised old bans on the employment of married women in teaching and other public jobs. Several state legislatures considered bills to prohibit hiring wives in private industry (Smuts, 1971:45). Yet, some women did not leave the labor force and instead remained working in industry in the low-paying, unskilled positions (Hattaway, 1976:21).

The depression that followed, however, further reversed whatever economic gains women had made. Women's labor force participation increased very slowly until the early 1940s; between 1940 and 1945, however, this rate changed again.

World War II brought a tremendous change in the status of working women. No previous war had had the same impact on women's labor force participation. During the war large numbers of women, including married women with children, entered the labor force in male-dominated industries. Prior to 1940, the typical woman worker was young, single, and poor. During the war years, nearly three out of four single women workers were married and the number of wives (particularly those over 35) in the labor force doubled (Chafe, 1976). Women from all social backgrounds went to work in order to contribute to the war effort.

> The greatest increase was in the durable goods manufacture. By June, 1943, over 22 percent of all women working were involved in such production. At the height of the war production, these industries had the highest percentage of women workers: communications, equipment, small arms ammunition, electrical equipment, professional and scientific equipment, rubber products and weapons under 20mm. Women became welders and shipbuilders, they built airplanes and produced ammunition [Trey, 1972:44].

Glancing back at Table 1, we can review the dramatic statistical changes in the number of working women after 1940. Table 1 reveals that, in 1940, 29 percent of the entire population of women 16 and over participated in the labor force, while in 1974 this figure rose to almost 46 percent, and in 1978 to 49 percent. In 1940, women workers constituted one-fourth of all persons employed; by 1974, they represented nearly two-fifths of the working population. The greatest increases occurred between 1940 and 1945—the war years—when the number of women in the labor force grew by 5.5 million workers. Women workers represented 38 percent of the entire female population. The war years also gave women access to skilled, higher-paying industrial jobs for the first time. Many women occupying these new industrial positions had worked before, but had been restricted to the lower-paying, unskilled service jobs. Women now worked as switchmen, precision tool makers, overhead crane operators, lumber jacks, drill press operators, and stevedores (Baxandall et al., 1976). The following is an account of a woman welder, Augusta Clawson, who was a federal employee working in an Oregon shipyard in 1944. She wrote about her life experience as a welder in order to encourage other women to enlist. The following excerpt describes part of her work:

> And it isn't only your muscles that must harden. It's your nerve too, I admit quite frankly that I was scared pink when I had to climb on top deck today. It's as if you had to climb from the edge of a fifth story to the sixth of a house whose outside walls have not been put on. Even the scaffolding around the side is not very reassuring, for there are gaps between, where you are sure you'll fall through. The men know their muscles are strong enough to pull them up if they get a firm grip on a bar above. But we women do not yet trust our strength, and some of us do not like heights. But one does what one has to. And it's surprising what one can do when its necessary [Clawson, 1975:134].

The war also changed other traditional female roles. Black women were suddenly able to find employment outside of their typical domestic work—manufacturing became available to them for the first time.

Equal work did not mean equal pay for the women in these varied wartime occupations. Even though the National War Labor Board issued a directive to industries that stipulated equal pay for equal work, the order contained "enough loopholes so that employers in most cases could continue to discriminate in their wage scales" (Chafe, 1976:19). Women not only continued to receive lower wages, but they were typically denied opportunity to advance in their newly acquired occupations (Baxandall et al., 1976).

POST-WORLD WAR II:
THE CHANGING COMPOSITION
OF WOMEN IN THE LABOR FORCE

At the war's end, with the return of men to civilian life, there was tremendous pressure on women to return to their former positions; this also occurred after World War I.[3] A new social ideology began to emerge during this time—"the feminine mystique" (Friedan, 1963). This cult of the early fifties brought together social workers, educators, journalists, and psychologists, to convince women that their place was again in the home. It was not unlike the "cult of domesticity/womanhood" advanced in the late nineteenty century to differentiate the middle- from the working-class woman. Friedan notes that in the 15 years after World War II the image of "woman at home" rather than "at work" became a cherished and self-perpetuating core of contemporary American culture:

> Millions of American women lived their lives in the image of those pretty pictures of the American suburban housewife, kissing their husbands goodbye in front of the picture window, depositing their station wagons full of children at school, and smiling as they ran the new electric waxer over the spotless kitchen floor. . . . They had no thought for the unfeminine problems of the world outside the home; they wanted men to make the major decisions. They gloried in their role as women, and proudly wrote on the census blank, "Occupation: housewife" (Friedan, 1963:15).

Behind these efforts to bring women back to the home, some historians note, were important economic considerations. The revival of the conception that women's place was in the home was integrally linked to women's postwar economic role as consumer:

> On the one hand the system couldn't provide full employment; on the other hand, continued industrial profits required the diminution of military spending, an expansion in the consumption of household durable goods. An emphasis on "homemaking" encouraged women

to buy. To increase private consumption families were encouraged to leave the cities for the suburbs by low-cost Federal Housing Administration loans and miles of commuter highways subsidized by the government (Baxandall et al., 1976:282-283).

Yet, despite barriers to women's employment outside the home, many did not return to their former way of life, even though they were displaced from heavy industries by men. Instead, women found employment in the more "traditional" women's jobs that became available in the expanding service sector of the economy. The rapid growth of the service sector, especially clerical and sales positions, created an increasing number of white-collar jobs. Those responding to such employment opportunities were often middle-class, married women in midlife, returning to work as family responsibilities lessened, though younger women with children were also driven into the work force by economic necessity:

> I hear on all sides that I should go back to the kitchen. . . . Do they think I'm working just for fun or pin money? They should know that it's no easy task for a woman to take care of her husband and her young children and at the same time keep a job. I am fearful with all these cutbacks that because I am a woman I will be among the first to go (Young and Shouse, 1945:274-275).

Oppenheimer (1973) analyzed the increased needs of industry for women workers, especially the need for married women with children. She notes that demographic factors—a shortage of male and single female workers to fill this newly expanded service sector—were one important reason why married women, especially older women with no preschool children, entered the labor force. The birth rate, which had been 30.1 per 1,000 in 1910, declined to 21.3 in 1930, and to 18.7 in 1935, where it remained unchanged until 1945. As a consequence, beginning in 1945, there was a scarcity of young workers which continued into the 1960s. Coupled with this was the decrease in the age at which women married, as well as an increase in the number of children per family. These demographic factors tended to open up opportunities for the employment of older mothers with no preschool children. The declining birth rates in the years

TABLE 3: Women in the Labor Force, 1940–1972

Marital Status	Employed Women							
	1940	1944	1948	1955	1960	1965	1971	1972
	Number (Millions)							
Single	6.7	7.5	5.9	5.1	5.4	5.9	7.2	7.5
Married, living with husband	4.2[a]	6.2	7.6	10.4	12.3	14.7	18.5	19.2
No children under 18 years	2.7	b	4.4	5.2	5.7	6.8	8.4	b
Children 6–17 only	1.5[a]	b	1.9	3.2	4.1	4.8	6.4	b
Children 0–5			1.2	2.0	2.5	3.1	5.5	b
Widowed, divorced, living apart	2.9	4.7	3.7	4.6	4.9	5.4	6.0	6.2
All women	13.9	18.5	17.2	20.1	22.6	26.0	31.7	32.9
	Percent							
Single	48.1	58.6	51.1	46.6	44.1	40.5	52.7	54.9
Married, living with husband	14.7	21.7	22.0	27.7	30.5	38.3	40.8	41.5
No children under 18 years		b	28.4	32.7	34.7	34.7	42.1	42.7
Children 6–17 only	8.6[a]	b	26.0	34.7	39.0	42.7	49.4	50.2
Children 0–5			10.7	16.0	18.6	22.8	29.2	30.1[c]
Widowed, divorced, living apart	35.4	42.0	38.3	38.5	40.0	35.7	38.1	40.0[d]
All women	25.7	35.0	31.0	33.4	34.8	36.7	42.5	43.6

[a]Estimated. Source: U.S. Department of Labor, Women's Bureau (n.d.). Data for 0–5 and 6–17 are combined for 1940.

[b]No information available.

[c]With no children under three, 36 percent were employed; with children under three, 27 percent.

[d]For 1972, the proportions employed were: widowed, 27 percent; living apart, 42 percent; divorcees, 70 percent (with preschool children, 62 percent).

Source: Hoffman and Nye, 1974.

1930-1945 left a shortage of men for these positions (Hoffman and Nye, 1974).[4]

The most recent years have witnessed increasing work-force participation of women in their twenties and thirties with young children. Table 3 shows that, since 1965, the increase in working women with school-age children was from 43 percent to 50 percent. Those with preschool children went from 23 percent to 30 percent. Several factors increased the participation of women in this age group:

> Women were having fewer children of pre-school age for whom care was required, more financial support of day care became available, and a much larger proportion of young mothers, because of divorce, or separation, needed to supplement their income by taking employment. Since half of all divorces and more than half of all terminal separations occur in the first seven years of marriage, younger mothers were affected disproportionately [Hoffman and Nye, 1974:14].

BARRIERS TO WOMEN'S PARTICIPATION
AND TO THEIR ECONOMIC AND SOCIAL STATUS
IN THE LABOR FORCE

In spite of a historical trend toward increased participation of women in the labor force, there are still many barriers to women's equal position in the workplace. One of the major problems is that, while the volume and composition of women in the labor force has changed dramatically, there are other aspects that remain stubbornly resistant to change: the clustering of women in sex-typed jobs, the disproportionate number of women in low-ranking positions and their comparatively low earnings in relation to men with the same training and experience. Although the women's movement and recent legislation have produced pressures for change, there still remains resistance to the enforcement of laws that run counter to deep-rooted attitudes and institutionalized conventions about differential treatment of women and men. Equal opportunity and equal pay remain to be established.

Women are still clustered in occupations where historically they have been dominant. From Figure 1, we note that the

Figure 1: Employed Persons in 1975

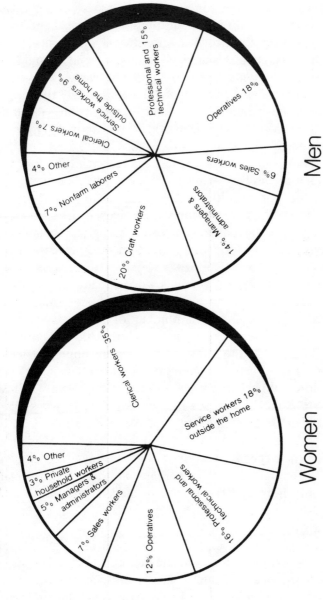

Men

Professional and 15% technical workers

Operatives 18%

6% Sales workers

14% Managers & administrators

20% Craft workers

7% Nonfarm laborers

4% Other

Clerical workers 7%

Service workers 9% outside the home

Women

Clerical workers 35%

Service workers 18% outside the home

16% Professional and technical workers

12% Operatives

7% Sales workers

5% Managers & administrators

3% Private household workers

4% Other

Source: U.S. Department of Labor, 1976.

majority of women are concentrated in the clerical positions. While women make up two-fifths of all professional and technical workers, they tend to be concentrated in the more "nurturant" professions as teachers (2.1 million women) and health workers (1.4 million). There is limited movement of women into male-dominated fields.[5] Women are less likely than men to be managers and administrators, and represent only about one-fifth of these workers (U.S. Department of Labor, 1976).

Besides occupational sex-typing of jobs, there is another form of segregation which is apparent in the hierarchical structure of occupations themselves. Women are given jobs that tend to lack advancement opportunities, while men usually hold the top positions in the hierarchy. Women are given little or no on-the-job training and are therefore often ineligible to apply for higher positions—a "Catch 22" situation that prevents upward mobility.

The list of barriers to women's work equality is still longer; we have only touched the surface of some major impediments. One could easily point to a number of others, such as the unequal burden placed on women who work and also have families to care for, the inflexibility of work hours, difficulties in obtaining child care, underemployment, and unemployment. Other, more subtle barriers are produced by various forms of discimination inherent in sex-role stereotyping of life skills—in differences in child rearing and educational instruction, both at home and in school. Attitudes and orientations of men and women to their specific economic roles are ingrained early and have persistent effects. It is perhaps in this area, especially, where a shift in perspective is most needed—a perspective which will underline the importance of women's work as a "career," not just a "job."

A recent conference on "Young Women and Employment: What We Need to Know About the School to Work Transition" underlined the need for such a career perspective. The conference participants pointed to inadequate vocations and career counseling and sex-role stereotyping by adults and peers, as well as to the unrealistic ideas women have about their own futures:

most young women still approach the school-to-work transition with little realization of the fact that they will spend 30 or more years of their adult lives in the labor force. That is the vital information that we must get across to young women today. When that fact is accepted by young women, efforts to encourage them to make serious occupational choices and to pursue education and training for jobs that will interest them and pay adequately [U.S. Dept. of Labor, 1978:2].

The Conference on Women in Transition stressed the responsibility of those who socialize women (family, school) to develop a new outlook for their economic role; to impart the notion that women should not just have a job, but should place emphasis on having a career. Career education is an emerging concept to provide women with suitable direction and focus in their lives, to have them look with healthy skepticism at the traditional roles to which they have been confined. Career education will help each woman to make a series of education and work decisions in the pursuit of concrete work goals (Regan, 1977). On the individual level, one's career has been described as:

The moving perspective in which the person sees his life as a whole and interprets the meaning of his various attributes, and the things which happen to him [Hughes, 1958:63].

Such an emphasis on career would begin to require women and those who socialize them for economic roles to examine the work chosen in terms of a long range pattern: does this occupation begin a series of stages? What are the possibilities for advancement? Finally, the notion of career would require women to think in terms of their life context: is this where I want to be in a given career pattern at this particular point in my life?

SUMMARY AND CONCLUSION

Historically, we have observed at first the slow, but then increasingly rapid employment of women in the labor force from colonial times to the present. During colonial times, women held a critical economic position, carrying on the production of food, goods, and services, as well as having responsibility for bearing and rearing children. Some colonial women were engaged in a variety of occupations outside the home, but the predominant pattern was that of women working at home. The transformation of society from an agrarian rural economy to an urban industrial one ushered in a new era of roles and definitions of women's work. At first women's work at home expanded to include production of goods and services for market sale. This "putting out" system, however, became obsolete with the entry of single women into the textile factories. Demographic changes also served to propel this outward shift. Labor, especially that of males, was in short supply. Men were needed in the fields to tend to the needs of a still largely agrarian society. Single, unmarried women filled industrial positions instead, viewing their work as a temporary interlude before marriage. As the economy expanded, more and more jobs opened up to women, such that by the turn of the nineteenth century they were found in a variety of occupations.

The turn of the century also brought on ever-changing composition of the female work force, as waves of immigrants replaced native American women in factories. As the economy expanded and prosperity came to more and more middle-class families, middle-class women could, in Lerner's words (1976), "become Ladies"—a rank formerly reserved for upper-class women. Once again "women's place" was defined to be at home. If these women did work outside the home, the appropriate work position was a white-collar job (sales, clerical, or professional occupations). Middle and working-class employment became more distinct; factory work was now identified as undesirable.

Although women did go out to work and made substantial inroads into a variety of occupations, their work was still largely confined to a few occupations, where they were primarily employed in unskilled, low-paying jobs (even when "white-collar"). While World War I accelerated the entry of women into new fields of industry, the depression soon wiped out such gains. World War II brought a tremendous increase in the women's labor force, one which continued to accelerate after the war. The composition of the work force also changed dramatically as more and more older married women with nonpreschool children, and later married women in their twenties and thirties with preschoolers, entered the labor force.

Women's place in the labor market of today is one of higher visibility and their employment is expected to increase further in the near future. The United States Department of Labor has suggested that in 1980 the labor force will expand to 100 million workers, 40 percent of which will be women. Other labor analysts, in view of the current female labor force growth, feel that even these projections will be surpassed.

Yet, even with these impressive statistics, women still face tremendous occupational barriers. Their work capacity is funneled into gender-stereotyped jobs—largely clerical and sales positions—and their pay is unequal to that of men by a large margin. While several legislative inroads have been made toward breaking down discrimination in the work world—especially by federal nondiscrimination laws which urge employers to treat men and women without sexual distinction in terms of job assignments, pay, fringe benefits, and other employment conditions—these laws largely remain unenforced. Even though changing norms and values in society and the women's movement have helped set the pace for change toward legitimate and viable options—alternatives to women's traditional role—much still remains to be done if women are to enjoy access to a full range of work and career options.

NOTES

1. Partly in response to the growing female labor shortage, an indenture system was established whereby poor and unmarried men and women in Europe sold their labor for a certain number of years in exchange for their passage across the Atlantic. By the time of the American Revolution, this system of indenture brought between one-half and two-thirds of all immigrants to America (Wertheimer, 1977).

2. The experiences of slaves in the colonial period differed depending on the economic status and individual personality of the slave owner. Before the Civil War a black woman in one of the "cotton states," working on one of the larger plantations,

would have been either a "house servant" or one of several million slaves who produced the major cash crops of Virginia, North Carolina, Maryland, Delaware, Kentucky, Tennessee, or Missouri. The following advertisement was typical of the time:

> Negroes for Sale: A girl about twenty years of age (raised in Virginia) and her two female children, one four and the other two years old—remarkably strong and healthy—Never having had a day's sickness with the exception of the smallpox in her life . . . She is prolific in her generating qualities and affords a rare opportunity to any person who wished to raise a family of strong and healthy servants for their own use [Flexner, 1959:21].

3. Some industries, for example, knowingly hired the wives of their employees, reasoning that these women would not be reluctant to yield their jobs to their own husbands (Trey, 1972:18). Other practices, such as the shutting down of day care facilities, was another tactic which helped to hasten women's movement back to the home. Union seniority policies often discriminated against the female war workers because of the recency of their employment status (Hattaway, 1976:97).

4. Additional factors account for the shortage of males in the service sector; many considered these jobs to be "female occupations" and the low wages in these positions tended to underline the fact that they were "for women only." Besides this, men had more opportunities for educational advancement through the G.I. Bill.

5. While women have been substantially underrepresented in such traditionally male-dominated professions as law, medicine, architecture, and engineering, there is some indication that for certain professions this may be changing. This change is reflected in the increasing number and percentage of women enrolled in professional training. The most notable increases in professional training of women have been in the fields of law, pharmacy, and medicine (Parrish, 1974).

REFERENCES

Abbott, E. (1910) Women in industry. New York: D. Appleton and Co.

Axelson, L.J. (1963) "The marital adjustment and marital role definitions of husbands of working and nonworking wives." Marriage and Family Living 25.

Baker, E.F. (1964) Technology and women's work. New York: Columbia University Press.

Baxandall, R., L. Gordon, and S. Reverby. (1976) America's working women: A documentary history—1600 to the present. New York: Vintage Books.

Brownlee, W.E. and M.M. Brownlee. (1976) Women in the American economy: A documentary history, 1675-1929. New Haven, Connecticut: Yale University Press.

Bularzik, M. (1978) "Sexual harrassment at the workplace: Historical notes." Radical America 12.

Chafe, W.H. (1976) "Looking backward in order to look forward: Women, work, and social values in America." In J.M. Kreps (ed.), Women and the American economy. Englewood Cliffs, N.J.: Prentice-Hall, Inc.

Clawson, A. (1975) "Shipyard diary of a woman welder." Radical America 9.

Dexter, E.A. (1924) Colonial women of affairs: A study of women in business and the professions in America before 1776. Boston: Houghton Mifflin Co.

Flexner, E. (1959) Century of struggle: The women's rights movement in the U.S.Cambridge: The Belknap Press.

Freidan, B. (1963) The feminine mystique. New York: Norton.

Gordon, A.G., M.J. Buhle, and N. Schrom (1971) "Women in American society: An historical contribution." Radical America 5.

Hamilton, A. (1964) Report on the subject of manufactures, Vol. I, 1791. In E.F. Baker, Women in technology. New York: Columbia University Press.

Hattaway, K. (1976) "Did Rosie the riveter give up her job? Women war Workers during and after World War II." In D.G. McGuigan (ed.), New Research on women and sex roles. Ann Arbor: University of Michigan, Center for Continuing Education of Women.

Havener, H. (1972) "Prepare for peace." In J.E. Trey, "Women in the war economy – World War II." The Review of Radical Political Economics 4.

Hoffman, L.W. and F.I. Nye. (1974) Working mothers. San Francisco: Jossey-Bass.

Hughes, E. (1958) Men and their work. Glencoe, Illinois: Free Press.

Larcom, L. (1976) "A New England girlhood." In W.E. Brownlee and M.M. Brownlee, Women in the American economy: A documentary history, 1675-1929. New Haven, Connecticut: Yale University Press.

Leonard, E.A., S.H. Drinker, and M.Y. Holden. (1962) The American woman in colonial and revolutionary times, 1565-1800. Philadelphia: University of Pennsylvania Press.

Lerner, G. (1976) "The lady and the mill girl: Changes in the status of women in the age of Jackson." In J.E. Friedmand and W.G. Shade (eds.), Our American sisters. Boston: Allyn and Bacon.

Morgan, J.N. et al. (1966) Productive Americans. Ann Arbor: University of Michigan.

Oppenheimer, V.K. (1973) "Demographic influence on female employment and the status of women." American Journal of Sociology 78.

Parrish, J.B. (1974) "Women in professional training." Monthly Labor Review, May.

Regan, B. (1977) "De facto job segregation." In American women workers in a full employment economy. A compendium of papers submitted to the Subcommittee on Economic Growth and Stabilization of the Joint Committee of Congress of the U.S. Washington, D.C.: U.S. Government Printing Office.

Ross, H.L. and V. Sawhill. (1975) Time of transition. Washington, D.C.: Urban Institute.

Smuts, R.W. (1971) Woman and work in America. New York: Schocken.

Stromberg, A.H. and S. Harkness. (1978) Women working: Theories and facts in perspective. Palo Alto, California: Mayfield Publishing Co.

Trey, J.E. (1972) "Women in the war economy – World War II." The Review of Radical Political Economics 4.

United States Department of Labor. (1978) Women and work. Washington, D.C.: Office of Information, Publications and Reports.

United States Department of Labor. (1978) Women and work. Washington, D.C.:
    Office of Information, Publications and Reports.
——— Employment Standards Administration, Women's Bureau. (1976) Women
    workers today. Washington, D.C.: U.S. Government Printing Office.
Wertheimer, B.M. (1977) We were there: The story of working women in America.
    New York: Pantheon Books.
Young, R. and D.F. Shouse. (1945) "The woman worker speaks." Independent
    Woman, October.

3

OCCUPATIONAL VALUES
AND FAMILY ROLES:
WOMEN IN BLUE-COLLAR
AND SERVICE OCCUPATIONS

MARY LINDENSTEIN WALSHOK

The changing position of women in the workplace and the family has been the focus of a great deal of public discourse, considerable legislative activity and a growing amount of social science research. The initial focus of attention in this area has tended to be on the work and family experiences and problems of women working in white-collar and professional positions and of homemakers dealing with returning to work or school (Friedan, 1963; Rossi, 1965; Bernard, 1965; Ginzberg, 1966; Epstein, 1970; Theodore, 1971). While these are pressing and legitimate areas of concern, as important are the changing circumstances of women in working-class positions and the

AUTHOR'S NOTE: This research is supported by Grant Number 1R01MH 2768-5-01-02-03, Center for the Study of Metropolitan Problems, NIMH. Elements of this article appeared earlier in "Nontraditional Jobs for Women: The Blue Collar World," a paper presented at the Annual Meetings of the American Association for the Advancement of Science, February 1976, and in "The Integration of Employment and Family Roles Among Women in Blue Collar and Working Class Jobs," a paper presented as a seminar at the National Institutes of Mental Health, February 1977.

consequences of these changes for the individual, the family, and society. There are a few sensitive and insightful studies on working-class women, particulary in the context of the blue-collar family (Komarovsky, 1967; Rubin, 1977). However, careful studies of the occupational values and on-the-job experiences of women in blue-collar and service occupations and of the ways in which such women integrate employment and family roles are much more difficult to find.

There is clearly a need for more data on working-class women for a variety of reasons. First, generalizations about the social, economic, and psychological implications of the changing nature of women's roles in American society can only be tentative until a more cross-sectional portrait of the female experience is available. Given the critical importance of structural characteristics such as class, race, ethnicity and place of residence to our understanding of social experience in general, the female experience specifically needs to be studied in its broadest social outlines. Secondly, changes in educational, economic and employment policies run the risk of being unresponsive or ill-suited to significant sectors of the American population if the nature of their experience of social change is not fully understood. Finally, the development of a reliable body of empirical data and a systematic approach to theory in the Sociology of Work and the Sociology of the Family depends on a firm base of descriptive data on diverse populations.

Given these concerns, I will provide an overview of what is currently known about working-class women and working-class work based on census data and the body of basic research currently available to us. I will then move into a discussion of findings emerging from an ongoing study of women in blue-collar and service occupations in three urban centers in the West. The data under discussion relate to the significance of paid employment in the lives of these working women and to the ways in which women working in blue-collar and service occupations integrate employment and family roles. The larger study of which these findings are a part deals generally with the employment experiences of women in blue-collar and service occupations and specifically with the experiences of women entering nontraditional blue-collar occupations such as welding or auto mechanics.

CURRENT PERSPECTIVES ON WOMEN
IN BLUE-COLLAR AND SERVICE OCCUPATIONS

In addition to the fact that the overall participation of women in the labor force has increased dramatically since World War II, the internal character of the female labor force is changing. Forty-six percent of all women 16 years of age and over are currently in the labor force accounting for 39 percent of the civilian labor force of this country. This compares with 1940 when approximately 29 percent of all women 16 years of age and over were in the labor force representing 25 percent of the total labor force. In 1940, however, women in the labor force tended to be characteristically young and single (18 to 24) with the rates for women 35 and over with school age children increasing as they returned to work. In the 1950s and 1960s the return to work of older women with school age children kept increasing, but the highest proportion still was younger women and the lowest, women in the childbearing ages and women over 60. By 1974, however, a new pattern was emerging. Fully 61 percent of women 20 to 24 were in the labor force and participation during the childbearing years remained high (52 percent) with increases to 55 percent among women 35 to 54 years of age. These figures indicate that today a majority of women in the early years of marriage and child rearing continue their full-time participation in the labor force. In fact, the greatest increases have been among married women and young mothers, groups which 35 years ago represented the lowest participation groups.

The U.S. Department of Labor suggests a variety of reasons for these changes:

> The economic climate during most of this period was a major contributor to the sharp increase in the labor force participation of young mothers. The availability of jobs, particularly in the expanding service sector, undoubtedly attracted many married and other

young women into the marketplace. It would also appear that generally good job opportunities for young married women, particularly in clerical, sales, and service fields, may have played a part in the decisions of many young couples to postpone the timing of their first child or to have fewer children. On the other hand, the movement into the labor force may have followed rather than contributed to declining fertility of these women. The birth rate per thousand population during the latter 1960s fell from 19.4 in 1965 to 17.5 in 1968. Although it showed some indication of picking up in 1969 (17.8) and 1970 (18.4), the rate fell again, and in 1973 it was 15.0. Advances in birth control techniques facilitated the decline in the birth rate and consequent increase in women's labor force participation [U.S. Department of Labor, 1975: 13-14].

Department of Labor statistics also indicate that women had an average income of less than $6,500 a year in 1973 with the percentage of women workers in the higher income categories being quite small; 41.8 percent of women workers earned $10,000 to $14,999 compared to 22.3 percent of men; 1.3 percent of women earned $15,000 or more compared to 16.9 percent of men. These income figures are important to note because, as we shall demonstrate later, systematic social science research has tended to focus on the more affluent, and thus the smallest minority of female workers.

Of equal interest for our purposes is the occupational distribution of women. Although women's increased labor force participation is due largely to the increased demand for women workers in female jobs (Oppenheimer, 1970), there also appear to be some shifts. The Department of Labor reports that as of 1974, 35 percent of all employed women were in clerical jobs, 21 percent were service workers, 15 percent professional and technical workers and 13 percent were operatives. Within these categories women tend to cluster in "female" fields such as cosmetology or nursing. In fact, women workers cluster in a fairly limited number of fields as reported by the Department of Labor.

Although increasing numbers of women have become employed in traditionally male career fields in the last decade and a half, women are still concentrated in a relatively small number of occupations.

For example, in 1973 more than two-fifths of all women workers were employed in ten occupations—secretary, retail trade sales-worker, bookkeeper, private household worker, elementary school teacher, waitress, typist, cashier, sewer and stitcher, and registered nurse. Each of these occupations employed more than 800,000 women.

There were 57 occupations in which at least 100,000 women were employed. About three-fourths of all women workers were employed in these 57 occupations. Thirty of these occupations were white-collar, 14 were service, and the remaining 13 were blue-collar or farm. The number of occupations in which 100,000 or more women were employed increased to 57 in 1973 from 36 in 1960 and 29 in 1950.

An indication of the continued occupational concentration of women's employment can be seen by examining the percentage women make up of all employees in the 57 occupations. In 17 of the occupations, women accounted for 90 percent or more of all employees. In more than half of the occupations (31 of the 57), women made up 75 percent or more of all employees.

Male employment showed much less occupational concentration. The ten largest occupations for men employed less than 20 percent of all male workers, and 52 percent of the men were employed in the 57 largest occupations. (As indicated previously, the comparable proportions for women were about 40 percent and 75 percent) [U.S. Department of Labor, 1975:91-92].

Despite the continued concentration of women in a relatively small number of traditionally women's fields, important shifts appear to have taken place during the 1960s with women workers entering male fields in large numbers.

Perhaps the most dramatic shift that occurred between 1960 and 1970 was the large influx of women into the skilled trades. In 1970 almost half a million women (495,000) were working in the skilled occupations (craft and kindred worker group), up from 277,000 in 1960. The rate of increase (nearly 80 percent) was twice that for women in all occupations. It was eight times the rate of increase for men in the skilled trades.

Employment increased in almost all the skilled trades—in construction, mechanic and repair, and supervisory blue-collar occupations.

In fact the increase for women exceeded the rate of growth for men. For example, the employment of women carpenters increased by nearly 8,000 (from about 3,300 to about 11,000), compared with a growth of less than 6,000 among male carpenters. In employment of women were: electricians from 2,500 to 8,700 (0.7 to 1.8 percent); plumbers from about 1,000 to 4,000 (0.3 to 1.1 percent) [U.S. Department of Labor, 1975:92].

The Census reports that women have also made significant though overall, not as dramatic employment gains in some predominantly male *professions.*

Employment of women lawyers grew from less than 5,000 to more than 12,000 between 1960 and 1970 and women nearly doubled their proportion of all employed lawyers (2.4 to 4.7 percent). Similar gains in employment were made in the medical professions. The number of women physicians increased from about 16,000 to nearly 26,000, and the proportion of doctors who were women rose from 7 to 9 percent. The number of women dentists increased from about 1,900 to more than 3,100 (from 2.3 to 3.4 percent of all dentists) [U.S. Department of Labor, 1975:93].

An awareness of recent labor market trends and employment characteristics is important when examining the existing research and literature on women and work. Understandable, but nonetheless problematic, is the emphasis in the literature on women college students, women scientists, attorneys, academics, business executives and other high earners, and on dual-career families in which both partners are professionals or high earners (Rossi, 1965, 1974; Ginzberg, 1966; Astin, 1969, 1972; Epstein, 1970; Theodore, 1971; Holmstrom, 1972). Although all are excellent studies, they tend nonetheless to focus on a narrow range of social background characteristics, career-choice processes, actual work experiences and family and lifestyle concerns. In addition, despite the new employment trends reported by the Department of Labor, the literature focuses on the problems of entering and succeeding in predominantly male fields such as law, business, medicine and college teaching, even though the gains in these fields have not been as significant as in many blue-collar and technical occupations.

This apparent research bias undoubtedly results to some extent from the ease with which academic social scientists can study and gain access to other professionals. However, it also reflects a more general inattention in the literature on work and career choice processes to the experiences of female skilled and semiskilled workers. In addition, while social scientists have given valuable attention to questions of worker organization, morale and alienation among male blue-collar workers, there appears to be little concern with studying the development of career and vocational commitment, the workplace experience, or the integration of work commitments with community and family roles among women workers. The sociology of work tends to be a sociology of the male workplace, the culture of the male work group or the lifestyle of the male worker. In fact, from the current literature one would assume that were no such thing as a significant and varied group of working women in the blue-collar world (Herrick and Shepherd, 1971; Le Masters, 1975; Kornblum, 1976). Census data suggests quite the contrary.

The virtual absence in the literature on women working in blue-collar and service occupations results in the persistence of a number of common-sense assumptions about the occupational values, work experiences and importance of family roles to large numbers of women in the labor force. Most problematic is the minimal importance attributed to paid employment in the lives of anyone other than well-educated, professional women and, of course, men (Blauner, 1964; Safilios-Rothschild, 1974). Paid employment is commonly represented as a choice which must be balanced against the more primary role of wife and mother or as a simple extension of the family role for the lower-income or poverty-level woman who, out of economic necessity, is forced to contribute to family maintenance. The kind of work and its personal rewards are seen as less important than money, if important at all. However, there are increasing indications that for many women paid employment is not perceived as a simple extension of family roles or as a problematic alternative to, or a source of conflict with, marriage and family roles. For

many women it is a "taken for granted" aspect of adult experience. It is regarded as a typical and predictable fact of life
whether or not one faces dire economic necessity, marries or
has children. In fact there is much to suggest that paid employment is as significant to the personal satisfaction of the blue-
collar women as the literature suggests it is for men, or for more
affluent professional women, although perhaps for different
reasons. Mirra Komarovsky's early observations about the
restricted nature of the role of housewife in the working class
are useful here.

> The greater sense of pressure experienced by the college-educated
> mother is not due to the time spent on housework and care of young
> children. The fact is that working-class life is more restricted. There
> is no chauffeuring of children to and from art or dancing classes, no
> rushing with the children's dinner before the baby-sitter takes over
> the parents' night out. There are no books to be finished or current
> magazines to be read. There is very little club work and little social
> life with other couples. Visiting with relatives is informal, and meals
> away from home are usually at the home of one of the couple's
> parents. Women friends and relatives occasionally drop in for coffee
> and then continue visiting as their hostesses iron or mend. In
> comparison with college-educated women, then, the lives of these
> homemakers are narrow in range of activities and interests. For
> educated women, a sense of pressure is generated by the sheer
> volume of the stimuli to which they respond and by their conse-
> quent awareness of the many uses to which they might put free time
> [Komarovsky, 1967].

Komarovsky comments not only on the more elaborate nature
of middle-class homemaking but goes on to describe the greater
ambivalence towards paid employment felt by middle-class
women in comparison to blue-collar women.

> In one earlier study, college-educated mothers appeared more defen-
> sive and guilt-ridden about their desire to work. This was substan-
> tiated in another investigation of middle-class working mothers who
> insisted to their children that they work only because they need the
> money, a statement they acknowledge to be untrue. "Otherwise
> what excuse could I give . . . for working?" The self-doubts raised by
> the spread of psychoanalytic theory ("What is wrong with me that

motherhood and homemaking do not suffice?") do not plague our respondents. The desire to work "for a change of atmosphere" was expressed by them without any embarrassment or defensiveness. The working-class housewife is so tied down that to work in order to "get out of the house" is an acceptable motive even when it may occasionally disguise a wish for independence or adventure. But the prosperous housewife who wants to work can hardly claim that this is her only way to get "out of the house." She must acknowledge that she wants to "realize her potentialities" or be a "person in her own right." Such individualistic drives have however been made suspect by the doctrine that the truly feminine woman finds ample rewards in her familial roles and does not crave individual achievement [Komarovsky, 1967].

It is likely that the pressures and satisfactions experienced by middle-class women in homemaking roles are decreasing given that increasing numbers of middle-class women are currently in school or the work force. Nonetheless the relatively greater isolation and dissatisfaction experienced by working-class women in homemaking roles has been convincingly supported in recent works on the blue-collar family, and on northeastern, urban, working-class neighborhoods (Rubin, 1977; Ferree, 1976). The full significance of this for women's motivations to work, their experience of the workplace and the meanings they attach to employment, as well as the ways in which they manage to balance multiple role commitments are just beginning to be explored.

Our three-year study of urban women in blue-collar and service occupations is an effort to provide valuable data and fresh perspectives on this topic.

RESEARCH FINDINGS ON WOMEN
IN BLUE-COLLAR AND SERVICE OCCUPATIONS

The data under discussion are preliminary findings from intensive case studies of 120 women in working-class jobs (approximately 75 percent of which are nontraditional) in three major cities in California. These women are being followed over a three-year period with consideration given to their personal and work histories; their current work or training situation; their continuing employment experiences; and the manner in which they combine work roles with marriage, family and community roles. In addition, we are collecting a variety of information on political and social attitudes, including attitudes towards sex roles and the women's movement.

Our sample is drawn primarily from work and training settings. The first two years of data collection have involved two separate, lengthy, tape-recorded, semistructured interviews. In this way we have been able to capture a longitudinal picture of the experience of the women as described and interpreted through their own language and framework of understandings.

Sixty-nine percent of the sample are Caucasian, 13 percent Black, 12 percent Latina, and six percent Other. The majority (73 percent) are 30 years and under. Fourteen percent never completed high school, 20 percent finished their schooling with high school, 44 percent have some college, and 15 percent have bachelors' degrees. Twenty-five percent of the respondents are currently married (another 20 percent are separated or divorced) and 30 percent currently have children at home. The over-representation of younger women in our sample in part accounts for the under-representation of married women and women with children. The pioneering nature of movement into nontraditional fields may also attract single women with fewer responsibilities who can afford to take risks.

In the first year we interviewed approximately 30 women in traditional fields, close to half of whom were cosmetologists, and 90 women moving into nontraditional fields including occupations such as pipefitting, auto mechanics, small appliance repair, aircraft, instrument mechanics, cabinet making, welding and over two dozen other skilled trades and crafts jobs. We reinterviewed more than half of our first year group in the second year. Many of the women entering nontraditional fields have extensive work experience in primarily traditional fields such as electronics assembly, clerical work and housekeeping. The general comments about work reflect the total work experiences of the full sample. Data on work and family roles are based on comments from about half of our total sample, of whom about half again are working in the nontraditional fields.

THE SIGNIFICANCE OF PAID EMPLOYMENT

Based on a small number of interviews with blue-collar working wives in the late 1950s Komarovsky observed that the women clearly worked for money but that the "sheer pride of earning" was itself "another reward" (Komarovsky, 1967:68). She also noted that apart from money there are "other rewards of working; the enjoyment of social life on the job, the pleasures of workmanship, the bracing effect of having to get dressed up in the morning, some relief from constant association with young children and having something interesting to tell my husband." Komarovsky concluded that a "job need not be a highly skilled one to yield the worker some satisfaction from its execution" (Komarovsky, 1967:70). Our findings suggest these sentiments as well as a number of other values are crucial to an understanding of the general benefits of paid employment in women's lives. Women entering nontraditional fields additionally experience more intense and often special kinds of challenges and rewards from employment which need to be noted.

In the most general terms we have been able to identify the following cluster of motives or rewards that can describe the ways in which paid employment is significant to the women we have interviewed.

1. Economic benefits defined in terms of:
    —need for money; for basic support; for supplemental income;
    —self sufficiency or independence from husband or others;
    —enhanced sense of self worth;
    —opportunity for increased income as a function of promotions;
    —increasing earnings;
    —desire for fair compensation for contributions made, or work done.
2. Desire to get out and do something; escape boredom.
3. Desire for outside communication and friendship.
4. Desire for challenge and personal satisfaction defined in terms of:

    —learning new things;
    —meeting clear expectations; i.e., output;
    —mental challenge;
    —physical challenge;
    —proving to others one is capable of unusual accomplishments;
    —enjoying change;
    —desire for independence/autonomy in work.
  5. Need for achievement and recognition.

These women work for complicated reasons and derive multiple rewards from their employment. Employment does not appear to be a peripheral activity in their lives, but a central activity tied to their sense of self, independent of its clear economic benefits or its relationship to family life.

A few quotes from the respondents are illustrative of this. One woman stated the economic independence point this way:

> I've never been good for asking my husband for anything. I don't want to have to ask anybody for anything. And I don't have to say "Well, honey, can I have this or can I spend that." It gives me more money, even though what I'm making now isn't that much more. I feel a lot more independent.

Over 90 percent of the women interviewed indicated that money was the most important positive thing about working, with approximately half going on to frame their statements in terms of the feelings of independence and self worth that come with earning your own money.

A prevailing sentiment among another significant percentage of the women is that employment is desirable because it gets them out of the house and doing something. One woman talked at length about how she "let's herself go" unless she has some kind of job.

> Well, obviously the first plus is having money of your own, which makes a hell of a difference and just being occupied. I said before I was lazy and I am in a sense that if I sit home and I have nothing but housework, it just seems like my day gets longer and longer and I do less and less and less and I escape more. I watch television, or read. I also drink more.

Another woman stated it this way:

> I'm a very independent person so it has—that's my income you
> know, and I lose by dependence on other people and I don't like,
> you know, being around the house, you know, I'd rather be out
> doing something constructive, something that I can account for all
> my time and you know, I just enjoy it. I really enjoy it . . .

The third most frequently mentioned benefit is the communication and friendships that develop in the work setting.

> I do like it because of the people and I get along with most
> everybody and have a good time, you know, it's pretty lax type of
> atmosphere and I don't go out very often or do anything socially too
> often, so here is where I get contact with people—adults that I can
> talk to, other than my kid. No, that would be the first thing, the
> contact with other people.

Many of the women go on to mention the importance of the challenges and personal satisfactions that come with their accomplishments in the workplace. Such statements were especially frequent among the women in nontraditional occupations. A woman in appliance repair stated:

> Right now I really want to get into something that was interesting to
> me. Waitressing is not in a way bad, but it is dull, you know, it's the
> same old stuff, plus it was very physically wearing and this is why I
> decided I wanted training in appliance repair. I had been thinking
> about some kind of trade I could get in, and this seemed like it was
> the most interesting. I enjoyed the training—there's enough to fixing
> machines so that it's a something to work at, you know, it's just not
> something you automatically do, you think it over and figure it out
> and this is the kind of work I want to get into because I think I'll
> enjoy it more than just more routine, routine—put it into a slot and
> turn it over and stamp it—that sort of a thing.

It's not just the challenge of the job itself. For many of the women a nontraditional job changes what they enjoy off the job as well. A woman working at an air rework facility has discovered a whole new world of interests.

> The good things about working at this job is that I'm really learning
> a lot, like I said, every week I change what I'm doing and if I don't

learn it well, they keep me there an additional week. They make sure that we know what we're doing and I really enjoy that because I feel like I'm accomplishing something, whereas before where I was working it was routine and you could not see anything from it, you know, you were helping somebody else, but you weren't helping yourself. With the training program, you really feel like you're learning something so you're helping yourself, you feel good about it.

With the job itself, the parts that we're doing, they go in the airplane and I've really been getting into airplanes and old movies and go to library and look at the books there. I've really taken notice of this type of thing a lot more so that's good, too, because I never really had a special interest that I really got into like I am with that.

The desire to do physical work, to use your hands, and use your body is a work value only recently acknowledged in women. Many women have long been interested in vigorous physical activity and see this as a positive characteristic of many traditionally male jobs. Over a dozen women made comments similar to this one:

I found what I really liked when I was working in the shop was that my body felt better, I was getting exercise and I need exercise really bad because I'm so out of shape and that was really important to me that my job wasn't a sit-down job, I liked that. It got hard at times, you know, where your body was pooped out, but then it feels good because you felt like you had exercise so you had more energy in the long run. And doing something with your hands was kind of cool, because you could see what you were doing. Actually see the results—when you fixed a car it ran—the immediate satisfaction, and that's something I never have had in a job. In a factory you don't see where it's going or anything, so that's cool, plus you know that you did it. It's like solving a puzzle—when you get the answer, yea!

Another woman stated directly that she likes "hard" work.

Well, just that it's different. You don't find too many women that do shipfitting. And I thought—I'm always a hard worker, I don't like to brag, but I like to work hard. If I make up my mind, I know I could do it. And I wanted to do this because I figure it's different from the piddle-peddle with the women's jobs. Those little tiny things in electronics and it's just kind of boring all the time but this is hard. It's hard work.

Finally, distinct from a desire for challenge and personal satisfaction, many of the women express high needs for achievement and recognition which they feel might be satisfied through good employment. One respondent stated it this way:

> I wanted my career to be real important to me and to mean something to me emotionally—satisfy a need in me—not just factory work. Making money—I didn't want to just make money. I wanted a career that was important to me, you know what I mean.

Another expressed it this way:

> A high paying job. I would like a job with a position. I mean if I'm going to be in this type of work I'd like to be a supervisor or something. Something that—and I don't have any idea what their pay scale is, or maybe have the opportunity to become an electronics technician. Something so that I know more than they do, I know why it's being done and I know all about it.

A black female apprentice told us:

> I've always wanted to get ahead. All my life I've wanted to do something—like whatever I start, even today, I want to finish it, whether I'm right or wrong. I started the apprentice program and that's another four years I took contract and I don't really like contracts, but I started it and I want to finish it.

What is important about these statements is that, taken together, they highlight the diversity of sentiments and motives women in blue-collar and service occupations bring to their work or, more accurately, want from their work. It is interesting to note that, with a few exceptions, none of the women indicated they would stop working even if they did not need the money. It is clear that, at least at this particular time in the history of women, the benefits of paid employment outweigh the benefits of homemaking, particularly in light of the decreasing demands on the homemaking role and the decreasing importance of the social and familial ties which have traditionally provided some rewards for domestic roles. Working-class women arc feeling this acutely as our research and the research of Ferree (1976) and Rubin (1977) reveal.

INTEGRATING EMPLOYMENT AND WORK ROLES

A realization of the significance of paid employment in the lives of the women we are studying is essential to an understanding of how they integrate work roles and family roles. If we believe, as the conventional literature suggests, that paid employment for most women is simply an extension of family roles, our understanding of its meaning in their lives and the way they combine it with other commitments will take one form. If, on the other hand, we see paid employment as central to identity and ultimately personal satisfaction, our understanding of its meaning in the lives of women and the manner in which they integrate it with other roles may take quite a different form.

The women in this sample who are married and/or raising children appear to be living with contradictory attitudes and practices when it comes to combining employment and family roles. Our data indicate that working women, cosmetologists and welders alike, express extremely egalitarian attitudes

TABLE 1: Response to Short Fixed-Alternative Questionnaire

	Agree	*Disagree*
Most girls become housewives and rarely work outside the home.	16.7%	74.1%
Women should stick to "women's jobs" such as teaching, nursing, secretarial work, and not compete with men.	1.9%	93.5%
Women should avoid politics and community activities and put more time into doing a better job with their own families.	4.6%	86.1%
It is difficult for a woman to have a career and still keep her femininity	6.5%	86.1%
Most jobs can be done as well by women as men	93.5%	4.6%

TABLE 2: Response to Specific Questions Dealing with Roles in the Family

	Agree	Disagree
There is nothing more fulfilling to a woman than the raising of her children.	20.4%	69.4%
A woman's greatest natural ability lies in being a mother	20.4%	74.1%
Raising children is more a mother's job than a father's.	6.5%	87.0%
Having a challenging job or career is as important for women as being a wife and mother.	81.5%	8.3%
A man ought to feel free to relax when he gets home from work	61.1%	24.1%
Except in special cases, the wife should do the cooking and housecleaning and the husband should provide the family with money	9.3%	86.1%
If the husband is working to support the family, his wife has no right to expect him to work while he's home . . .	3.7%	92.6%
A man who helps around the kitchen is doing more than should be expected. .	3.7%	93.5%
A husband has more respect for his wife if she has a career	33.3%	38.0%

towards male-female roles in general, and towards conjugal roles in particular. In response to a short fixed-alternative questionnaire at the end of the interview, the respondents replied with the answers shown in Table 1.

In response to specific questions dealing with roles in the family, we got the distributions in Table 2.

The ambivalence about husbands expressed in the last item becomes quite clear as we look carefully at the interview data. It is clear that general attitudes are not so easily transformed into practice. Many of the women describe themselves as taking responsibility for a wide range of household activities in addition to their full-time employment and though many believe a woman's job may be as important to the family and to her own sense of fulfillment as a man's, they nonetheless often have to struggle to combine their work roles with their love and marital relationships. So, for example, when asked who takes responsibility for major household tasks, there are clear differences in the types of activities husbands help with and those they do not. Husbands—in small numbers compared to wives—are reported as taking responsibility for such things as meal preparation, shopping and some housecleaning. However, with the diversity of other homemaking tasks which need to be done, there appears to be little help. This is particularly true with such tasks as washing and ironing and the more integrative activities such as entertaining, gift giving and taking care of family crises. In fact, when asked to describe a typical weekday, some women give rather grueling descriptions, particularly the married women in nontraditional jobs. An electronics mechanic-apprentice described her typical day in the following manner:

> I get up usually at a quarter to five or five in the morning, take a shower and wash my hair. My brother works at North Island; he was riding with me for a while, but he's not riding anymore. So I don't have to pick him up. And I usually get to work about 45 minutes early and they have a cafeteria right in the building and I usually eat breakfast there so I don't have dirty breakfast dishes to do when I get home. I'll read the paper. Then just regular working, depending on where I'm working, like I said I move every three or four months to a different shop, to different duties. But now I'm out climbing on airplanes and I usually get home about 4:30 or 4:45 and I pick Peter up and go home and let the animals in or out or wherever and cook dinner, clean up and he sits glued to the TV and I yell, "Dinner" and he says, "Oh, no."

> I: You yell what?

> R: I yell, "Dinner," and he doesn't want to stop watching TV.

> I: How do you feel your working combines with your family responsibilities and the other responsibilities you have? Are you able to make it mesh together or is there a lot of conflict or what?

> R: Yeah, it's tough—it gets really hard to come home, you know; you leave the house at six and get home at five—that's 11 hours. And then to have to try to figure out something to eat and then have to do the dishes—it just gets to be a drag. I think that's mainly why I

get tired of getting up for work, because of what I know I have to come home to after. Like just—simple things—like having to remember to put the trash out for Wednesday and that type of thing. It just makes me so mad—I'm on my way out to work on Wednesday mornings and I think, "Goddam, I forgot to put the trash out last night" and then I have to go back and take it out. Just little things like that. It's tough, it's hard to do.

These comments are not very different from those expressed by a woman in a more traditional field, electronics assembly.

R: I get up in the morning and I usually start screaming because I've overslept, and I jump in the shower—then I'm out there slamming things around, trying to make some lunches and cussing at the kids—not swearing, but hollering at them. Try to get them in gear, throw their breakfast together, try to get in my car and leave by 6:30 to come down to school, drop them off at the babysitter's, come down here. I'm in school for about six hours, then I get in my car and go home, pick up the kids, look at the house which is a total wreck, and usually fall asleep in the chair for a couple of hours, or start cleaning it up—one or the other, it depends on how tired I am. And I never really sleep because I have a six year old and he has to be watched. The ten year old, he's pretty independent. Fix supper, which seems to never get fixed until about 8:00, never get my dishes done, fall asleep on the couch—maybe I'll run through some wash or something like that, and my husband goes to bed and I usually wake up at 5:00 in the morning on the couch and then I go into bed, and get up at 5:30 or 6:00. I mean it's terrible really, but . . .

In addition to describing typical days in which they combine major amounts of time and energy both at home and at work the women also report varying degrees of support from their husbands for the kind of work they are doing. The following comment by an auto-mechanic trainee captures the spirit of many of the respondents who feel their husbands *are* supportive.

I: How does your husband feel about your work?

R: Oh, he loves it, especially when he looks at the money I've saved. Sometimes it gets to him because someone will start bugging him. "Oh, your wife's an auto mechanic." Then the neighbors—the girls—frown on it. The guys don't, but the girls think my place is in the home. I can see their point of view. Every once in a while everybody will get on his case and then he'll snap at me, but that usually doesn't last more than one day. Basically, he enjoys it. He wants me happy. He kind of laughs and makes a remark to the guys, "I don't care what she does as long as she brings home a paycheck."

The manner in which more negative feelings are communicated is well expressed in the following statement from a fork-lift operator.

I: How does your husband feel about your work?

R: I think he's jealous, just like all the other men I work with. They can't take it when a woman—they'll be nice to you until you get the same paycheck that they get and you do the same work they're doing, then they don't like it. They treat you different, they're very mean. Not my boyfriend—my boyfriend doesn't like me to talk about it—he says, "You leave work at work." He says, "You're the one who wanted to work like that, so it's your fault." 'Cause I used to complain sometimes and say, "Guy, they don't have to be so mean to me."

CONCLUSION

It is clear that even though the respondents express high levels of work interest and commitment, and regard employment as a major source of personal satisfaction, large numbers of them continue to perform conventional roles at home and receive only mixed support from their husbands or lovers.

What is of critical interest at this phase in the analysis is the contrast between the apparent satisfactions and rewards the women as individuals are deriving from their employment and the seemingly conventional reservations and expectations they report significant others as having. It is clear that one of the critical dilemmas for the modern woman, including the woman in the blue-collar world, is how to preserve her identity and opportunities for nonalientating labor in spite of her family commitments, rather than how to endure alienating labor to earn the necessary money for a family with whom she prefers to spend all her time. It is important to recognize the extent to which women in this mechanized century have become alienated from their work at home and socially isolated because of increasingly suburban lifestyles. In this regard working-class women are clearly similar to more affluent, educated professional women workers. Under such conditions, any outside work becomes attractive. In addition, given current inflation and other economic pressure, paid employment for blue-collar women is essential to family well-being.

REFERENCES

Astin, H. (1969) The woman doctorate in America. New York: Russell Sage Foundation.
–––. (1972) Women: A bibliography on their education and careers. New York: Behavioral Publications.
Bernard, J. (1964) Academic women. University Park, Pennsylvania: Pennsylvania State University Press.
Blauner, R. (1964) Alienation and freedom. Chicago: University of Chicago Press.
Ferree, M. (1976) "Working class jobs: Housework and paid work as sources of satisfaction." Social Problems, Vol. 23, No. 4.
Epstein, C. (1970) Woman's place. Berkeley, California: University of California Press.
Ginzberg, E. (1966) Educated american women. New York: Columbia University Press.
Holmstrom, L. (1972) The two-career family. Cambridge, Massachusetts: Schenkman Publishing Company.
Komarovsky, M. (1964) Blue-collar marriage. New York: Random House, Inc.
LeMasters, E.E. (1975) Blue-collar aristocrats. Madison, Wisconsin: University of Wisconsin Press.
Oppenheimer, V. (1970) The female labor force in the United States. Berkeley, California: Institute of International Studies, University of California.
Rosenberg, M. (1957) Occupations and values. New York: The Free Press.
Rossi, A. (1965) "Barriers to the career choice of engineering, medicine or science among American women." In J. Matfield et al. (eds.) Women and the scientific professions. Cambridge, Massachusetts: MIT Press.
Rubin, L. (1969) Worlds of pain. New York: Basic Books.
Safilios-Rothschild, C. (1974) Women and social policy. Englewood Cliffs, N.J.: Prentice-Hall.
Theodore, A. (1971) The professional woman. Cambridge, Massachusetts: Schenkman Publishing Company.
U.S. Department of Labor. (1975) Handbook on women workers.

4

RACIAL DIFFERENCES IN
FEMALE LABOR-FORCE PARTICIPATION:
TRENDS AND IMPLICATIONS FOR THE FUTURE

F R A N K L. M O T T

It is generally acknowledged that in recent years female attachment to the labor force has increased dramatically, particularly for women of childbearing age. This trend has reflected not only demographic factors but also fundamental changes in how women's roles are viewed in our society (U.S. Dept. of Labor, 1975). What is less well known is that this trend has not equally affected all women. Whereas white labor-force participation levels for women between the ages of 20 and 44 have consistently risen since 1960, black labor force rates have levelled off in recent years. As a result, there has been a major racial convergence in work participation. For example, as recently as

AUTHOR'S NOTE: The author wishes to thank Jean Haurin, Sylvia Moore and Pat Rhoton for their helpful suggestions and outstanding research assistance on this project. This paper was prepared under a contract with the Employment and Training Administration, U.S. Department of Labor, under the authority of the Comprehensive Employment and Training Act. Researchers undertaking such projects under Government sponsorship are encouraged to express their own judgements. Interpretations or viewpoints stated in this document do not necessarily represent the official position or policy of the Department of Labor.

1960, black women 35 to 44 years of age were almost 50 percent more likely to be working than their white counterparts; by 1975, this racial gap had narrowed considerably (Sweet, 1973).

This paper will examine in some detail certain aspects of this racial convergence utilizing a unique data set, the National Longitudinal Surveys of labor market behavior. These surveys encompass a series of interviews with four different population cohorts, although the focus of this paper will be on the interviews with nationally representative samples of black and white women 14 to 24 and 30 to 44 years of age.[1] In particular, detailed information about the labor-force attitudes and behavior of women 20 to 24 years of age in 1968 and 1973 and 35 to 39 and 40 to 44 in 1967 and 1972 are currently available from these surveys. Thus, it is possible to examine minutely the dynamics of the above-noted racial convergence in labor-force behavior (for women almost a generation apart in age) and to suggest what this convergence implies for the future labor-force behavior of black and white women.

TRENDS IN LABOR-FORCE PARTICIPATION BETWEEN 1967 AND 1972: A DETAILED EXAMINATION

Even a cursory examination of Table 1 suggests that there are major differences between black and white labor-force trends over this 1967 to 1972 period.[2] For the most part, labor-force participation rates (the percentage of the population group either working or looking for work) for white women of all ages and marital statuses increased. In contrast, declining patterns of participation may be noted for most of the black groups, with the notable exception of young, married, black women. The 35- to 39-year-old group can be used to demonstrate this convergence phenomenon; in 1967, the black and white labor-force participation rates for this age group were about 70 and 46 percent, respectively. By 1972, the white rate had increased to about 54 percent and the black rate had declined to 62 percent. As a result, the difference between the black and white rate narrowed from about 24 points to only eight points. Similar patterns were evidenced for the other two age groups here under discussion, although the pattern is less pronounced for the 20 to 24 year olds.[3] During this five-year period, there were also significant declines in the proportion of women of child-bearing age with children of preschool age in the home. Thus, the increasing work participation of white women is consistent with this changing childrearing pattern whereas the black labor-force trend is in apparent contradiction with the fertility trend. Indeed, the percentage of black 35- to 39-year-old women with a preschool child in the home declined from 43 to 29 percent during the half decade at the same time that their labor force attachment *also* was declining.

Examining Table 1 more carefully, one finds that for white older (35- to 44-year-old) women, the most notable increases in work participation were among women who either were sepa-rated or divorced. In contrast, the sharpest declines for black women were also for this same marital category. As a result, while black labor-force participation rates for separated or divorced mature women were well *above* the white rates in 1967, by 1972 they were far *below* the white rates. From a policy perspective, this trend needs to be carefully considered. Not only has the maritally disrupted group been growing in recent years as a percentage of the total population, but in addition, this is the group which is in greatest need of the financial remuneration which gainful employment can best pro-vide (Mott and Moore, 1977; McEaddy, 1976).

The changes in rates described in Table 1 disguise the actual dynamics behind the 1967 to 1972 transition. That is, the changes described represent "net" changes during the period and mask the considerable movement in and out of the labor force during the period. For example, it would be possible for the overall labor-force participation rate for a group to remain unchanged simply because the same large number of individuals entered as left the labor force during the period. Table 2 decomposes the labor force transition process of the three groups of women. First, it may be noted that the percentage of all black women employed at both points in time is substan-tially above the percentage of white women employed. This is consistent with the "net" statistics which show higher black

TABLE 1: Labor-Force Participation Rates in 1967 and 1972 by Age, Race and Marital Status[1]

| | White | | | | | Black | | | | |
| | 1967 | | 1972 | | Change in rate 1967 to 1972 | 1967 | | 1972 | | Change in rate 1967 to 1972 |
	Number of respondents	Labor force rate	Number of respondents	Labor force rate		Number of respondents	Labor force rate	Number of respondents	Labor force rate	
Ages 20 to 24[2]	1,235	57.4	1,396	65.9	+ 8.5	379	62.1	585	62.4	+ 0.3
Married, spouse present	766	48.0	821	58.4	+10.4	176	57.3	220	63.7	+ 6.4
Separated or divorced	76	67.9	88	68.6	+ 0.7	41	55.1	78	55.3	+ 0.2
Never married	392	73.3	485	77.5	+ 4.2	162	69.9	286	63.3	– 6.6
Ages 35 to 39	951	46.4	968	53.7	+ 7.3	367	70.4	338	62.3	– 8.1
Married, spouse present	835	43.1	832	49.6	+ 6.5	243	66.3	185	62.2	– 3.8
Separated or divorced	53	62.9	80	78.8	+15.9	86	84.8	104	63.0	–21.8
Never married	49	81.5	45	87.1	+ 5.6	16	3	35	56.9	–
Ages 40 to 44	1,086	50.3	951	55.9	+ 5.6	405	70.0	367	64.0	– 6.0
Married, spouse present	949	46.7	797	51.7	+ 5.0	267	66.4	234	63.4	– 3.1
Separated or divorced	81	72.3	81	81.5	+ 9.2	79	87.1	81	68.9	–18.2
Never married	28	89.1	44	80.6	– 8.5	28	80.4	13	3	–

1. Sample limited to women interviewed in all survey years.
2. All estimates for the 20- to 24-year-old group are for early 1968 and early 1973. For ease of presentation the table headings indicate only 1967 and 1972.
3. Rates are not calculated where sample size is under 25.

labor-force participation rates at both points in time. However, for the older women, it may be noted that larger proportions of the black women left the labor force and larger proportions of the white women entered during the five-year interval. However, most of this difference simply reflects the different labor-force mix of the two racial groups in 1967. That is, since a larger proportion of all black women were in the labor force in 1967, it is not surprising that a larger proportion left following that point in time. Conversely, since a larger proportion of white women were not working in 1967, everything else being equal, one would expect a larger proportion of all white than of all black women to enter between 1967 and 1972. As indicated in Table 2, if one takes into account this difference in labor force "mix" between the races in 1967, there are no major racial differences for the older women in the probability of entering or leaving the labor force.

However, for the youngest age group, the 20 to 24 year olds, a significant racial difference in probabilities may be noted as the average white working woman was much more likely to withdraw from the labor force than her black counterpart. This is consistent with other evidence which documents conclusively that young white women are much more likely to leave a job when they have their first child than are prospective black mothers (Mott and Shapiro, 1977).

CHARACTERISTICS OF LABOR FORCE "STAYERS" AND "LEAVERS"

If the recent narrowing of the differential in labor force participation rates between black and white women were solely a reflection of the fact that a larger proportion of black women have been in the labor force (and thus "eligible" to leave the labor force), the phenomenon would perhaps only be of marginal interest. However, an examination of the characteristics of those who have been leaving employment and, conversely, the characteristics of those remaining at work, suggests that the trend has certain major implications for both social policy and social programs.

Table 3 compares a number of basic sociodemographic attributes and work attitudes for the four categories of women described in Table 2. Among the young 20- to 24-year-old women (most of whom are in a different life-cycle stage), certain dramatic differences between the workers and nonworkers are apparent. Some of these patterns are consistent across racial lines and others are not. First, all women, but particularly those women 35 to 44 years of age, who had left the labor force had significantly less education than women employed both in 1967 and 1972. The educational differences between the stayers and leavers was much greater for black women than white women. Second, paralleling the educational differences, older women who left employment had been earning lower wages than those who stayed on the job. In addition, for the older black women, the leavers were much more likely to have been receiving welfare than the stayers. Thus, those women leaving the labor force were, on average, of lower socioeconomic status and had been less "successful" in terms of wages when they were working.

Shifting from the behavioral to the attitudinal side, several additional discrepancies are apparent. First, there was significantly greater agreement with the statement "work of both parents is necessary to keep up with the high cost of living" among white women who were job stayers than among the job leavers. This is certainly not surprising and suggests a greater degree of economic need for the working group. In contrast, undoubtedly reflecting the lower average level of economic well-being among the black women, there was far greater consensus among both the job stayers and leavers that "work of both parents is necessary." This suggests that, for the most part, the black job leavers who have little education and low wages nonetheless felt (*after* having left employment) that *their* employment was *necessary* to keep up with the high cost of living. Thus, there is an apparent inconsistency between the attitudes and behavior of many of these women.

It should also be noted that the older white women who maintained ties with the labor force were more likely than their exitting counterparts to feel that "a working wife feels more

TABLE 2: Gross Changes in Employment between 1967 and 1972, by Race and Age in 1967

	Number of respondents	Percent of distribution	Employed in 1967 and 1972 (Stayers)	Employed 1967 and not employed in 1972 (Leavers)	Not employed 1967 and employed in 1972 (Entrants)	Not employed in 1967 or 1972 (Nonworkers)	Probability of Exit	Probability of Entrance
White								
20—24	1,356	100.0	29.5	19.6	18.7	32.2	.40	.37
35—39	1,008	100.0	30.2	10.8	21.1	37.9	.26	.36
40—44	1,163	100.0	35.1	9.4	17.2	38.3	.21	.31
Black								
20—24	440	100.0	34.5	14.6	18.8	32.0	.30	.37
35—39	400	100.0	44.7	16.0	12.9	26.4	.26	.32
40—44	431	100.0	45.6	16.6	11.8	26.0	.27	.31

NOTES: See Table 1.
1. Probability of exit is equal to the employed 1967/not employed 1972 group divided by the total employed in 1967 group.
2. Probability of entrance is equal to the not employed 1967/employed 1972 group divided by the total not employed in 1967 group.

useful than one who doesn't hold a job." In contrast, there was no such contrasting pattern evidenced for the older black women. Not only were the job leavers as likely to respond positively that "working wives feel more useful" as the job stayers, but, in addition, their responses were much more positive than for the white women (Shea, 1970). To the extent that this item measures something more than just the need to work due to economic necessity, the result, on the surface, is perhaps surprising. The principal point, however, remains that whereas white women show fairly large differences in attitudes between stayers and leavers in the expected direction, no similar systematic differences appear for most black women; that is, those blacks who left employment surely were not doing so because of any strong preference for not working.

Whereas Tables 2 and 3 focus on the characteristics of women in 1967, Table 4 compares women (of a given age) who were employed in 1967 and 1972. As highlighted earlier, black labor-force participation rates have been declining and white rates have been increasing. In contrast, among those women who continue working there is evidence of increasing commitment to the work force between 1967 and 1972 on the part of black women relative to their white counterparts. As may be noted in Table 4, for those white women who were working, there were systematic declines in the proportion working full-time, particularly at the older ages. Black working women, on the other hand, were more likely to be working full time in 1972 than in 1967. Thus, while a smaller percentage of black women were working, those who were working were working more hours.

In addition, it may be recalled that black women from broken marriages were most likely to have withdrawn from the work force. This is also the demographic group which did the poorest in terms of maintaining full-time employment (see Table 4). This then offers further evidence of the inability of this high-employment-need group to maintain much needed employment ties.

Those black women who remained employed from 1966-71 were also generally successful in improving their earning power.

Black working women increased their real annual earnings from 27 up to 37 percent, depending on age group.[4] White working women were not as successful in increasing their real annual earnings. As a result, there was a dramatic convergence in annual earnings between black and white working women over the half decade. Part of this narrowing reflected the increase among black women in hours worked, and part reflected a possible lessening of wage discrimination during the period. Undoubtedly, however, a significant part of the narrowing in earnings differential also reflected the fact that the black women who left the labor force were those who had had, on average, less education and lower hourly wages.

Thus, two divergent trends may be noted. From an overall perspective, participation of black women in the work force is lessening in comparison with white women. However, those black women who continue to work appear to be relatively successful, reflecting to some extent a selection process whereby the black women with the least job skills are the ones most likely to have left the labor force. By "success," the reference here is both to the extent of attachment to the work force as well as the earnings associated with the employment.

SOME INTERPRETATIONS OF THE TREND AND IMPLICATIONS FOR THE FUTURE

It is clear that substantial proportions of black workers have in recent years been withdrawing from the labor force. It is also evident that the vast majority of these women have only limited education and had been earning relatively low wages. Table 3 also suggests that the majority of black women who were not employed either in 1967 or 1972 also have similar characteristics.

Job leaving may be either voluntary or beyond the control of an individual. In the case of these women, the reasons for withdrawal are undoubtedly mixed. The period 1967 to 1972 (as well as most years since then) represented a deteriorating period for the American economy. Typically, such a deterioration is accompanied by employment cutbacks, and these cutbacks tend to disproportionately affect those with the least experience, job skills and job tenure. Beyond this cyclical factor, there undoubtedly is also a secular trend operative. That is, we are in the midst of a long-term decline in the demand for many less skilled workers who have historically comprised a relatively large sector of the American labor force.

From the perspective of the individual, there may well be other forces at work. First, many American workers may be increasingly unwilling to accept the tedious, dirty, and unchallenging jobs at the bottom of the occupational ladder.[5] This attitude is undoubtedly enhanced by the relatively low wages which many of these jobs pay. Indeed, there are not an inconsequential number of jobs in our society which do not provide a wage above the poverty level—even if the worker is employed full-time, year-round! Under such circumstances, it is difficult to anticipate great demand for such jobs.

For at least some of these low-wage workers, one certainly needs to raise the question of whether or not they are worse off not working than working. Their choice may simply be between being "working poor" or "nonworking poor." The earnings they can draw from low-paying employment may not far exceed the "nonearnings" they can receive from welfare or various other transfer payments. Also, employment often entails a number of expenses which a nonworker can avoid such as transportation expenses, child-care costs and other items such as clothing and grooming costs.

The recent patterns of withdrawal probably reflect a mixture of both these demand and supply forces. Between 1967 and 1972 there was a sharp increase in the proportion of black families which received welfare, primarily AFDC. This receipt is most pronounced for women who are separated or divorced, the group we know has evidenced the sharpest decline in labor-force participation. On the other hand, the average annual AFDC payment during that period was well below the annual earnings level for most unskilled jobs and the increase in AFDC payments over the 1967 to 1972 period was below the average increase in real wages over that period (see Table 5). In fact, the

TABLE 3: Selected Behavioral and Attitudinal Characteristics, by Race, Age in 1967 and Labor Force Status

	20 to 24 years of age				35 to 44 years of age			
	Employed 1967 and 1972	Employed 1967, not employed, 1972	Not employed 1967, employed 1972	Not employed 1967, not employed 1972	Stayers	Leavers	Entrants	Nonworkers
	("Stayers")	("Leavers")	("Entrants")	("Nonworkers")				
White								
(1) Percent with less than 12 years of school	8.7	10.2	18.9	31.2	29.5	40.0	31.7	35.7
(2) Mean hourly wage in 1967	2.09	2.13	–	–	2.21	2.01	–	–
(3) Percent receiving welfare	0.9	1.0	3.0	4.0	1.5	1.5	4.1	3.1
(4) Percent agreeing "work of both parents necessary to keep up with high cost of living"[1]	57.2	39.1	56.4	42.5	75.0	65.6	72.4	46.6
(5) Percent agreeing "working wife feels more useful"[2]	45.8	34.1	53.5	35.6	62.8	50.5	55.1	35.8
Black								
(1) Percent with less than 12 years of school	27.4	35.7	38.7	51.6	52.7	74.2	56.7	70.2
(2) Mean hourly wage in 1967	1.71	1.76	–	–	1.75	1.52	–	–
(3) Percent receiving welfare	11.6	12.0	13.2	28.8	7.2	16.6	14.6	22.0
(4) Percent agreeing "work of both parents necessary to keep up with high cost of living"[1]	79.4	76.7	85.2	85.4	86.3	83.7	88.5	72.3
(5) Percent agreeing "working wife feels more useful"[1]	63.0	51.2	65.3	63.1	73.4	72.1	69.0	54.2

NOTES: See Table 1.
1. Attitudinal items were asked in 1972 for the 20 to 24 year old women and in 1974 for the women who were 35 to 44 years of age.

increase in average AFDC payments during that period was significantly below the increase in the general cost of living.

As may be noted in Table 5, the ratio of the average blue-collar wage to both the poverty-level estimates and average welfare payments *increased* over the half decade. By 1972, the average female "blue-collar" worker in our sample earned a wage which would have left her family about 22 percent above the poverty line *even if* no one else in her family was working. Her year-round, full-time wage would have earned her more than twice the amount she would have received from welfare.

These are average estimates, of course, which means that there are many individuals well below the average who might not have been able to earn above a "poverty wage." The data, however, do suggest that for most women the economic incentive was probably sufficiently strong to push or keep her in the labor force. Of course, for many of the black women not working or leaving work, the situation was beyond their control; either they were laid off from their job or they could not find employment commensurate with their limited job skills.

It is useful to note that the attitudinal data reinforce much of the above theme. For example, among black women who were *not* working, or who were laid off from work, there was substantial agreement with the propositions that work is necessary for economic reasons and that working women feel more useful. These are ideas expressed by the vast majority of the less skilled black women who *left* the work force between 1967 and 1972.

Increasingly, the vast majority of both black and white women felt it was acceptable to work if their husband approved. By 1972 about 30 percent of black women and between 20 and 25 percent of white women felt it was all right to work even if their husband disapproved! Indeed, sympathy with this attitude increased sharply for black and white women over the five-year period. To the extent that positive attitudes reinforce work behavior patterns and vice versa, one may anticipate some escalating of both white and black work attachment in the years ahead just on the basis of these apparent normative shifts (Macke, Hudis, and Larrick, 1978).

TABLE 4: Percentage of Employed Women Working 35 or More Hours Per Week in 1967 and 1972, by Marital Status, Race and Age[1]

	1967						1972					
	No. of respondents	Total marital status	No. of respondents	Married, spouse present	No. of respondents	Other marital status	No. of respondents	Total marital status	No. of respondents	Married, spouse present	No. of respondents	Other marital status
White												
20 to 24	839	80.8	442	81.6	397	79.9	831	78.6	426	80.0	405	77.3
35 to 39	362	75.7	288	71.2	74	93.7	438	61.2	341	61.5	97	80.0
40 to 44	450	80.0	359	76.3	91	94.3	454	75.9	346	73.2	108	84.1
Black												
20 to 24	280	74.8	122	70.2	158	78.6	303	87.9	115	88.3	188	79.5
35 to 39	215	72.8	138	69.5	77	79.5	192	75.8	105	77.2	87	73.8
40 to 44	252	72.3	155	69.8	97	77.5	206	81.9	128	85.1	78	77.8

NOTES: See Table 1.

1. Refers to "usual hours worked" on job.

The data gathered here suggest that there probably is a large and growing pool of nonworkers in our society ready and willing to work if the proper conditions (including rational pay levels) for employment exist; if appropriate guidance, skill training and other assistance are made available; and, most importantly, if jobs become available.

Largely because the basic determinants of the work participation of these women is so complex, the future labor-force-participation levels of black and white women are hard to predict. It is likely, however, that in the short run the racial convergence in the rates will continue to the point where white participation rates may exceed the black rates. However, this trend will ultimately cease for a number of reasons. First, as the proportion of black women who are employed declines, and the proportion not employed increases, the numbers eligible to leave employment will naturally decline and the numbers eligible to enter will increase. This highly mechanistic interpretation suggests that, if everything else were equal, an equilibrium in participation rates between the races should occur when the rates for blacks and whites attain equality.

Second, and perhaps more important, recent young cohorts of black women are completing, on average, much more schooling than their mothers' generation. For example, whereas about 50 percent of black 40- to 44-year-old women had not completed high school, the comparable figure for 20 to 24 year olds is only 25 percent (U.S. Bureau of the Census, 1977). Indeed, it may be recalled that black 20 to 24 year olds were the one age group in this study where the probabilities of black women leaving the labor force were lower than the corresponding probabilities for white women. Thus, the more alike black and white women become in their sociodemographic characteristics in the future, the greater the likelihood that they will behave similarly in the labor market.[6]

As a final note, it is useful to recall that for both economic and noneconomic reasons most black women prefer to work—whether they are working or not. This is the surest evidence that, if jobs are available, the future of most black women lies in the labor market.

TABLE 5: Selected Economic Indicators, 1967 and 1972[1]

	1967	1972	Percent change
Consumer price index (1967 dollars)	100	125	+25.0
Minimum wage	$ 1.40	$ 1.60	+14.3
Annual average AFDC payment per family	$1,940	$2,290	+18.0
Low income threshold for a nonfarm family of four	$3,410	$4,275	+25.0
Blue collar mean annual income	$3,897	$5,228	+34.2
Ratio of mean blue collar wage to low income threshold	1.14	· 1.22	
Ratio of mean blue collar wage to average family AFDC payment	2.01	2.27	

1. Sources of Estimates: Consumer price indices from Table 699 of the *1976 Statistical Abstract of the United States*, Washington, U.S. Government Printing Office, 1976. Minimum wage estimates from Table 6.4 of the same volume. AFDC estimates (monthly average) are from Table 140 in the 1972 Annual Supplement to the *Social Security Bulletin*. The 1967 and 1972 low income threshold estimates are from Table A-1 of U.S. Bureau of the Census, *Current Population Reports P-60 No. 91*, "Characteristics of the Low-Income Population 1972," Washington, D.C.: U.S. Government Printing Office, 1973.

NOTES

1. Under Labor Department sponsorship, four nationally representative samples of 5,000 respondents each have been interviewed by the U.S. Bureau of the Census for a decade with interviews continuing for at least five more years. Young men 14 to 24 years of age were first interviewed in 1966, reinterviewed each year through 1971 and then reinterviewed in 1973, 1975 and 1976. Men 45 to 59 years of age were first interviewed in 1966 and reinterviewed in 1967, 1969, 1970, 1971, 1973, 1975 and 1976. Women 30 to 44 years of age were first interviewed in 1967 and reinterviewed in 1967, 1971, 1972, 1974, 1976 and 1977. Women 14 to 24 years of age were interviewed annually between 1968 and 1973 and reinterviewed in 1975, 1977 and 1978. Each cohort included approximately 1,500 black and 3,500 white respondents and appropriate weights are available for combining the separate racial groups into an overall nationally representative population sample. See *The National Longitudinal Surveys Handbook,* Center for Human Resource Research, The Ohio State University, Revised November 1977, for further details about the surveys. This *Handbook* is available gratis from the Center.

2. The reader may note that the labor force estimates from the National Longitudinal Surveys (NLS) differ somewhat from comparable data from the Labor Departments' sponsored monthly Current Population Survey (CPS)—the survey which generates the monthly national employment and unemployment estimates. A

number of reasons have been advanced for these differences including the following: (1) all of the NLS interviews are with the respondent herself whereas the CPS interview may be with any responsible adult in the household, (2) the obvious labor force focus of the NLS survey may elicit more information about marginal labor force activities, and (3) there are seasonal differences between our results and many of the published CPS estimates. Most of suggested reasons for the differences are consistent with expected higher reported labor force activity levels for the NLS compared with the CPS data.

All of the results for the 20- to 24-year-old women in this report reference interviews which took place in early 1968 and early 1973. The interviews with the 35- to 29- and 40- to 44-year-old women were during the summers of 1967 and 1972. For ease of presentation, all of the above time periods shall be referred to simply as "1967" and "1972."

3. It should be emphasized here that other data sources indicate that this convergence pattern holds for virtually all age groups. We focus here on these three five-year age groups because they are the only age groups for which we have detailed work data. See, for example, The *1975 Manpower Report* cited above.

4. Reynolds Farley in his paper "Trends in Racial Inequalities: Have the Gains of the 1960s Disappeared in the 1970s?" in the *American Sociological Review*, April 1977, Vol. 42, No. 2, and Stuart Garfinkle, "Occupations of Women and Black Workers, 1962-74" in the *Monthly Labor Review*, November 1975, Vol. 98, No. 11, considered carefully the occupational concommitant of this trend noting the increasing occupational level of those black women in the labor force.

5. See *Work in America*, a report of a Special Task Force to the Secretary of Health, Education, and Welfare, Cambridge, Massachusetts, the M.I.T. Press, January 1973.

6. There is some disagreement about the relative importance of supply and demand factors as future determinants of the volume of lower level manpower. Harold Wool in "Future Labor Supply for Lower Level Occupations" in the *Monthly Labor Review*, March 1976, Vol. 99, No. 3, feels that there will be substantial reductions in the proportion of lower level workers who will be available in the years ahead. He, of course, includes the basic caveat that the size of the available pool is of course partly a function of the wages these jobs will pay. Other suggestions include restructuring of lower level jobs to increase the level of responsibility and variety associated with these jobs.

REFERENCES

Blau, F.D. (1975) "Longitudinal patterns of female labor force participation." In H.I. Parnes et al. (eds.) Dual careers, volume IV. Columbus, Ohio: Center for Human Resource Research, The Ohio State University.

Macke, A., P. Hudis, and D. Larrick. (1978) "Sex-role attitudes and employment among women: A dynamic model of change and continuity." A paper presented at the Secretary of Labor's Invitational Conference on the National Longitudinal Surveys of Mature Women, Washington, D.C., January 26.

McEaddy, B.J. (1976) "Women who head families: A socioeconomic analysis." Monthly Labor Review, Vol. 99, No. 6.

Mott, F.L. and S.F. Moore. (1977) "The determinants and consequences of marital disruption." In Years for decision, Vol. IV. Columbus, Ohio: Center for Human Resource Research, The Ohio State University.

Mott, F.L. and D. Shapiro. (1977) "Work and motherhood: The dynamics of labor force participation surrounding the first birth." In Years for decision, Vol. IV. Columbus, Ohio: Center for Human Resource Research, The Ohio State University.

Shea, J.R. (1970) "Work attitudes, satisfaction and job attachment." In Dual careers, Vol. I. Columbus, Ohio: Center for Human Resource Research, The Ohio State University.

Sweet, J.A. (1973) Women in the labor force. New York: Seminar Press.

U.S. Bureau of the Census. (1977) Current population reports, Series P-20, No. 314, "Educational attainment in the United States: March 1977 and 1976." Washington, D.C.: U.S. Government Printing Office.

U.S. Department of Labor. (1975) "The changing economic role of women." In U.S. manpower report of the President, 1975. Washington, D.C.: U.S. Government Printing Office.

5

WOMEN, WORK, AND WELFARE:
THE FEMINIZATION OF POVERTY

DIANA PEARCE

Poverty is rapidly becoming a female problem. Though many women have achieved economic independence from their spouses by their participation in the labor force (and in some cases, by divorce), for many the price of that independence has been their pauperization and dependence on welfare. In 1976, nearly two out of three of the 15 million poor persons over 16 were women (Bureau of the Census, 1976). In certain groups, the imbalance was even greater: over 70 percent of the aged poor are women. Black women, who comprised only 6.1 percent of the population in 1975, accounted for 17.0 percent of the poor that year (Women's Bureau, 1977).

The economic status of women has declined over the past several decades. At the same time, a number of important and relevant demographic changes (the increase in longevity, the increase in divorce, the increase in illegitimate births) have occurred. Perhaps the most striking of these trends is the increasing numbers of female-headed[1] families; the percentage of all families that were female-headed rose from 10.1 percent

AUTHOR'S NOTE: The author is indebted to Frank Munger, who sparked interest in this problem, and Baila Miller and George Wright, who reviewed early drafts.

in 1950 to 14 percent in 1976, an increase of almost 40 percent in a single generation (Bureau of the Census, 1976; Women's Bureau, 1977). At the same time, the economic well-being of this growing group has eroded. The ratio of median income of female-headed families to male-headed families has declined steadily from 56 percent in 1950 to 47 percent in 1974. Moreover, between 1950 and 1976 the number of families with incomes less than the poverty level that were female-headed doubled. Today almost half of all poor families are female-headed (Bureau of the Census, 1976; Women's Bureau, 1977).[2]

Paradoxically, this decline occurs in a period when other trends would suggest potential for improving women's status— trends such as the increase in women's labor-force participation, the mandating of affirmative action, and the increasing employ-ment of better-educated women. Yet, women's earnings, rela-tive to those of men, have decreased; the female/male ratio of full-time, year-round, civilian earnings has fallen from .61 to .57 between 1960 and 1974.[3] Larger differences are harder to explain. Whereas in 1950, the unemployment rate of women was only slightly larger than that of men (5.7 vs. 5.1), by 1976 it was 8.6 compared to the male rate of 7.0 (Women's Bureau, 1977). Moreover, if one does not include workers under 20, for whom unemployment rates are high for both sexes, the dis-parity becomes much greater; in 1974 the unemployment rate of women 20 years old and older was almost one-and-one-half times that of men (Bureau of the Census, 1976).

In sum, it is women who account for an increasingly large proportion of the economically disadvantaged. What these sta-tistics do not reveal is that while many women are poor because they live in poor male-headed households, an increasing number are becoming poor on their own. I will concentrate here on the latter group, that is, those women who are poor because they are women. While many women are poor for reasons other than, or in addition to, their gender, in this paper I will focus on the question: what are the economic and social consequences of being female that result in higher rates of poverty? This does not mean that the problems of the millions of women in poor male-headed households are insignificant or unimportant; on the contrary, much of what is said here can be applied to their problems as well. In particular, I will explore two aspects of the feminization of poverty: (1) the role of different sources of income—earned income, public and private transfer income—in allowing women's poverty, and (2) the role of the welfare system in perpetuating women's poverty.

INCOME AND POVERTY

Unlike earlier immigrant groups, who entered the urban labor market at the bottom and gradually improved their position, women have remained at the bottom (Coser and Rokoff, 1970; Darian, 1976; Oaite, 1976; Treiman and Terrell, 1970; Suter and Miller, 1973; Blinder, 1973; Sorkin, 1973). As Oppenheimer (1970) has cogently argued, women's entry into the labor force in steadily increasing numbers, from less than one-fifth of the work force in 1920 to nearly two-fifths today, has been bought at the price of economic advancement for women workers. That is, within occupationally segregated "ghettos," the demand for *cheap* labor and the demand for *female* labor become synonymous. The rapid growth of jobs, particularly since World War II, has been in industries and occupations that are low wage and dead end—and open to women. Once in the labor force, women are confined to these jobs, and are restricted from moving into better paid (but traditionally male) jobs, or moving up career ladders. As a result, women are much more concentrated in fewer occupations than are men; 60 percent of all women are in ten occupations. Moreover, this concentration has remained stable over time. Fourteen of 17 occupations that were predominantly female in 1900 are still predominantly female, and a segregation index developed by Gross (1968) indicates that women are as occupationally segregated today as they were at the end of the Victorian era.

Not only do women suffer limited occupational opportunity, but economic well-being is a price paid by women in the pink-collar (Howe, 1977) and other female ghettos (textile and electronics factories, banks and offices, household service and day care). Sometime ago, Knudsen (1969) showed that the

TABLE 1:   Weekly Wages and Percent Female for Selected
Industries, Jan., 1973

	Average weekly earnings	Percent Female
Apparel manufacture	$ 93	81
Transportation equipment	210	10
Malt liquor	229	7
Motor vehicles sales	152	11
Construction	223	6
Transportation & utilities	196	21

Source: E. Waldman and B.J. McEaddy, "Where Women Work —
An Analysis by Industry and Occupation," Monthly Labor Review
May, 1974, p.10.

higher the percentage of workers that are female in an occupation, the lower the average income in that occupation. Fuchs
(1971) maintains that most of the earnings gap between men
and women can be accounted for by the different jobs held by
men and women. In short, women are concentrated in relatively
few, generally low-paying, occupations. Some specific examples
are given in Table 1.

The cost to women of occupational segregation is difficult to
grasp. In 1970, when the poverty level income for a family of
four was about $3,700, there were six million women who
worked full-time, year-round, and earned less than $4,000 per
year. Such women were concentrated in a few of the lowest-
paying jobs: household-service workers, farm workers, sales-
workers (Shortridge, 1976).

In terms of increased poverty of women, Sawhill (1976)
presents two sets of findings that put a price tag on occupational segregation. First, a study done by The Urban Institute
calculated the earnings functions of female heads of families as
if they were males, but otherwise with the same age, race,
education and residence characteristics. It was found that
women who head families would receive 36 percent more
income if they were men, other things equal. If male labor-force
participation characteristics, such as hours worked, are also
added into the equations, the women's incomes would also
increase, but by much less (13 percent). Sawhill also calculated

what could be considered to be the long-term institutional constraints on women's income imposed by occupational segregation. Classifying occupations from the detailed (three-digit) census code as predominantly male (80 percent or more of all workers are male), predominantly female (30 percent or less of all workers are male), or mixed, she calculated the number of occupations in which a female high-school graduate, age 25-34, would make less than $3,000 per year working full-time. She found that while only 20 percent of the predominantly male occupations were ones with such poverty-level wages, over half (54 percent) of the female dominated occupations were ones with poverty-level wages (Sawhill, 1976).

Although similar in their role in the labor force to previous ethnic, immigrant, and racial groups who were exploited for their cheap labor—particularly in the first generation of their participation in the urban industrial labor force, in at least one respect women are different from such past groups of new entrants to the labor force. Women are permanent temporary workers. That is, employers can and do take advantage of women by simultaneously enticing them to enter the labor force (the help-wanted ads read "varied, interesting work, young company on the move"), but at the same time minimizing their commitment to the idea of an individual career ("earn that Acapulco vacation, send your kids to college"). As long as women, as well as their employers, view their work as temporary/secondary while their home and family is their permanent/primary commitment, they are less likely to engage in expensive-to-the-employer type activities such as participating in labor unions and affirmative-action suits, making demands for advancement or skill development, and even simply working long enough to be eligible for a pension.

This interest on the part of employers in obtaining loyal but not long-term employees also accounts for their lack of interest, much less enthusiasm, for developing quality day care, even for welfare mothers. Such a service might permit a nearly uninterrupted worklife, and/or commitment to the individual employer over a period of time long enough to acquire seniority, to demand a promotion, or otherwise to become expensive. Providing day care implies support for the permanent participation of women in the labor force, as well as acceptance of women, including mothers, as workers whose primary economic contribution is not that of child care. Without the provision of quality day care, on the other hand, women who drop out of the labor force or quit a job because of child-care problems can be seen as "less committed" workers. In turn, their lesser attachment to the labor force is identified as the cause of their disadvantaged status. Their interrupted worklives also make upward mobility difficult; they never achieve seniority, and career development suffers. Particularly, as fringe benefits become an increasingly large proportion of the employers's labor cost (estimates run as high as 40 percent), workers who are denied such benefits because of their temporary and/or part-time and/or short-term status are increasingly attractive economically. Temporary workers are *cheap* workers.

Related to the "temporary" status of women is their tendency to be employed in part-time work. Although clearly part-time work is the preference of many women, particularly middle-class women, there are many women who would prefer to work full-time, but are unable to do so. In part, this is because the structure of the economy has changed. Many of the service industries that account for much of the recent increased labor demand, and especially for female labor,[4] are ones that have hours that require one or two part-time shifts of workers rather than a single eight-hour shift (for example, restaurants, transportation service, and retail stores). Such places frequently differentiate between part-time and full-time workers, not only in wages and benefits, but in terms of opportunities for advancement and for upgrading of skills.

In addition to lower wages, women suffer from higher rates of unemployment and must wait longer periods of time between jobs. These patterns of instability, or what Wilensky (1961) called "disorderly work history," lead many women to become disillusioned, and leave the labor force. Almost twice as many women as men are classified as discouraged workers: neither working nor actively looking for work (Women's Bureau, 1977).

Finally, it should be noted that the effects of occupational segregation and wage discrimination are so strong that they tend to mask other kinds of disadvantages. Thus, there is evidence that black women earn somewhat more than white women of comparable education and occupation, apparently because black women tend to have more economic return-to-work experience than do white women (perhaps because their work history is less interrupted than the average white female's (Farley, 1977). Apparently, for a woman, race is a relatively unimportant consideration in determining economic status.

PRIVATE TRANSFER INCOME

The second source of income to be considered here is that of private transfers. At one time, most of the private transfer was indeed private, that is, within the nuclear family. Working husbands gave their nonworking wives some portion of the paycheck to pay for the expenses of the home and child(ren). The rising divorce rate is such that it is estimated that about one in three marriages will fail; moreover, they will fail sooner, resulting more often in the early marriage/early divorce young mother with very young children. The internal transfer of resources for housekeeping and the needs of the children becomes institutionalized in the form of child-support payments (and, sometimes, alimony). For many women, the price of freedom from the marriage bond is therefore very steep, for the likelihood of the same rate of transfer of economic support continuing is very low. In one study, done on behalf of the public welfare office charged with enforcement of child support for welfare mothers, it was found that a minority of only 22 percent of spouses were fulfilling all of their obligations fully; half were contributing nothing. Moreover, in two out of three AFDC cases, there was *no* child-support agreement, formal or informal to be enforced (NCSS, 1977). In part because of this problem, in part because the fathers are either not accessible or do not have the resources themselves, concentrated efforts at increasing child-support payments on behalf of women on AFDC have very little effect. The total money collected in December 1976, after nearly a year of increased nationwide efforts, averaged about $6 per recipient, and only one percent of the AFDC cases closed that month were closed because of receipt of child support (Ibid.).

It is clear that in the case of AFDC mothers the lack of child support is in part due to the fathers' own poverty, for one study estimated that over one-third were unemployed, almost one-fifth had criminal records, and the majority had unskilled or semiskilled occupations (Nicol, 1975). Potential for support exists; a third of the AFDC parents providing no support had some college education and a third had their high school diplomas (Nicol, 1975). This potential for support will not be realized because the social norms permit men to cease support of their children when they leave their children. The poor father has no monopoly on nonsupport, for the failure to provide (or cease to provide after a few years) is a practice widespread thoughout American society. Forty percent of absent fathers contribute nothing, while the average payment provided by the other 60 percent is less than $2,000 per year (The Urban Institute, 1976); this is at a time when the median income for all families is about $13,800. Thus, the poverty among female-headed families resulting from lack of child support will not decrease unless there is real change in the societal context that condones and even encourages the absent father's neglect of his financial responsibilities to his children.

Finally, women who head households are less likely to be the recipients of intergenerational transfers of resources. While many parents help adult children in times of financial need or crisis, the single or divorced daughter is less likely to be the recipient of these transfers. In addition, the dissolution of a marriage often includes selling the house and other property. It is also true that while women have the same overall median level of education as men, the distribution is much more clustered around the median. Thus, not only do fewer women have very low levels of education, but also fewer women than men continue their education beyond the high school level. The lesser investment in daughters' than in sons' higher education robs women of a source for intergenerational transfer of resources.

WOMEN AND PUBLIC TRANSFERS

Public transfers include all unearned income received from the government and can be divided into two basic types: that which is received as a consequence of participation in the labor force, and that which is received as minimal income support, regardless of previous employment status.

Work-related benefit systems tend to discriminate against women. While women are 52 percent of the beneficiaries of Social Security (which is underrepresentation because of the highly skewed sex distribution of the aged), they receive only 46 percent of the benefits (Bell, 1973).

Unemployment insurance, however, is somewhat more of an enigma. Figures cited by officials state that women make up 38 percent of the total recipients (Dahm, 1973), a figure which compares favorably with their percentage (40 percent) in the labor market. Yet, many factors indicate that a much larger number of women are not covered at all, or are covered in a very limited way. First, there are certain occupations that are entirely excluded, such as household service workers (that is, almost all women, or 1.7 million workers), and farm workers (who number .7 million). Second, unemployment insurance is predicated upon "willingness to work" which is usually defined as "willingness to work full-time." Since many women work in industries that structurally require part-time workers, many of them are excluded. Third, many states using the same kind of rigid logic, disenfranchise pregnant women entirely without considering individual differences in physical ability or willingness to work, and regardless of month of pregnancy. Fourth, many women work in the "irregular economy," doing work that is not covered because it is semilegal or illegal, marginal, or bartered (prostitutes, babysitters, women who type at home). Finally, many women workers seem to use AFDC as unemployment insurance (see below).

Other forms of "work"-related, income-transfer programs support so few women that it becomes difficult to compare the relative inequality created thereby. How much, for example, is the free medical care and educational benefits available to veterans directly or indirectly a reason for their lesser rates of male poverty? A corollary question of policy interest is whether the incidence of poverty is reduced for those *women* who serve in the armed forces, as apparently it may be for men who enter the labor force via the armed forces (Ornstein, 1976). As Black Lung coverage does for mineworkers, would "Brown Lung" legislation and benefit programs for the largely female work force of textile mills have a measurable impact on women's poverty (due in this case to work-related ill health and consequent uncompensated unemployment)?

In discussing public assistance, that is, public transfers not conditioned on previous labor-force experience, it is necessary first to establish the extent and the adequacy of such public assistance. Although the number of AFDC recipients has risen dramatically in the last decade, as a percentage of the population it has remained stable at about five percent (NCSS, 1977). Benefit levels, however, have been declining; using 1967 as the base (=100), benefits declined from $139 to $135, from 1974 to 1976, or about 1.4 percent per year. The actual average payment per family in 1977 was $235, or about $75 per recipient. By even the very conservative standards of state governments, benefit levels are inadequate. Each state determines its own standard of need based on cost-of-living estimates, but this standard is not necessarily tied to the Bureau of Labor Statistics poverty-level income cutoffs. Even so, the state is not required to provide families on relief with the full amount that the state has determined as their minimum need. Further, many states set an arbitrary top figure regardless of family size. The result is that, nationally, 23 percent of the AFDC caseload receives cash benefits that total less than 40 percent of the poverty line (adjusting for family composition, etc.), and 24 percent were given benefits that put them between 40 and 70 percent of the poverty line, of that nearly half of all AFDC recipients were receiving benefits that were less than 70 percent of the poverty line. (Joint Economic Committee, 1976; figures refer to 1974) Even including the cash equivalent of Food Stamps in the calculations, ten states in 1974 had *maximum* benefit levels less than 75 percent of the poverty line (Joint Economic Committee, 1976). Finally, if one compares the poverty level of recipients before and after receiving welfare, there is relatively little escape from poverty via AFDC: whereas 92 percent of the families receiving AFDC were poor before, 76 percent of AFDC families remain poor after receiving aid (Bell and Bushe, 1975).

It seems clear, then, that whatever the source of income considered, women are likely to receive less than they need, often much less than a poverty-level income. Child-support payments are, with rare exceptions, received irregularly; very often the payments are inadequate and are subject to premature demise. Welfare payments are below even that state's own determination of need in almost half the states, leaving almost all welfare families below poverty-level cash incomes. Even earned income, largely because of occupational segregation as well as discrimination, fails to provide above poverty level incomes for many women. In 1976, almost 20 percent of employed, female family heads were poor—and one-third of black employed females who headed families were in poverty (Women's Bureau, 1977).

As we have seen, each of the sources of income—and, therefore, of potential economic well-being—is likely to be inadequate and thus to contribute to women's poverty. The process of feminization of poverty is also a process of institutionalization of sexual inequality, focused in particular around the institution of public welfare. In order to understand, however, the role of public welfare in both the deterioration and the maintenance of women's poverty, it is necessary to put the role of welfare in historical perspective.

THE HISTORY OF THE AMERICAN WELFARE SYSTEM

Over time, the American welfare system has moved through three stages of development, each of which can be characterized by its role in the larger society, in particular its role *vis-à-vis* the labor market. In the first stage of this federally-constructed and subsidized system, welfare was conceived as a *means to protect an already glutted Depression-era labor market from being further flooded by would-be workers,* widows and deserted wives, the disabled, and the aged. Even the titles of the original state assistance programs revealed that welfare was predicated on motherhood: "Mothers' Pensions," "Mothers' Aid." By the 1950s, however, the problem became not one of two many workers, but of too much dependency. At this stage, welfare was seen as a *temporary expedient, necessary to ease the transition from rural to urban* (for example, for Southern black and white migrants), *and from home to work* (for the woman who heads the family). Welfare recipients at this juncture were not so clearly "deserving" as those in the first stage. Nevertheless, much of the policy debate centered on the adjustment problems of these families. Indeed, much of the rhetoric that frames today's policy questions comes out of this "tiding over" model of welfare; the "problem" of second-generation welfare families, the "vicious circle" of poverty, all imply that welfare had failed in its function as temporary expedient to tide one over a rough spot. This stage culminated in the 1962 Amendments which established social services for the welfare recipient. The object of these new services was to enhance the positive aspect of welfare, its role in easing the adjustment of the individual in crisis (for example, to urban life, to single parenthood, or both), while preventing the development of permanent dependency.

The third stage is somewhat more difficult to discern, for it continues to be clouded by the leftover rhetoric of the "tiding over" stage; the dominant policy question is, "Why don't welfare recipients work and get off welfare as quickly as possible?" If instead we turn it around and ask, "Why are so many welfare recipients working?", we will be better able to comprehend the way in which welfare is not simply a temporary aid during a crisis or adjustment phase, but a system that is creating a permanent underclass of welfare recipient/low-wage workers. For in spite of the enormous disincentives and severe labor-market handicaps of most recipients, an increasing proportion are working. Although, at any one point in time, only about 15 percent are working as well as receiving welfare, surveys indicate that the true percentage is at least 25 percent, to which one must add those in training, awaiting training, or looking for work (Williams, 1975).[5] Moreover, if one looks at even a relatively short span of time, it is clear that most welfare recipients in fact alternate between welfare and work, or combine both in a bewildering and rapidly shifting pattern. Of currently active AFDC recipients in 1973, Williams (1975) found that almost one-third had worked 13 months or more in the past three years, and only one-third were dependent *solely* on welfare over the entire 37-month interval. Like the ex-convict, the ex-welfare recipient is "at risk"; consigned by prejudice, discrimination, institutional constraints to a narrow range of opportunities to "get a living" by combining or alternating work and welfare. Put more graphically, *the third stage of welfare can be described as a "workhouse without walls."*

A WORKHOUSE WITHOUT WALLS

What are some of the elements that underpin the development of welfare as a "workhouse without walls"? Without trying to exhaust all possibilities, we will devote the remainder of this paper to a brief discussion of several of these elements: (1) the increase in labor-force experience of welfare recipients, (2) the change in welfare rules related to income disregarding, (3) the effects of the WIN program, (4) the skill levels and occupational status of welfare recipients, and (5) indirect effects of welfare/single mother status.

As with most mothers, the labor-force participation rate of welfare mothers was low in the past, but today over 90 percent have worked at some time, and fully three-fourths of AFDC recipients worked full-time at a regular job at some time in the past. Most began regular work early, almost half starting their first regular job by the time they are 17, including 18 percent who began regular work when they were 15 years or younger (Williams, 1975). Together with the figures cited above, it is clear that the typical woman on welfare is, or has been, a worker. If instead of viewing welfare recipients as single mothers who have "lost" their (male) source of economic support, one views welfare recipients as disadvantaged workers who are unemployed, then welfare takes on a different character. Essentially, welfare viewed this way is a kind of poor woman's Unemployment Compensation, but with a difference. Although serving the same economic function as Unemployment Compensation, that of temporarily supporting workers who have become involuntarily unemployed and thereby easing for both the individual and the economy the stress of being out of work, welfare is a privilege (however dubious) and not a right. This has important consequences for both recipient and the prospective employer; welfare supports a low-wage, predominantly female, labor pool that is so stigmatized, harassed, and degraded, that many eagerly seek to exchange welfare poverty for wage poverty.

Making the transition permanently from welfare recipient to worker is becoming increasingly difficult because of the way in which income disregards work. In 1967 Congress required that states not tax the recipient's earned income at 100 percent, but rather that they disregard one-third of all earned income plus employment-related expenses. While this reduced the effective tax rate to about 40 percent, the rest of the population does not face this steep rate until their income is above $40,000 (Levitan, Rein and Marwick, 1972). Even so, the tax rate forces recipients into a position whereby it is almost impossible for them to work their way off of welfare. It does this in two ways: first, the combined value of welfare's cash benefits, food stamps and medical benefits, plus the income disregards, make it necessary for recipients to earn quite a bit more than the maximum allowable amount to achieve an equivalent standard of living; second, the tax rate subsidizes and rationalizes the payment of poverty-level wages. Appel (1971) estimated that in Michigan, where one may earn up to $669 per month and sustain welfare eligibility, it would take $904 per month to buy the equivalent of welfare-subsidized food, child care and medical care. Likewise, there is a "notch" in terms of getting on welfare: it frequently is advantageous to quit work because one's earned income is too high to get *on* welfare, and then return to work at the same wage. Even with the high tax rate, the total welfare benefit package is higher than low or poverty-level wages without the nonmonetary benefits (Garfinkel, 1977). This should not be taken to mean that income disregards are not an improvement, but rather that they widen the group who work but do not earn enough to escape from welfare or poverty. As we shall see, few women on AFDC have the skills and education to earn their way to independence.

In addition to incentives to go on or stay on welfare while working, welfare systems offer incentives to work while on welfare simply by giving recipients less than the state has declared that they need. About half the states do not pay the full standard of need, resulting in over 62 percent of AFDC families having budgets that recognize unmet needs (NCSS, 1974, Table 55): any amount earned up to the level of need is usually totally disregarded.

Altogether, the income disregards and notches that push welfare recipients to work, and low-wage workers to get onto welfare, could potentially be the modern equivalent of the Speenhamland Plan (Polanyi, 1969). That is, employers have no reason to raise wages, for there is no scarcity of low-wage workers and much incentive for those who are on welfare to seek employment. But there is much incentive to lower wages below subsistence level, since the worker will be paid the difference, at least minimally, by welfare. Thus, the creation of low-wage jobs is subsidized by welfare, making profitable manufacture and services that would otherwise be too costly to produce. This creates a class of workers who are forced onto welfare because their work pays too little, and a class of welfare recipients who are forced to work because welfare is inadequate.

THE WORK INCENTIVE PROGRAM (WIN)

Since the days of the Poor Laws, welfare has sought to force people to work. This has been done not only by stigmatizing the poor, as when seventeenth-century Pennsylvanians had to wear a "P" on their sleeves (for Pauper), and by benefit inadequacy, as in the principle of "less eligibility" wherein no recipient receives more than the lowliest worker. It has also been done by coercion. The workhouse and poorhouse were the nineteenty-century means; today's poor are coerced through

TABLE 2: Comparison of Occupational Distribution of AFDC Mothers,
          Female Family Heads, and WIN Institutional Training
          Positions

	Ever Employed AFDC Mothers (1967)	Fem. Fam. Heads With Work Experience (1970)	% In Occupational Group in Poverty	WIN Training Positions (1971-2)
Professional, technical managerial, official	2	17	9	10
Clerical and sales	14	33	12	41
Craftsman and operatives	12	12	46	22*
Private household workers	20	8	56	23
Other service workers	28	22	34	

*Listed separately in occupational training distribution as "processing, machine trades, bench work, structural work"
Source: Levitan, et al. (1972); Bureau of the Census (1976)

forced registration in the WIN program. Although WIN does not force all recipients to work, its implied promise of a route out of poverty is, for many, a cruel hoax. WIN contributes to the poverty of women in several ways, each of which is a variation on the theme of reinforcing rather than removing the handicaps that women face in the labor market.

First, WIN has promised much but delivers little for most women. Although many women on welfare are required to register for WIN, there are a number of stages between registering for WIN and obtaining employment: certification, determination of need for services, training, job placement, etc. Thus while there were 1,175,800 ongoing mandatory registrants in November, 1975, there were only 6,900 who left WIN that month for employment (including those who became employed on their own and not through or because of WIN: NCSS, 1976). The relatively small numbers who do reach training are disproportionately male and white, for example, those with the least handicaps in terms of race and sex in the labor market (Levitan et al., 1972).

Once in training, WIN enrollees find that the jobs that they are being trained for are ones that will not remove them from poverty.

As can be seen from the table above, almost half the training slots are for jobs which are in sectors that have very high poverty rates for women who head families.[7]

Third, in addition to placing small numbers of women, and providing them in occupations that frequently do not pay a living wage, WIN has been moving towards direct job placement (sometimes with "on-the-job" training), in spite of the fact that women in particular benefit from even minimal skill upgrading (Smith et al., 1975; U.S. Commission on Civil Rights, 1974). Most job training under WIN was classified as minimum—less than six weeks—or moderate—up to several months.

The bottom line in assessing WIN, however, is its ability to prepare participants to earn a living wage; in that it has failed. Those recipients who are able to find employment do not usually earn even a poverty-level wage.[8] Smith (1975) reported that the average salary was $5572 for women, and $6306 for men; perhaps even more discouraging was the fact that the net average increase in earnings for all program participants was $676 per year for women with little or no recent work experience and $41 for women with recent work experience. (Figures are from the Dept. of Labor, 1976, cited in Gordon, 1978; figures are similar for men.)

Since WIN does not train women for jobs that provide the means to economic self-sufficiency, it is not surprising that one of its outcomes is increased caseloads, and/or an increase in working welfare recipients. The study by Smith et al. of Chicago (1975) found that two-thirds of the ex-WIN female participants who were working received supplementary welfare grants, but only one-third of the male recipients. About a year and a half after completing the WIN program, a majority were working (58 percent) or had worked (16 percent), yet a majority were also still on welfare (70 percent).

The WIN program, whatever its phase, is thus a cornerstone of the "workhouse without walls." By taking a group of women who are already handicapped by low educational levels, low skill and occupational status, and giving them either no training or minimal training in fields that do not pay a living wage, and forcing them to work, WIN has created for many women a "no-win" situation. They cannot use welfare training programs to get decently paid employment, nor can they use paid employment to get off of welfare.

CONCLUSIONS AND IMPLICATIONS FOR POLICY

The problem of women in poverty has many aspects that should be mentioned. First, many of the disadvantages suffered by poor women are exacerbated by racism and prejudice for minority women. Such effects, however, are complex and uneven. Second, many of the economic problems of women are reinforced or increased by the indirect effects of being female and/or a single mother; for example, housing discrimination forces many women to live in "ghettos" which are far away from the better-paying jobs in the new suburban industrial parks.

Even without having explored the added handicaps of minority status or the additional indirect effects of gender, it is clear that the relative economic status of women is declining. This is true regardless of the income source. In spite of increased labor-force participation, the occupational ghettoization and discrimination has prevented any improvement in women's earnings relative to men. Child support, which rapidly increasing divorce and illegitimacy rates makes more important, is so minimal in reality that even the one- or two-child family runs a high risk of becoming poor if the father leaves. And welfare, although it supports more of the eligible population than ever before, does so at an even more penurious level than in the past (relative to the current incomes of American families in general).

Welfare's role in women's poverty is much more than simply one of penny pinching in payment levels, for it plays an important part in perpetuating women's poverty. We have maintained here that the Work Incentive Program and income-disregard programs are creating a "workhouse without walls," from which escape is increasingly more difficult. The welfare system has not only "bureaucratized" inequality (Street, 1978), it has institutionalized it. By uniting inequality in the labor market with the pauperization that is endemic to public welfare, the American system is creating a set of forces that oppress all women, as well as those that are already in poverty. For the same work incentives that "encourage" women on welfare to work at poverty-level wages are also the means of subsidization of a low-wage labor force enabling entire industries to pay poverty-level wages. By "training" and/or placing AFDC women in traditional, low-paying, predominantly female occupational ghettos, WIN programs not only perpetuate their poverty, but reinforce the barriers that many women face as they try to get jobs that pay a living wage but are traditionally male.

The major implication for policy of both the feminization of poverty and the increasing labor-force participation of welfare mothers is that gender cannot be ignored. That is, the poverty of men and the poverty of women are different problems, requiring different solutions. For men, the problem is more one of a high-dependency burden: in the New Jersey income experiment, the average number of children per family was four (Holimer, 1976), while nationally the AFDC-UP family averaged 4.4 persons. In contrast, an average AFDC female-headed family was 3.1 persons (NCSS, 1976; see also Ferman, n.d.). Male poverty is thus more often a welfare problem, that is, supplementing wages with some kind of family allowance for those with heavy dependency burdens. For women, however, the problem lies more with the labor market. Going to work, even full-time, is not likely to be the means of escape out of poverty for most welfare women.[9] Once welfare policy begins to treat female welfare recipients as disadvantaged workers, then it can begin to develop appropriate programs of intervention at the individual level (for example, training in traditionally male blue-collar occupations) and at the institutional level (aggressive action by the federal government against sex segregation of enterprises and even entire industries). Without such changes, we will continue to build a "workhouse without walls," and its inhabitants will become even more predominantly women who are trapped in a life of poverty by welfare penuriousness and institutionalized work-force marginality.

NOTES

1. This term will be used to connote those families in which there is only an adult woman and no adult male; likewise, "male-headed" will be used to refer to families in which there is an adult male, and perhaps an adult female. These are official Census Bureau terms, and not descriptions of intra-family dynamics.

2. This is probably an underestimate, for the poverty levels established by the Census Bureau assume that a male-headed family needs more money than a female-headed family of the same size; thus in 1972 the poverty threshold for a family of four (with three dependent children was $3902 if the family was headed by a male, but only $3715 if it was headed by a female (U.S. Commission on Civil Rights, 1974).

3. The ratio of female to male changes in an uneven pattern over time, as well as across industries.

4. Why is it that in a society that constantly investigates welfare recipients for fraud, no one enforces child support? It may be that this reveals something about the way in which marriage is still an economic institution. It is as if the husband's economic support before divorce was in "payment" for the wife's housekeeping, emotional support, and sexual access, but not for her childrearing activities, for it is only the childbearing activity that is continued after divorce, typically by the wife—93 percent of mothers receive custody of the children (The Urban Institute, 1976).

5. This does not include those who are: in training, awaiting training, awaiting placement, or looking for work. Thus the employment of a broader definition of "in the labor force" not limited to those currently and officially working would result in a much larger percentage of welfare mothers in the work force (however marginally).

6. Two caveats about this anomaly should be noted, however. First, there is little evidence that people consciously act in this way; rather it is probably an unconscious move that is difficult to reverse. Second, and perhaps more important, it only applies to women workers; men have an hours limitation (100 per month) on the amount that they can work and stay on welfare, whereas for women the only limitation is total earnings.

7. Of course, this table is only a gross indicator; it is expected that more detailed breakdown on both occupational distribution of AFDC mothers and WIN training positions would reveal even more reinforcement of occupational segregation. In addition, this limitation is carried through at the individual level.

8. By law, WIN participants may be placed in jobs that pay as little as 75 percent of the minimum wage (U.S. Commission on Civil Rights, 1974).

9. On the basis of a number of studies that the work ethic is alive and well among the poor, it is assumed that they want to work, so that what is taken as problematic is not whether the poor (or welfare mothers) are willing to work, but whether they can find jobs by which they can support themselves. See especially Goodwin (1972) and Holimer (1976).

REFERENCES

Appel, G. (1971) "The AFDC work incentives in Michigan." In Research and statistics as a management tool, proceedings of the eleventh workshop on public welfare research and statistics, August 8-11, Las Vegas, Nevada.

Bell, C. (1973) "Women and social security: contributions and benefits." In Economic problems of women. Hearings before the Joint Economic Committee, 93rd Congress of the United States, 1st Session, July 24-26, 30.

Bell, W. and D.M. Bushe. (1975) "The economic efficiency of AFDC." Social Service Review 49.

Blinder, A.S. (1973) "Wage discrimination: Reduced form and structural estimates." Journal of Human Resources 8.

Bureau of the Census, U.S. Department of Commerce. (1976) A statistical portrait of women in the U.S. (Current Population Reports, Special Study Series P-23, No. 58.)

Child support payments in the United States. (1976) Washington, D.C.: The Urban Institute.

Coser, R.L. and G. Rokoff. (1970) "Women in the occupational world: Social disruption and conflict." Social Problems 18.

Dahm, M.H. (1973) "Unemployment insurance and women." In Economic problems of women. Hearings before the Joint Economic Committee, 93rd Congress of the United States, 1st Session, July 24-26, 30.

Darian, J.C. (1976) "Factors influencing the rising labor force participation rates of married women with preschool children." Social Science Quarterly 56.

Farley, R. (1977) "Trends in racial inequalities: Have the gains of the 1960s disappeared in the 1970s?" American Sociological Review 43.

Ferman, L.A. "Welfare careers, low wage workers and sexism." New Research on Women (University of Michigan, n.d.).

Fuchs, V. (1971) "Differences in hourly earnings between men and women." Monthly Labor Review.

Garfinkel, I. (1977) "Welfare, what's right and wrong with it." Paper presented at The Center for the Study of Democratic Institutions, Chicago, Illinois, November 22.

Goodwin, L. (1972) Do the poor want to work: A social-psychological study of work orientations. Washington, D.C.: The Brookings Institution.

Gordon, N. (1978) "Women's roles and welfare reform." Challenge 20.

Gross, E. (1969) "Plus ça change . . . ? The sexual structure of occupations over time." Social Problems 16.

Holimer, M.R. (1976) "Excerpts from HEW, 'Synopsis of selected findings to date from the income maintenance experiments.' " In Research and statistics to meet today's needs and tomorrow's challenges: Papers from the sixteenth annual conference on welfare research and statistics, New Orleans, Louisiana, August 15-18.

Howe, L.K. (1977) Pink-collar workers: Inside the world of women's work. New York: Putnam.

Joint Economic Committee. (1976) "Welfare alternatives: A report with recommendations based upon the public welfare study of the subcommittee on fiscal policy." 99th Congress, 2nd Session, August 5.

Knudsen, D.S. (1969) "The declining status of women: Popular myths and the failure of functionalist thought." Social Forces.

Levitan, S., M. Rein, and D. Marwich. (1972) Work and welfare go together. Baltimore: The Johns Hopkins University Press.

NCSS (National Center for Social Statistics) Social Rehabilitation Service, U.S. Department of Health, Education, and Welfare. (1977) "Public assistance statistics, December, 1977." Washington, D.C.: U.S. Government Printing Office.

–––. (1977) "Public assistance statistics, February, 1977." Washington, D.C.: U.S. Government Printing Office.

–––. (1974) "Findings of the 1973 AFDC study, Part II-A: financial circumstances."

Nicol, H. (1975) "Preliminary findings of child support enforcement research." In Papers from the fifteenth annual conference on welfare research statistics, San Francisco, California.

Oppenheimer, V. (1970) The female labor force in the United States: Demographic and economic factors governing its growth and changing composition. Berkeley, Califirnia: Institute of International Studies, University of California.

Ornstein, M.D. (1976) Entry into the American labor force. New York: Academic Press.

Polanyi, K. (1957) The great transformation. Boston: Beacon Press.

Sawhill, I. (1976) "Women with low incomes." In M. Blaxall and B. Reagan. Women and the workplace: The implications of occupational segregation. Chicago: University of Chicago Press.

Shortridge, K. (1976) "Working poor women." In J. Freeman (ed.). Women: a feminist perspective. Palo Alto, California: Mayfield Publishing Co.

Sorkin, A.S. (1973) "On the occupational status of women, 1870-1970." American Journal of Economics and Sociology 32.

Smith, A.D., A.E. Fortune, and W.J. Reid. (1975) "Notes on policy and practice: WIN, work and welfare." Social Service Review 49.

Street, D. (1978) "Bureaucratization, professionalization, and the poor." In K.A. Gronbjerg, D. Street, and G.A. Suttles. Poverty and social change. Englewood Cliffs, N.J.: Prentice-Hall.

Suter, L. and H.P. Miller. (1973) "Income differences between men and career women." American Journal of Sociology 78.

Stromberg, A. and S. Harkess, (eds.). (1977) Women working. Palo Alto, California: Mayfield Publishing Co.

Treiman, D. and K. Terrell. (1970) "Sex and the process of status attainment: A comparison of working men and women." American Sociological Review 40.

U.S. Commission on Civil Rights. (1974) Women and poverty. Washington, D.C.: U.S. Government Printing Office.

Waite, L.J. (1976) "Working wives: 1940-1960." American Sociological Review 41.

Waldman, E. and B.J. McEaddy. (1974) "Where women work–an analysis by industry and occupation." Monthly Labor Review.

Wilensky, H. (1961) "Orderly careers and social participation: The impact of work history on social integration in the middle mass." American Sociological Review 26.

6

HUSBANDS AT HOME:
ORGANIZATION OF THE HUSBAND'S
HOUSEHOLD DAY

SARAH FENSTERMAKER BERK

Any concern with the work lives of women would seem to demand that we pay attention not only to their activities (both within and without the household) but also to the day-to-day actions of other family members. An examination of husband's household activities can give a clearer picture of the possibilities of effecting change in a system which is currently organized so that women bear primary responsibility for household labor and child care.

Various measurements of household work contributions by family members provide overwhelming evidence that wives contribute significantly greater amounts of labor to the maintenance of the household and family than either their husbands or children. (For contrasting approaches, see Blood and Wolfe, 1960; Berheide et al., 1976; and Robinson, 1977.) This hypothesis, that women are uniquely tied to household labor and child

AUTHOR'S NOTE: Thanks go to Richard A. Berk for technical advice and the construction of the comparative data on the activities of wives. Additional thanks go to Anthony Shih for data processing and Ai Chao for typing the manuscript. The research itself was supported by a grant from the NIMH Center for the Study of Metropolitan Problems (#MH 27340-01).

care, is supported by a number of different methodological approaches studying several types of families. Sociological research efforts range from broadly descriptive treatments (see Komarovsky, 1962; Lopata, 1971; Oakley, 1974) to determinations of household apportionments of labor (for example, Pleck, 1977; Berk and Berk, 1978). Researchers specializing in time-budget descriptions of daily life have focused on the relative time allocations to household labor by family members (Robinson, 1977). Others have studied the effects of alterations in the extrahousehold commitments of family members and variable family types and class in predicting "who does what" in the home, and in explaining the overall lack of participation by husbands.

Aggregate cross-sectional assessments of time allocation by husbands or a more standard analysis of task allocation relative to wives leads to the conclusion that husbands' household time is dominated by many activities other than household labor and child care. The questions which follow from this are: what are the other activities of husbands?—how are these activities typically organized, sequenced, and grouped? Further, how is the content and organization of their household time altered (if at all) by the presence of small children or the employment of their wives?

Much earlier research has been limited in its power to describe the actual contributions of husbands and wives. One problem is that investigators begin by collecting data from which only *cross-sectional* estimates of effort can be calculated. The most common approach is to ask respondents how much total time they allocate to a range of activities (Morgan et al., 1966), or ask respondents what tasks they perform (Oakley, 1974). While collecting diary-level data on sequences of activities, other researchers nevertheless aggregate the material and work with cross-sectional estimates (Robinson, 1977). Finally, although qualitative observational studies often report in narrative form the household activities undertaken by various members, the data collection and analysis have examined the "texture" of daily life rather than determined precisely how the day is organized. In short, there is little or no description and analysis of household activities as a dynamic process.

Domestic life, however, is not a series of randomly assorted tasks, but an ongoing process in which actions are dependent on temporal extra-household contingencies, the time-bound demands of members, and the necessary sequential relations among actions. Thus, it is important to study the activities of any household member in relation to external constraints and to the internal imperatives of the activities themselves.

This chapter will examine the household activities of husbands as they are structured in time. Variation in the organization of household time associated with family composition and wives' employment will also be described. Finally, a comparison will be made between husbands and wives in the organization, sequencing, and interrelationship of their respective activities.

METHODOLOGY

The data analyzed below were gathered from a national probability sample of 748 intact households in moderate to large urban areas in the United States as part of a study on household labor. Two distinctive components of the larger study were the immediate source of the data analyzed here.

Diary report forms were prepared for respondent wives on which they could chronicle their household activities for one 24-hour period.[1] When applied to the national sample, this method generated a list of 41,346 household activities which were then coded into 650 unique items. These were further collapsed into 157 categories of household activities. "Diary" data for husbands were also gathered from a random subset for 50 percent of the 748 intact households, and 348 husbands participated. In contrast to the more open-ended and self-administered diary instrument from wives, husbands were asked to undertake a card-sorting operation. From a group of 81 household activities, husbands selected those which had been undertaken and placed the activities in their order of accomplishment. Like the wives, husbands were also asked to comment on each task along a variety of dimensions (for example, time spent on the activity, feelings attached to it and the like).

Husbands sorted the same list of activities for two separate time periods. One was described as "today after waking up, but before the time you would normally go to work." The other time period was described as "yesterday evening after the time you would normally return from work." For purposes of this analysis, these time periods will be referred to as "morning" and "evening," respectively. While the open-ended diary instrument supplied by the wives generated specific information on starting and ending times for activities, the result of the sorting and ordering operation for husbands was a data set roughly comparable to that of their wives'. It represents a retrospective accounting of the sequencing of their activities.

Table 1 lists the household activities sorted by husbands for construction of their retrospective diaries. Based largely on direct observation and interview in a pilot study of households (Berk, 1976), the activities sorted by husbands were designed to reflect the kinds of routine tasks which household members undertake. It should be mentioned, however, that neither husbands nor wives were asked about activities which occurred on weekend days. For this study, specific attention was given only to routine, day-to-day household work and child care as they are embedded in other weekday household behaviors. Despite this intentional omission, however, one will note in Table 1 that a vast array of household activities and household labors are represented by the broad categories listed (for example, yard work, banking and finances, household repair or remodeling, cooking meals, and so on). Further, respondents were given the opportunity to include a task or tasks which were not on the sorting list, and these appear in the analysis as "unspecified activity."[2] Finally, husbands were also allowed to rank order duplicate tasks, if they were accomplished more than once in the relevant time period.

This study examines the ways in which the household activities of husbands are structured through the day. Thus, primary focus will be on data from their retrospective diaries. Since specific concern is with household labor and child care, atten-

TABLE 1: Household Activities Sorted by Husbands In Order of Accomplishment

1. Ate breakfast
2. Ate dinner
3. Ate snack
4. Bathed children
5. Called (specify whom)
6. Cleaned kitchen
7. Cleaned up after breakfast
8. Cleared dinner table
9. Combed hair
10. Drank coffee
11. Dressed
12. Dressed children
13. Dried dishes
14. Drove children to school or bus stop
15. Emptied garbage
16. Fed pet
17. Went to bank
18. Went to gas station
19. Got phone call (specify from whom)
20. Did household repair or remodeling
21. Left for work
22. Let pet out or in
23. Loaded dishwasher
24. Made beds
25. Made breakfast
26. Made coffee or tea
27. Made dinner
28. Made part of dinner
29. Made sack lunch
30. Made snack
31. Paid bills/handled finances
32. Played with children
33. Prepared for bed
34. Put away dinner leftovers
35. Put children to bed
36. Put dishes away
37. Put dishes in sink
38. Read book
39. Read magazine
40. Read newspaper
41. Rinsed dishes
42. Ran errand (where?)
43. Served dinner
44. Set table
45. Shaved
46. Showered or bathed
47. Straightened house
48. Talked with children
49. Talked with wife
50. Washed dishes
51. Washed up, brushed teeth
52. Watched TV
53. Went out (visiting, bowling, movies, etc.)
54. Went out for entertainment (Other than theater, movie or concert)
55. Wiped dinner table
56. Wiped stovetop or kitchen counters
57. Woke children
58. Woke up
59. Woke wife
60. Did yard work
61. Anything else (specify)
62. Handled banking (checking, savings, and loans)
63. Did household budgeting
64. Planned change in or around the house
65. Planned family activities
66. Prepared household records or paperwork
67. Talked with friends or neighbors
68. Wrote a note or a letter
69. Wrote a greeting or condolence card
70. Went to store
71. Studied (what?)
72. Read brochures, articles, catalogs, etc.
73. Did arithmetic
74. Went to theater, concert or movies
75. Visited friends or neighbors
76. Friends or neighbors visited
77. Went to governmental or official event or location
78. Wrote a list
79. Copied a document
80. Filed household records or paperwork
81. Helped children with schoolwork

tion will be given not only to description of husbands' activities, but also to variation in the content and organization of their household labor contributions. To that end, households comprised of unemployed wives, wives who are employed full-time, childless household, and households with young children will be scrutinized for their impact on the organization of husbands' "household time." Once the activities of husbands are described and examined for variation, diary data supplied by employed wives about their own activities will be compared. Thus, through the analysis of specific activities of husbands and wives three general questions will be addressed. First, what are the routine activities which husbands undertake and which structure their morning and evening hours? Second, how does the content and organization of these activities vary with the composition of households and the employment status of wives? Third, how do husbands and wives compare in the structure of their household time when both of them are employed full-time?

Any data collection method which is designed to produce rich detail and specificity about human behaviors will also bring with it problems of data reduction. Both the husbands' and wives' diary techniques provided a unique glimpse of household activities and much-needed detail on the sequential ordering of household labor and child-care tasks when embedded within the myriad other activities of households. However, since the study is concerned with "routine" activities, many activities which occur infrequently go unmentioned in the analysis of patterned behaviors. For example, a tiny proportion of the tasks which husbands undertake in the morning hours might involve yard work. But since the unit of analysis will be the household *activity* rather than the respondent himself, in this instance yard work would go unanalyzed as a feature of the patterned behavior in the morning period. Therefore, for analysis of both the husbands' and wives' diary items, for each kind of household in each time period, not all reported activities are actually considered. Only activities which constitute at least one percent of all activities recorded will be included. For instance, for families where wives are employed full-time, husbands report undertaking a total of 1,064 activities for the morning period, and therefore only diary activities which were reported at least 11 times will be analyzed when attention is given to those families. While it may seem that much data are sacrificed with this inclusion rule, one should also remember that such a criterion is quite "generous" in the sense that some relatively nonroutine activities may emerge and be included. In fact, analytic "nets" are cast widely.[3]

CLUSTERING ACTIVITIES OVER TIME

In order to dispense routine activities over time and explore longitudinal patterns in the ways activities are organized, it was first necessary to develop some aggregate measure of "when" each of the activities typically occurred. For each husband, retrospective accounts of activities were simply ordered from first to last, and a mean rank across husbands was used to provide a "typical" rank for each activity. In other words, the reported ranks for each activity were simply summed and then divided by the number of times the activity was reported to be accomplished. For the wives' diaries, the mean starting time was similarly calculated.

While sequencing of activities for husbands is based on mean ranks and the sequencing of activities for wives is based on mean starting times, the two summary measures are more comparable than might first appear. The analysis will be more concerned with "substantive time" (for example, "dinner time," "before dinner," and so on) than with "real time." It is a concern more with what activities are undertaken and what their sequencing relationship is to one another, rather than precisely the real time at which activities occur. Other analyses are underway where real time is taken far more seriously.

After examining what activities are undertaken and the order in which they occur, I will consider the issue of whether some subsets of activities are similar in the ranks they obtain. Are there some activities which might be characterized by low average ranks and therefore as "early morning" activities? Are there others which might be characterized by high average ranks and therefore associated with getting ready to leave for work?

In other words, by examining the ways in which average ranks tend to cluster, some typology of household activities (resting on the order in which activities occur) can be extracted from the data.

There are a variety of existing cluster procedures (Hartigan, 1975; Ryzin, 1977), but to date none rest on firm statistical justifications (Baily, 1975). Hence, clustering techniques are perhaps best viewed as descriptive algorythms whose relative strengths and weaknesses depend on the substantive application and the kinds of data available. In this context, Johnson's (1967) "hierarchical clustering" approach was selected because it allowed not only for observation of some single "best" arrangement of the activities, but also careful examination of how that arrangement was produced.

Unfortunately, the clustering process itself leaves unanswered how many clusters one should ultimately report as the "best" representative (for example, typology) of the cases. There are no significance tests to assess the chance patterns and no a priori criteria for what "best" might mean. Hence, one must rely on substantive hunches and post hoc rules which trade parsimony (the number of clusters) for heterogeneity (dissimilarity in distances within clusters). One tries to achieve a sensible balance so that there is a relatively small number of clusters, each of which includes similar cases. In the data reported here, for instance, one cluster might reflect activities which occur on the average around breakfast time and another cluster that reflects activities which occur on the average around dinner time.

In the clustering applications which follow, several *caveats* should be kept in mind. First, the clusters rest on mean ranks and therefore show typical patterns only. Not every family is accurately described. Thus, on the average, one might find that husbands read the newspaper after dinner, but read magazines shortly before retiring. Still, many husbands may not subscribe to this routine. Second, just because one applies hierarchical clustering does not mean that "clean" clusters will appear or that they will necessarily make substantive sense. Indeed, later we will see that while some sets of activities do seem to occur around the same time and appear to "belong" together on substantive grounds, others will not cluster clearly and/or will seem anomolous. (Note, however, that "fuzzy" clusters constitute findings.) Finally, clusters will be formally considered after the kinds of activities undertaken and the sequence of activities are examined. In an important sense, they are an extension of earlier issues rather than the lynchpin of the entire analysis.

THE HUSBAND'S HOUSEHOLD DAY

MORNING ACTIVITIES:
A COMPARISON AMONG HUSBANDS

Table 2 compares the morning activities of husbands who are childless with husbands who have *at least* an infant (less than three years of age) in the household. There may be older children in the household as well, but for purposes of simplicity, attention here is directed to those fathers who have at least an infant child.

For those husbands without children, an activity had to be reported at least 17 times, and 26 activities emerged. One will recall that the clustering procedure results in the grouping of activities which tend to receive the same mean rank and thus gives a good indication of the sequencing of activities which occur in close succession. For this table, and the ones that follow, differences in the mean ranks of specific activities *within* a cluster greater than approximately .20 are not likely to occur from chance. Moreover, differences between the *cluster* means do not represent chance results. Thus, for example, when considering morning activities, one would not bother about whether husbands wash up and brush their teeth before or after waking the children. The ordering of these activities is probably arbitrary (for these data). However, the sequencing of activities which begins with waking up, waking wife, waking children, showering, shaving and dressing is probably an accurate reflection of the general time-ordering and sequencing of the first few morning activities of husbands.

Turning first to the morning time period before husbands normally leave for work, there are three clusters of activities

with quite clear differences among them. Naturally, the first
activity reported is "woke up." Unlike the other activities
reported by husbands, the rank orders reported for the action
of waking up is not subject to the variation which characterizes
other tasks and which is reflected in somewhat inflated mean
rank scores.[4] The activity of waking up is followed shortly by
the personal grooming undertaken by husbands prior to going

TABLE 2: Husband Morning Household Activities By Household
          Composition

	No Children (#of Activities = 1,727)			Infants and Other Children (#of Activities = 1,001)	
Cluster	Content	$\bar{X}$ Rank	Cluster	Content	$\bar{X}$ Rank
1	Woke up	1.00	1	Woke up	1.00
2	Showered or bathed	3.01	1	Woke children	2.82
2	Woke wife	3.25	1	Washed up, brushed teeth	2.99
2	Shaved	3.75	1	Woke wife	3.17
2	Washed up, brushed teeth	3.97	1	Shaved	3.67
2	Made coffee or tea	4.28	1	Showered or bathed	3.80
2	Combed hair	4.39	Cluster 1 $\bar{X}$ = 2.91		
2	Dressed	4.41	2	Talked with wife	4.60
2	Talked with wife	4.42	2	Combed hair	4.77
2	Ate breakfast	4.70	2	Dressed	4.89
2	Made breakfast	5.04	2	Drank coffee	5.84
2	Drank coffee	5.14	2	Unspecified activity	6.37
2	Unspecified task	5.52	2	Made breakfast	6.48
2	Let pet out or in	5.83	2	Talked with children	6.52
2	Made beds	6.07	2	Let pet out or in	6.54
Cluster 2 $\bar{X}$ = 4.55			2	Made coffee or tea	6.55
3	Rinsed dishes	6.69	2	Ate breakfast	6.64
3	Fed pet	7.13	Cluster 2 $\bar{X}$ = 5.92		
3	Read newspaper	7.31	3	Watched TV	7.88
3	Left for work	7.41	3	Put dishes in sink	8.06
3	Cleaned up after breakfast	7.42	3	Played with children	8.11
3	Put dishes in sink	7.76	3	Read newspaper	8.53
3	Emptied garbage	8.35	3	Left for work	8.54
3	Went to store	9.65	3	Emptied garbage	8.68
3	Watched TV	9.72	3	Cleaned up after breakfast	10.57
3	Ate snack	9.93	3	Ate snack	10.59
3	Dried dishes	10.18	Cluster 3 $\bar{X}$ = 8.87		
Cluster 3 $\bar{X}$ = 8.32					

to work. In fact, cluster 2 represents a combination of those activities which surround the actions of rising, getting dressed, and eating breakfast. One can also infer that while other household members are preparing for the day, some husbands have started the coffee or teapot. The last activity in cluster 2 may represent the transition from the more self-involved activities of rising to the household contributions which characterize cluster 3. Along with "making beds" in cluster 2, cluster 3 also contains tasks which we might more readily label "housework:" rinsing dishes, cleaning up after breakfast, putting dishes in the sink, emptying garbage, and drying dishes. One would also assume that cluster 3 includes husbands who have just returned from work and who are able to eat snacks and watch some television. Despite their presence, however, cluster 3 is primarily defined by after-breakfast chores and leaving for work.

While such description provides a unique glimpse into the routine of childless husbands, the question posed is whether with the presence of small children in the household the activities of fathers significantly depart from those of childless husbands. Table 2 presents comparative data for fathers with small children. Here we see three clusters of 24 activities that not only include waking up, but also attention to other family members. Cluster 1 also contains those tasks associated with grooming in the first moments of the morning. Except for the activities of waking up and talking with children, the first two clusters for both types of families are substantially identical. So far, it is difficult to perceive any major differences in the morning activities of fathers versus childless husbands. Cluster 3 contains eight activities and, with the exception of the activity of "played with children," provides much the same picture as that of husbands without children. Here too, the primary activities are represented by a few breakfast and kitchen-related chores and leaving for work.

The conclusion one would draw when comparing these sets of activities is that morning routines are marked by their non-random patterning and sequence. Further, there is some evidence to suggest that very little is undertaken that is not directly related to the immediate imperative of going to work.

In short, there is little "extraneous" activity which focuses on tasks one might call household labor or child care. Finally, the ordering of husbands' morning activities are not fundamentally altered by the presence of a family member assumed to be quite demanding and likely to shape the activities of all household members. One must necessarily conclude that if young children have an impact on the content and organization of household morning activities, their fathers are not the ones who are affected in any but the most incidental ways.

Turning to another domestic situation in which husbands' morning activities might show important variation, Table 3 is designed for a specific look at husbands whose wives are unemployed and husbands whose wives are employed full-time. One might hypothesize a major difference between these patterns, since, in this case, both adults must leave the house at a certain time. In short, one might assume that the demands of wives' employment would remove the kinds of flexibility which a household with an unemployed wife might enjoy. The set of 22 activities for husbands with unemployed wives shows quite familiar patterns associated with rising, getting dressed, eating breakfast, and leaving for work. The only discernible difference between those whose wives are not employed and those whose wives are employed full-time is that, in addition to cleaning up after breakfast, some husbands with employed wives undertake the chore of making beds. Interestingly enough, this activity was one of the few housework tasks in which childless husbands also engaged. This activity may be primarily one undertaken by husbands when both adults are leaving the house at about the same time.

Regardless of the type of family being examined, there is a systematic and seemingly invariant quality to the morning activities of husbands. The impression one gets from looking at the husbands' household life—at least in the morning—is that little impinges on the necessity for completion of those tasks attached to leaving for work.

To get a complete picture of the variation in the household activities of husbands when they include the presence of small children or employed wives, one must also turn to evening

TABLE 3: Husband Morning Household Activities By Wife Employment
Status

	Unemployed (# of Activities = 3,102)			Fulltime Employed (# of Activities = 1,064)	
Cluster	Content	X̄ Rank	Cluster	Content	X̄ Rank
1	Woke up	1.00	1	Woke up	1.00
2	Woke wife	3.06	1	Woke wife	2.96
2	Washed up, brushed		1	Woke children	3.08
	teeth	3.23	Cluster 1 X̄ = 2.35		
2	Showered or bathed	3.41	2	Showered or bathed	4.21
2	Shaved	3.50	2	Washed up, brushed	
2	Combed hair	4.15		teeth	4.69
2	Dressed	4.21	2	Shaved	4.88
Cluster 2 X̄ = 3.59			2	Talked with wife	5.17
3	Made coffee or tea	4.74	2	Talked with children	5.60
3	Talked with wife	5.07	2	Dressed	5.71
3	Ate breakfast	5.12	2	Made coffee or tea	6.11
3	Drank coffee	5.35	2	Combed hair	6.35
3	Made breakfast	5.53	2	Made breakfast	6.41
3	Let pet out or in	6.04	Cluster 2 X̄ = 5.46		
3	Talked with children	6.11	3	Ate breakfast	7.39
3	Fed pet	6.41	3	Drank coffee	7.52
3	Read newspaper	7.20	3	Let pet out or in	7.73
Cluster 3 X̄ = 5.73			3	Unspecified activity	7.80
4	Put dishes in sink	7.78	3	Read newspaper	9.02
4	Left for work	7.89	3	Fed pet	9.09
4	Cleaned up after		3	Made beds	9.96
	breakfast	8.11	3	Watched TV	10.06
4	Emptied garbage	8.32	3	Cleaned up after	
4	Watched TV	8.74		breakfast	10.35
4	Ate snack	9.71	3	Left for work	10.37
Cluster 4 X̄ = 8.42			Cluster 3 X̄ = 8.93		
			4	Put dishes in sink	11.02
			4	Emptied garbage	11.75
			Cluster 4 X̄ = 11.38		

activities. Perhaps it is the case that, regardless of household
composition, the structuring of husbands' household activities is
less constrained than the morning period and perhaps more
vulnerable to alterations by the demands of others.

EVENING ACTIVITIES:
A COMPARISON AMONG HUSBANDS

Table 4 compares the evening activities of childless husbands
with those of fathers. These activities begin at the time hus-

bands would normally return from work. One will note first that some of the lowest mean ranks for childless husbands are represented by what looks like "morning" tasks. This probably represents the small number of husbands who are getting up to go to work. Not surprisingly, they then prepare for their "work day" by also getting dressed and combing their hair. These first few tasks in cluster 1 resemble some of the routine activities engaged in by most husbands in the morning, and represent a good example of the social imperatives which serve to define and sequence the household day. Despite this, the first cluster for both types of families is more completely characterized by predinner chores and the eating of dinner. However, one will note that for fathers there are a wider variety of tasks which are reported during this period. Husbands with small children report not only eating dinner and having after-dinner coffee, but some go to the gas station, talk to their children and wives, straighten the house, play with the children, or clear the table. This is the first time, therefore, that the presence of children seems to have the potential for altering the routine of husbands. They do not necessarily take on *more* household activities in the same period of time, but for many, after-dinner routine includes attention to the task of fathering.

In the postdinner period, childless husbands engage in many of the same activities as those husbands with small children. The tasks of the second cluster for both kinds of husbands contain the chores of pet care, putting dishes in the sink, and personal grooming. Both sets of activities also include phoning and watching TV. In addition, childless husbands set the table, (presumably for breakfast the next morning) and this suggests that employed husbands and wives may seek to get a "jump" on the next day by preparing early for the morning routine.

A clear difference between the husbands is illustrated in the third cluster. For husbands without children, this after-dinner period is characterized by leisure activities which demand relatively uninterrupted attention. Here, childless husbands read brochures, books, and magazines. The pattern for husbands with small children present is quite different. During the later-evening hours after dinner, these husbands are still engaging in a

TABLE 4: Husband Evening Household Activities By Household Composition

	No Children (#*of Activities = 2,075*)			*Infants and Other Children* (#*of Activities = 1,327*)	
Cluster	*Content*	*$\bar{X}$ Rank*	*Cluster*	*Content*	*$\bar{X}$ Rank*
1	Combed hair	7.30	1	Went to gas station	5.80
1	Dressed	7.79	1	Ate dinner	7.30
1	Talked with wife	8.08	1	Talked with children	7.84
1	Ate dinner	8.16	1	Drank coffee	7.86
1	Let pet out or in	8.22	1	Dressed	8.22
1	Woke up	8.93	1	Talked with wife	8.39
1	Made coffee or tea	9.24	1	Combed hair	8.59
1	Drank coffee	9.34	1	Made coffee or tea	8.75
Cluster 1 $\bar{X}$ = 8.38			1	Fed pet	9.12
2	Emptied garbage	10.10	1	Straightened house	9.13
2	Washed up, brushed teeth	10.13	1	Played with children	9.54
2	Cleared dinner table	10.17	1	Cleared dinner table	9.61
2	Ate snack	10.40	Cluster 1 $\bar{X}$ = 8.35		
2	Paid bills/handled finances	10.50	2	Read newspaper	10.37
2	Set table	10.59	2	Let pet out or in	10.56
2	Made phone call	10.61	2	Watched TV	10.65
2	Fed pet	10.64	2	Washed up, brushed teeth	10.78
2	Shaved	10.70	2	Put dishes in sink	10.87
2	Read newspaper	10.76	2	Made phone call	10.95
2	Watched TV	10.78	2	Ate snack	11.06
2	Put dishes in sink	10.95	2	Went to store	11.61
2	Made snack	11.30	2	Showered or bathed	12.09
2	Showered or bathed	11.58	2	Read book	12.12
2	Unspecified activity	11.97	2	Read magazine	12.14
Cluster 2 $\bar{X}$ = 10.74			Cluster 2 $\bar{X}$ = 11.20		
3	Read brochures, articles, catalogs	12.97	3	Ran errand	12.59
3	Rinsed dishes	13.14	3	Got phone call	12.94
3	Put away dinner leftovers	13.44	3	Emptied garbage	12.97
3	Put dishes away	13.61	3	Made snack	13.80
3	Went to store	13.71	3	Unspecified activity	14.65
3	Prepared for bed	13.78	3	Planned family activities	15.25
3	Read book	13.86	3	Prepared for bed	15.32
3	Read magazine	14.80	3	Put children to bed	15.48
Cluster 3 $\bar{X}$ = 13.66			Cluster 3 $\bar{X}$ = 14.12		

variety of tasks which include errands, phone calls, emptying the garbage, and planning family activities. In addition, putting children to bed becomes the last task of the evening. What seems to distinguish the two types of households is that the routine for husbands without children centers on more kitchen-related chores later in the evening (rinsing dishes, putting away dinner leftovers, putting dishes away) *and* more solitary leisure pursuits (reading brochures, books, and magazines). It may be that husbands with small children have traded both kitchen-related and leisure-time activities for others related to the tasks of child care (planning family activities, putting children to bed, and the like). Further, fathers may be more "mobile" than mothers tending to infants, and thus more likely to run errands.

Table 5 compares the evening activities of husbands with unemployed wives with husbands whose wives are employed full-time. One would expect that perhaps husbands whose wives are employed full-time might engage in fewer overtly leisure activities in the evening. We might predict that if both adults had recently returned from work, there would be less opportunity for husbands to simply rest, relax, read the newspaper, or wait for dinner. When comparing the first cluster for both types of families, one immediately notices a difference in the timing of dinner-related activities. Both of the first clusters are represented by husbands who are presumably waking up to go to work. However, there is a greater variety of activities in the cluster immediately following the arrival of husbands whose wives are employed. Further, on the average, husbands whose wives are employed engage in five more activities in the evening hours.

If one compares the *kinds* of tasks engaged in by the two "types" of husbands, some similarities are striking. Specific attention to household work tasks indicate that almost all the tasks in which husbands with unemployed wives engage in the postdinner period are also undertaken by husbands with employed wives. However, one should not fail to notice that these evening activities are done considerably later for those husbands who have employed wives and perhaps cannot enjoy the fruits of wives' afternoon labors. Both sets of clusters

TABLE 5: Husband Evening Household Activities By Wife Employment
Status

Cluster	Content	$\bar{X}$ Rank	Cluster	Content	$\bar{X}$ Rank
	Unemployed (#*of Activities = 3,878*)			*Fulltime Employed* (#*of Activities = 1,440*)	
1	Woke up	6.85	1	Woke up	8.58
1	Talked with wife	7.64	1	Made coffee or tea	9.93
1	Ate dinner	7.71	1	Combed hair	10.10
1	Dressed	8.11	1	Drank coffee	10.15
Cluster 1 $\bar{X}$ = 7.58			1	Talked with wife	10.15
2	Combed hair	8.56	1	Dressed	10.24
2	Cleared dinner table	8.57	1	Talked with children	10.43
2	Talked with children	8.61	1	Went to gas station	10.65
2	Played with children	9.00	1	Ate dinner	11.25
2	Drank coffee	9.25	1	Left for work	11.31
2	Let pet out or in	9.67	1	Read newspaper	11.60
2	Made coffee or tea	9.76	1	Fed pet	11.67
2	Fed pet	9.79	1	Let pet out or in	11.68
2	Read newspaper	10.00	1	Made phone call	11.71
2	Put dishes in sink	10.21	1	Watched TV	11.86
2	Made phone call	10.38	1	Shaved	12.26
2	Shaved	10.67	1	Washed up, brushed teeth	12.32
2	Ate snack	10.68	1	Went to store	12.44
2	Unspecified delivery	10.75	1	Paid bills/handled finances	12.67
2	Got phone call	10.86	Cluster 1 $\bar{X}$ = 11.10		
2	Watched TV	10.89	2	Set table	13.20
2	Washed up, brushed teeth	10.99	2	Straightened house	13.25
2	Ran errand	11.07	2	Emptied garbage	13.44
2	Made snack	11.44	2	Showered or bathed	13.72
2	Emptied garbage	11.61	2	Read brochure, articles, catalogs	13.89
2	Showered or bathed	11.68	2	Cleared dinner table	14.07
2	Went to store	11.68	2	Ate snack	14.20
Cluster 2 $\bar{X}$ = 10.28			2	Unspecified activity	14.35
3	Read magazine	12.28	2	Played with children	14.65
3	Read book	12.53	2	Put dishes in sink	14.87
3	Read brochures, articles, catalogs	12.78	2	Ran errand	15.39
3	Prepared for bed	13.94	2	Got phone call	15.45
Cluster 3 $\bar{X}$ = 12.88			2	Read magazine	15.62
			Cluster 2 $\bar{X}$ = 14.31		
			3	Made snack	17.08
			3	Wiped stovetop or kitchen counters	17.44
			3	Put away dinner leftovers	17.50

TABLE 5: Husband Evening Household Activities By Wife Employment
Status (Cont)

	Unemployed (#of Activities = 3,878)			Fulltime Employed (#of Activities = 1,440)	
Cluster	Content	$\bar{X}$ Rank	Cluster	Content	$\bar{X}$ Rank
			3	Prepared for bed	17.55
			3	Planned family activities	18.06
			Cluster 3 $\bar{X}$ = 17.53		

include kitchen-related tasks such as clearing the dinner table,
making coffee or tea, putting dishes in the sink, making snacks,
and emptying garbage. In addition, both sets of clusters are
represented by the tasks of running errands and child care.

Similarities end as one progresses through the activities for
the postdinner period. Husbands with employed wives engage in
more chores during the period in which leisure activities predominate for husbands with unemployed wives. Husbands with
employed wives set the table for breakfast, handle family
finances, straighten the house, wipe off kitchen counters, put
away dinner leftovers, or plan family activities. The final cluster
for each kind of household in Table 5 reveals the differences
between the two. Both report the task of preparing for bed as
the last of the evening. However, while the husbands with
unemployed wives engage in those leisure activities which require uninterrupted time, (reading magazines, books, brochures), husbands with employed wives are more likely to
engage in the kitchen-related chores.

When comparing the morning and evening activities of husbands overall, one is struck by a major distinguishing pattern.
The structure of morning activities suggests that they are not
randomly distributed through time. There is a shape and
sequence to the clusters which conveys considerable time con-
straint. Most of the activities involve the process of getting up,
getting dressed, and getting out of the house. In addition, the
presence of others does not seem to fundamentally shape the
activities of husbands. With the exception of waking the family

and talking with them, there are few tasks which would necessarily be determined by family members. In the main, activities center on the respondent himself, with little likely variation in the sequence of most of the clustered activities.

In contrast, the evening hours are much less constrained, as evidenced by the greater variation in the sorts of activities in which husbands engage. During this period only a minority of husbands must operate "as if" it were morning and go through the preparations for work. The evening is centered primarily on the cluster of activities surrounding dinner and slowly shifts to a set of activities almost completely defined by their leisure components. Again, the presence of others seems marginal to the activities undertaken, especially in the later evening hours when there are large blocks of recreational time devoted to reading.

However, of all the comparisons made between husbands, the differences in the patterning of their household routines generated by the employment status of the wife is most striking. The morning activities of husbands in general may be so constrained as to allow little alteration in patterning and sequence, regardless of family composition or characteristics. In contrast, the evening, with its array of less unconnected (although systematic) patterns of tasks, may allow for more discretion on the part of husbands to respond to shifting demands from others (children) or to extrahousehold commitments on the part of wives. In fact, in a much more detailed and dynamic way, these differences may recapitulate a finding cited by many who are concerned with the division of household labor: when wives are employed full-time there is, *ceteris paribus,* a small increase in the household labor contributed by husbands (see Berheide et al., 1976; Berk, 1976; Vanek, 1977). Table 5 illustrates *how* such an increase is revealed.

A COMPARISON OF HUSBANDS'
AND WIVES' ACTIVITIES

So far we have been concerned with how husbands' household time is arranged and patterned and how it varies under the two household characteristics of family composition and wives' employment status. We have seen that morning tasks are structured such that husbands give attention primarily to the activities surrounding preparation for the workday. In contrast, evening activities seem to respond in part to the presence of children and to the added demands of wives' employment.

While it is clear that household labor tasks more likely characterize the evening activities of husbands whose wives are employed, one wonders how the structuring of household time compares for husbands and wives. A variety of comparisons could be made, of course, yet this kind of analysis is much less suited to an exact specification of the division of household labor between husbands and wives. Insofar as the clustering of activities through time provides a picture of the processual qualities of domestic work life, it is a useful approach. However, more powerful techniques are available for analyzing the factors which determine the apportionment of household labor among members (see Berk and Berk, 1978). Therefore, for purposes of this discussion, I will compare the activities of only those husbands and wives whom one would assume to be *most alike* in the kinds of extrahousehold constraints which face them; that is, I will compare activities of husbands with employed wives with the activities of employed wives.

Table 6 reveals some immediate differences between the data generated from the wives' open-ended diaries and the more structured counterpart supplied by their husbands. Up to now, I have been discussing the way husbands' tasks have been rank-ordered. Notions of when tasks begin and end have been a rough approximation at best, based on the general relationship among activities (for example, "before dinner," "after dinner," and so on). With the wives' diaries, mean starting time is used as a summary measure for a more exact picture of how household time is structured. Therefore, when one compares data from husbands and wives, one has the luxury of understanding more completely how husbands' tasks are situated in time. Yet, one also runs the risk of attributing much more specificity to the husbands' data than is warranted.

TABLE 6: Husbands and Wives Morning Household Activities: Families
with Employed Wives

	Husbands (#of Activities = 1,064)			Wives (#of Activities = 1,501)	
Cluster	Content	$\bar{X}$ Rank	Cluster	Content	$\bar{X}$ Starting Time
1	Woke up	1.00	1	Woke up	6:33
1	Woke wife	2.96	1	Made coffee and tea	6:43
1	Woke children	3.08	Cluster 1 $\bar{X}$ = 6:38		
Cluster 1 $\bar{X}$ = 2.35			2	Drank coffee or tea	6:54
2	Showered or bathed	4.21	2	Ran dishwasher	6:55
2	Washed up, brushed teeth	4.69	2	Groomed	6:58
			2	Made lunch	7:00
2	Shaved	4.88	Cluster 2 $\bar{X}$ = 6:57		
2	Talked with wife	5.17	3	Cleaned bathroom	7:03
2	Talked with children	5.60	3	Dressed	7:06
2	Dressed	5.71	3	Talked with husband	7:07
2	Made coffee or tea	6.11	3	Made breakfast	7:08
2	Combed hair	6.35	3	Ate breakfast	7:08
2	Made breakfast	6.41	3	Woke children	7:11
Cluster 2 $\bar{X}$ = 5.46			3	Served breakfast	7:12
3	Ate breakfast	7.39	Cluster 3 $\bar{X}$ = 7:08		
3	Drank coffee	7.52	4	Made beds	7:18
3	Let pet out or in	7.73	4	Left house	7:18
3	Unspecified activity	7.80	4	Pet care	7:22
3	Read newspaper	9.02	4	Went to work	7:25
3	Fed pet	9.09	Cluster 4 $\bar{X}$ = 7:21		
3	Made beds	9.96	5	Dressed children	7:28
3	Watched TV	10.06	5	Read Newspaper	7:30
3	Cleaned up after breakfast	10.35	5	Driving	7:32
			5	Cleaned up after breakfast	7:30
3	Left for work	10.37	Cluster 5 $\bar{X}$ = 7:31		
Cluster 3 $\bar{X}$ = 8.93			6	Chauffeured children	7:48
4	Put dishes in sink	11.02	6	Paid work	7:49
4	Emptied garbage	11.75	Cluster 6 $\bar{X}$ = 7:48		
Cluster 4 $\bar{X}$ = 11.38					

Moreover, when husbands and wives are compared, the morning and evening activities of wives are divided into three time
periods rather than simply dichotomized like those of husbands'. The first set of activities covers the starting time from
5 a.m.–8:59 a.m. The other two time periods encompass the
evening activities; one for the starting time from 5 p.m.– 8:59

p.m. and the other from 9 p.m.–12:59 a.m.[5] Hence, Tables 7 and 8 compare all the husbands' evening activities with the early and late evening activities for wives.

It should be remembered that these comparisons are made for adult household members whom one would assume have much the same "objective" constraints impinging on them; both have to get up and go to work, both arrive home at roughly the same time, and both must repeat the cycle the following morning. Further, the comparison is made not simply between husbands who are employed full-time and wives who are employed full-time, but between the reported activities of husbands who have wives employed full-time and the reported activities of employed wives. Generally speaking, then, one could say that the data for husbands represent a subset of the activities occurring in the very households reported on in the wives' diaries.

Recall that one of the observations made about the structure of husbands' morning activities was that there seemed to be little variation and flexibility in the time alloted to preparation for work. Across all types of families, the primary morning activities for husbands centered on preparing oneself for the day. A somewhat different picture emerges for the wives. In Table 6, for example, one sees that almost immediately on rising wives begin some kitchen tasks. This is illustrated in the second cluster for wives where before 7 a.m. many of them have already prepared coffee or tea, run the dishwasher, and made brown bag lunches for her husband and/or children. The comprative cluster analysis allows us to see that the second set of activities for wives is defined by kitchen chores, where for husbands it is defined by the activities of personal grooming.

The third clusters for both husbands' and wives' morning activities are roughly comparable. Here, wives serve and eat breakfast, in addition to getting dressed and waking children. Husbands engage in activities associated with eating breakfast and reading the newspaper. However, one should also note in cluster 3 for the wives that a wide variety of tasks are begun during the period shortly after 7 a.m. For example, while she is getting dressed, the employed wife may also begin some light cleaning in the bathroom. Further, she may engage in conversation with her husband, make, serve, and eat breakfast, as well as wake the children. All of these activities seem relatively unconnected, although the sheer number of activities begun also conveys the time pressure associated with the job of getting oneself and the family ready for the day.

Comparing the third cluster of activities for the husbands and the fourth and fifth for the wives, differences in "after-breakfast" time are apparent. Husbands and wives engage in bedmaking and pet care, and by 7:25 the activity of leaving for work first appears for wives. After-breakfast chores continue for wives, combining the child-care task of dressing children, reading the newspaper, driving, and cleaning up after breakfast. The only comparable task found for husbands is participation in a clean-up after breakfast, although the husbands' tasks found in cluster 4 (putting dishes in sink, emptying garbage) may occur at this time. The morning activities for wives end at 7:49 with the task of chauffeuring children (presumably to school or day care) and going to work.

Even a rough comparison between the clusters of morning activities for husbands and wives illustrates some stark differences. When the morning activities for husbands alone were examined, the impression was given that there was little flexibility in the way tasks could be structured in time. In short, one might conclude that it would be difficult to expect husbands to perform any activities other than those associated with getting up and out of the house. However, an examination of the employed wives' activities indicate that a variety of household work and child-care tasks are of necessity "sandwiched in" among the identical tasks in which husbands engage (grooming, eating, and so on). The two structures of household time associated with the morning chores related to breakfast and pets are quite comparable. What separates the two morning routines of husbands and wives and what constitutes the compelling difference between them are the chores associated with child care. For the wives (as opposed to the husbands), child care and other household activities are inextricably bound together: there are no separate clusters which are defined by child care.

While it is not surprising to learn that wives and husbands differ in their attention to and responsibility for the tasks of child care (Berk, 1976), the comparison of how such activities are clustered in time and incorporated within the imperatives of other tasks vividly underscores the way the household work process is differentially structured for men and women, regardless of the similarities in their "objective" constraints.

A comparison of evening activities for wives and husbands appears in Tables 7 and 8. Recall that because of the collapsing of all evening activities for husbands and the dichotomized evening time periods for wives, the data for husbands in Tables 7 and 8 are identical. Consequently, in Table 7 attention will be given to the first two activity clusters for husbands as compared to the wives' activities for the period 5 p.m.–8:59 p.m.

TABLE 7: Husbands Evening Activities and Wives Household Activities,
5 p.m. – 8:59 p.m.: Families With Employed Wives

	Husbands (#of Activities = 1,440)			Wives (#of Activities = 1,412)	
Cluster	Content	$\bar{X}$ Rank	Cluster	Content	$\bar{X}$ Starting Time
1	Woke up	8.58	1	Made dinner	5:52
1	Made coffee or tea	9.93	1	Home from work	5:56
1	Combed hair	10.10	Cluster 1 $\bar{X}$ = 5:54		
1	Drank coffee	10.15	2	Set table for dinner	6:04
1	Talked with wife	10.15	3	Washed dishes	6:15
1	Dressed	10.24	3	Served dinner	6:17
1	Talked with children	10.43	3	Supervised children	6:17
1	Went to gas station	10.65	3	Arrived home	6:19
1	Ate dinner	11.25	Cluster 3 $\bar{X}$ = 6:17		
1	Left for work	11.31	4	Talked with husband	6:22
1	Read newspaper	11.60	4	Drank coffee or tea	6:24
1	Fed pet	11.67	4	Ate dinner	6:26
1	Let pet out or in	11.68	4	Dressed	6:28
1	Made phone call	11.71	Cluster 4 $\bar{X}$ = 6:25		
1	Watched TV	11.86	5	Wiped up	6:33
1	Shaved	12.26	5	Read newspaper	6:33
1	Washed up, brushed teeth	12.32	Cluster 5 $\bar{X}$ = 6:33		
1	Went to store	12.44	6	Instructed children	6:46
1	Paid bills/handled finances	12.67	6	Relaxed, rested	6:46
			6	Laundry preparation	6:48
Cluster 1 $\bar{X}$ = 11.10			6	Cleaned up after dinner	6:51
2	Set table	13.20	Cluster 6 $\bar{X}$ = 6:48		
2	Straightened house	13.25	7	Groomed	6:53

TABLE 7: Husbands Evening Activities and Wives Household Activities,
5 p.m. − 8:59 p.m.: Families With Employed Wives (Cont)

Cluster	*Husbands* *(# of Activities = 1,440)* Content	$\bar{X}$ Rank	Cluster	*Wives* *(# of Activities = 1,412)* Content	$\bar{X}$ Starting Time
2	Emptied garbage	13.44	7	Washed dinner dishes	6:55
2	Showered or bathed	13.72	7	Unspecified activity	
2	Read brochures,			in kitchen	6:57
	articles, catalogs	13.89	Cluster 7 $\bar{X}$ = 6:55		
2	Cleared dinner table	14.07	8	Ran dishwasher	7:00
2	Ate snack	14.20	8	Cleaned kitchen	7:00
2	Unspecified activity	14.35	8	Drove	7:03
2	Played with children	14.65	8	Other talk	7:03
2	Put dishes in sink	14.87	Cluster 8 $\bar{X}$ = 7:02		
2	Ran errand	15.39	9	Left house	7:10
2	Got phone call	15.45	9	Hobby	7:11
2	Read magazine	15.62	9	Paid work	7:15
Cluster 2 $\bar{X}$ = 14.31			Cluster 9 $\bar{X}$ = 7:12		
3	Made snack	17.08	10	Watched TV	7:22
3	Wiped stovetop or		Cluster 10 $\bar{X}$ = 7:22		
	kitchen counters	17.44			
3	Put away dinner				
	leftovers	17.50			
3	Prepared for bed	17.55			
3	Planned family				
	activities	18.06			
Cluster 3 $\bar{X}$ = 17.53					

One might expect that with the pressures of the morning
behind them, employed husbands and wives would be on more
"equal footing" in the evening. The first two clusters for the
wives are defined by the activities of arriving home and making
dinner. Within the time period between 5:52 and 6:04,
employed wives have arrived home, started the process of making dinner, and set the table. This is followed closely by dish-
washing, serving the dinner, and supervising children. (Note
again the necessary incorporation of child care into the other
household activities accomplished during this period.) For the
time immediately preceding dinner, there is no such pattern for
husbands. The first cluster represents those husbands who are

waking up to go to work, some who are talking with their children, or running an errand to the gas station.

Shortly after dinner, wives begin the process of cleaning up. Husbands have either begun to watch television, have left the house to go to the store, or are turning to household paperwork. Also during this period (at approximately 6:30), wives may take some time to read the newspaper. Examination of clusters 5 and 6 for the wives indicates that household work chores of dinner-related tasks and child care are embedded in periods of rest, relaxation, and reading. Four activities are begun during the period between 6:46 and 6:51: the instruction of children (perhaps with homework as the focus), relaxation, *and* the tasks associated with doing laundry and cleaning up after dinner.

Cluster 2 for the husbands also contains activities which involve household labor: emptying the garbage, straightening the house, and setting the table. However, cluster 7 for the wives, beginning at 6:53, includes after-dinner clean-up in earnest; washing the dinner dishes is begun, as well as another kitchen-related chore of a more general nature. These tasks are associated with the "husband" chores of clearing the dinner table and putting dishes in the sink.

Cluster 8 for the wives continues after-dinner cleanup with the tasks of running the dishwasher, cleaning the kitchen, and what one would assume is conversation after dinner occurring with kitchen chores. The third cluster for the husbands is represented by similar activities, with the tasks of wiping the stovetop or counters and putting away dinner leftovers dominating this cluster. The early evening ends for wives with some women leaving the household for paid employment and others alloting time to hobbies or watching television.

One of the most obvious findings from a comparison between husbands' and wives' early evening activities is that the clusters for husbands do not represent "clean" groupings of tasks. Unlike their wives, husbands have a wide variety of activities which can structure their routines, indicating the more flexible household responsibilities of husbands. In contrast, the clusters for wives represent clear and easily distinguishable clusters which seem much more ordered by the external constraints of household "events" (dinner, for example) and by the internal constraints of the tasks themselves (such as cooking a meal, followed by serving, eating, and cleaning up). In short, activities for sample wives do not exhibit the variation in a household routine where some wives watch TV, shower, bathe or read, while others set the table, straighten the house, and empty the garbage. What is clear from this comparison is that while some husbands with employed wives do considerably more household work than those whose wives are unemployed, there are still marked differences between husbands and wives in the flexibility of their routine activities through the day.

Table 8 compares the husbands' evening activities just reviewed with the late evening (9 p.m.−12:59 a.m.) activities of wives. Specific attention will be given to clusters 2 and 3 of the husbands' activities, since they represent the after-dinner period and are more comparable to the late evening activities of wives.

TABLE 8: Husbands Evening Activities and Wives Household Activities,
9 p.m. − 12:59 a.m.: Families With Employed Wives

Cluster	Husbands ($\#$ of Activities = 1,440) Content	$\bar{X}$ Rank	Cluster	Wives ($\#$ of Activities = 659) Content	$\bar{X}$ Starting Time
1	Woke up	8.58	1	Put children to bed	9:42
1	Made coffee or tea	9.93	1	Other talk	9:51
1	Combed hair	10.10	Cluster 1 $\bar{X}$ = 9.47		
1	Drank coffee	10.15	2	Watched TV	10:05
1	Talked with wife	10.15	2	Ate snack	10:09
1	Dressed	10.24	Cluster 2 $\bar{X}$ = 10:07		
1	Talked with children	10.43	3	Folded clothes	10:15
1	Went to gas station	10.65	3	Affect with husband	10:17
1	Ate dinner	11.25	Cluster 3 $\bar{X}$ = 10:16		
1	Left for work	11.31	4	Dressed	10:21
1	Read newspaper	11.60	4	Relaxed, rested	10:22
1	Fed pet	11.67	4	Read newspaper	10:25
1	Let pet out or in	11.68	4	Groomed	10:27
1	Made phone call	11.71	Cluster 4 $\bar{X}$ = 10:24		
1	Watched TV	11.86	5	Washed dishes	10:29
1	Shaved	12.26	5	Arrived home	10:30
1	Washed up, brushed teeth	12.32	5	Talked with husband	10:31
			Cluster 5 $\bar{X}$ = 10:41		

TABLE 8: Husbands Evening Activities and Wives Household Activities,
          9 p.m. − 12:59 a.m.: Families With Employed Wives (Cont.)

| | *Husbands* | | | *Wives* | |
| | *(#of Activities = 1,440)* | | | *(#of Activities = 659)* | |
Cluster	*Content*	*X̄ Rank*	*Cluster*	*Content*	*X̄ Starting Time*
1	Went to store	12.44	6	Went to bed	10:41
1	Paid bills/handled		Cluster 6 X̄ = 10:41		
	finances	12.67	7	Read − general	10:53
Cluster 1 X̄ = 11.10			7	To and from work	10:57
2	Set table	13.20	7	Slept	10:58
2	Straightened house	13.25	Cluster 7 X̄ = 10:56		
2	Emptied garbage	13.44			
2	Showered or bathed	13.72			
2	Read brochures, articles, catalogs	13.89			
2	Cleared dinner table	14.07			
2	Ate snack	14.20			
2	Unspecified activity	14.35			
2	Played with children	14.65			
2	Put dishes in sink	14.87			
2	Ran errand	15.39			
2	Got phone call	15.45			
2	Read magazine	15.62			
Cluster 2 X̄ = 14.31					
3	Made snack	17.08			
3	Wiped stovetop or kitchen counters	17.44			
3	Put away dinner leftovers	17.50			
3	Prepared for bed	17.55			
3	Planned family activities	18.06			
Cluster 3 X̄ = 17.53					

Beginning at 9:42, wives start the task of putting children to
bed. This is followed shortly by general family communication
and a transition to many more leisure activities than were
present earlier. What is striking about this period for the wives is
how much things have calmed down. Much of this probably has
to do with the absence of child-care tasks which tend to assume
a peremptory status over other tasks. In sum, in the seven
clusters which describe the wives' late evening routine, only

three activities could be roughly characterized as household work or child care.

While we have little way of knowing from this analysis exactly when husbands' activities occur in relation to their wives', one might infer that those husbands who engage in household labor in the evening may do some of their chores after the period when the wife has completed her work and left the kitchen. For example, in cluster 3 we see the tasks of wiping the stovetop or kitchen counters and putting away dinner leftovers. While this may represent the families who eat dinner later, and therefore clean up at a later time (there are wives who are washing dishes at 10:29 p.m.), it may also be that the household work of husbands is less constrained by pressure toward completion in order to do other tasks. For instance, if wives are primarily responsible for child care in the evening, they may feel compelled to complete their work in the kitchen prior to the childrens' bedtime demands. In the main, one must conclude that the late evening period is marked by leisure activities and the choice of husbands *and* wives to read, plan family activities, or watch television. As a parenthetical addition, I might add that despite the fact that the wives' activities represented here are those of employed women, there is little sense that late evening hours are the time to "catch up" on household labor. Such catching up may well be undertaken on weekends, as has been reported elsewhere (Robinson, 1977).

SUMMARY AND CONCLUSIONS

Detailed evidence from the literature on how Americans use time strongly supports the conclusion that wives allocate more total time to a large variety of household labor and child-care tasks. What this chapter sought to describe and clarify was the household time allocation by husbands; how the dynamics of such allocation varies among households, and how the structure of the household day differs for husbands and wives who are most similar in their extrahousehold responsibilities.

An examination of the retrospective diary accounts of husbands revealed activity around a great many tasks, even if one limited analysis to household work and child care. Among other activities, husbands engage in errand-running, planning family activities, kitchen chores, general straightening, and bill-paying. However, such diversity does not mean that household time is unordered, or the activities are randomly distributed through time. Indeed, one of the compelling findings which emerge from use of the clustering technique is that mornings and evenings take on distinctive patterns; these patterns seem determined both by household "events" (mealtimes) and events in the larger world which affect household arrangements (such as work, school, opening of shops, and so on).

One can conclude that the structuring of the husbands' household day is determined by many different forces. First, and especially in the morning periods, clusters of frequent activities reflect extrahousehold constraints. For husbands generally, the morning period of household time was almost exclusively devoted to the activities necessary to leaving the house. Second, a large variety of individual needs structure the dynamics of time use and sequencing. Need for sleep is an obvious example, but one would also include the allocation of time surrounding meals, as well as that of the "personal" tasks of getting up and getting dressed. Third, household time is also structured by the demands of the activities themselves. For example, a variety of kitchen tasks depend for their meaning on a relatively rigid sequence (for example, husbands cannot put the dishes in the sink until the meal is finished, or dry the dishes until they are washed). Fourth, some activities engaged in by husbands require a prolonged segregation from other tasks. While husbands may be able to eat breakfast, drink coffee, read the newspaper, and feed pets all in relatively quick succession, reading books demands more protracted attention. Consequently, some household time becomes structured around the demands of the activities themselves.

The factors described above generally apply to all household members; they can affect the structure of household time for husbands, wives and children. However, there are some distinctive characteristics of husbands' activities which also emerged. The general picture of all of the husbands' activities indicated that there was little flexibility in the ordering of their morning tasks, particularly those connected with preparing to leave for work. What the morning clusters illustrated was the process behind a conventional situation: husbands are fundamentally dependent on the household labor of wives. A comparison of childless husbands and fathers with at least small children showed too that this patterning and sequence of morning activities stood firm, despite the presence of small children. While the impact of children was hard to discern, this is not to say that some husbands engaged *only* in the more self-involved tasks of grooming and eating. Significant mention was made of the tasks of cleaning up after breakfast, putting dishes in the sink, and emptying garbage. Morning activities of husbands with employed wives were also compared to those of husbands with unemployed wives. Little difference between the two emerged, other than in the task of making beds.

Evening activities showed considerable variation among husbands across different family types. For example, childless husbands have a much less complicated predinner evening period than fathers with small children. Fathers undertook more different kinds of activities during this period and, in addition, the fathers' tasks of child care (although they were primarily recreational) indicate a significant difference in the structure of household time between childless husbands and fathers. What also distinguishes these husbands is that for post-dinner activities, husbands without children included more kitchen chores and more solitary leisure pursuits. It was concluded that husbands with small children may have traded both kitchen chores and leisure activities for some attention to child care.

Evening activities for husbands with employed wives also illustrated that the structure of the husbands' household day can be variable. Most obviously, the timing of evening activities suggests that husbands with employed wives begin all tasks later and crowd more activities into the evening than do husbands whose wives are unemployed. Interestingly enough, the husbands with employed wives do not include those recreational tasks which demand uninterrupted attention. They are more likely to be engaged in postdinner kitchen chores than those with unemployed wives.

Consequently, while the morning activities of all types of husbands show real similarities, evening activities show great variability. Clearly, the evening is the time when the demands of extrahousehold commitments may not loom so large and when the demands of other family members might show their effects. Both the presence of small children, as well as the outside employment of adult household members, could (in theory) show some impact on the husbands' evening activities. Attention exclusively to husbands suggest that their household "days" are not so harried, or rigidly demanding to preclude additional tasks or a fundamental rearrangement of task sequence. Moreover, while this paper did not take as its mission the comparison of husbands' and wives' relative *task* allocation, a brief comparison between the household days of husbands and wives revealed two clear differences.

First, the tasks and activities associated with child care invade the structuring of both morning and evening activities of employed wives. One gets the impression from the clusters describing the time allocation process for wives that at any moment a child-care task may preempt both the order and arrangement of other activities. This is not the pattern for husbands, who (especially in the morning) seem impervious to the demands of children and their impact on the ordering of other household activities.

Second, if one compares the sheer numbers of household work tasks undertaken by husbands and wives in the evening, they seem on more equal footing. While there are still obvious differences in the ways child-care tasks structure (and restructure) evening hours, both adult members arrange most of their evening activities around kitchen-related chores. However, the dinner-related tasks which appear for the wives represent a much more homogenous patterning. A wider range of activities appear for husbands during this period. Consequently, the patterning of the husbands' household day, regardless of the constraints placed on them by other household members, may be more flexible. In principle, the husbands' household day could be subject to more significant alteration than that of their wives.

This analysis implies a great deal about the possible changes which might be associated with husbands' household activities. Clearly, husbands are often constrained by their responsibilities to the outside world. Yet, we have seen that their wives are also constrained. And, one may conclude that the structuring of domestic life for husbands illustrates the secondary investment made to household labor and child care. However, one must also conclude that it is not primarily the imperatives of the outside world, nor the kinds of household activities undertaken, which most significantly generate the shape and sequence of their domestic lives.

Most important, the analysis of the longitudinal dynamics of household time allocation shows that there are both limits to and points of possible change where husbands might respond to additional and more "productive" uses of their household time. Specifically, this analysis clearly reveals that the household time of husbands could well include more attention to the demands of children, which at present do so much to interrupt, deter-mine, and reorder the activities of their wives. Finally, the differences between husbands with employed wives and those without suggest a relatively vast yet untapped potential for social change requiring a reorganization of much of the hus-bands' household day.

NOTES

1. The diary report form required respondents to write down each of their household activities in as much detail as they could manage. For *each* activity listed they were also asked: (a) starting and ending time; (b) whether they felt the activity was work, leisure, a combination of both, or neither; (c) who, if anyone, was with them when this activity was accomplished; (d) who, if anyone, was helping them; (e) who, if anyone, was just keeping them company; (f) whether they were watching or listening to television, radio, etc.; (g) whether they felt the activity was pleasant, tiring, boring, satisfying, difficult, unpleasant, frustrating and/or one with no feeling attached.

2. These additions were too few in number and too diverse in character to warrant separate categories of activities.

3. In addition, the one percent rule provides a modicum of stability in the estimates used in the analysis.

4. This results from the existence of a lower bound of 1.0. Hence, it is "harder" to obtain a low mean rank.

5. This was necessary to reduce the chance of using a single mean starting time to inaccurately reflect a bimodal distribution. Wives, for example, might set the table for dinner at 5:30 p.m., and again (for breakfast the next morning) at 9:30 p.m. This was not a problem in the husbands' data, since few activities were repeated.

REFERENCES

Baily, K.D. (1975) "Cluster analysis." In D.R. Heise (ed.), Sociological methodology. San Francisco: Jossey-Bass.

Berheide, C.W., S.F. Berk, and R.A. Berk. (1976) "Household work in the suburbs: The job and its participants." Pacific Sociological Review 19.

Berk, R.A. and S.F. Berk. (1978) "A simultaneous equation model for the division of household labor." Sociological Methods and Research 6.

Berk, S.F. (1976) "The division of household labor: Patterns and determinants." Unpublished Ph.D. dissertation, Northwestern University.

Blood, R.O. and D.M. Wolfe. (1960) Husbands and wives: The dynamics of married living. Glencoe, Illinois: The Free Press.

Hartigan, J. (1975) Clustering algorithms. New York: John Wiley.

Johnson, S.C. (1967) "Hierarchical clustering schemes." Psychometrica 32.

Komarovsky, M. (1962) Blue-collar marriage. New York: Random House.

Lopata, H.Z. (1971) Occupation: Housewife. London: Oxford University Press.

Morgan, J.N., I.A. Sirageldin, and N. Baerwaldt. (1966) Productive Americans. Ann Arbor: Institute for Social Research, University of Michigan.

Oakley, A. (1974) The sociology of housework. New York: Pantheon.

Pleck, J.H. (1977) "The work-family role system." Social Problems 24.

Robinson, J.P. (1977) How Americans use time: A social-psychological analysis of everyday behavior. New York: Praeger.

Ryzin, T.V. (1977) Classification and clustering. New York: Academic Press.

Vanek, J. (1977) "Housewives as workers." In A.H. Stromberg and S. Harkess (eds.), Women working. Palo Alto: Mayfield Press.

7

JOB-SHARING COUPLES

WILLIAM ARKIN and
LYNNE R. DOBROFSKY

In industrial societies part-time employment is the most common paid work arrangement of women. In the 1970s, 67 to 90 percent of part-time workers are women. The International Labor Office reports that in Austria women compose 78 percent of the part-time labor force; in Australia, 447,000 women and only 110,600 men work part-time; in Canada, 67 percent of the part-time workers are women; 85 percent of the part-time workers are women in Japan; in Norway, almost 90 percent are women; and in the United States, out of almost 11,000,000 part-time workers in 1971, 7,241,000 are women; France has 977,000 part-time women workers contrasted to 215,000 part-time working men (International Labor Office, 1973). The majority of part-time working women are married; in the United States, 4,500,000 of the 7,241,000 were reported married and a majority have dependent children.

Along with women, young students, the elderly, and the disabled dominate the part-time work population. Looking at the demographic characteristics of those who engage in part-time employment, it becomes obvious that the social status assigned the part-time worker in industrial societies is low. This is a function of the work ethic which values full-time (that is, maximum) productivity measured by hours and pay. The low status of most-part-time work fills the dual purpose of providing workers for disvalued work and providing some work for disvalued individuals whose productivity is not highly respected. The opportunity to ascend the work-status ladder—which provides upward social mobility—is denied them.

Although part-time work can and does occur at all levels of employment, it mainly occurs at lower levels of status and pay and involves monotonous work. Pressures from the feminist movement in the form of legislative and judicial action mandating equal pay for equal work, and affirmative action to rectify past discrimination, have forced a reexamination of the relationship between work and "feminity." It is apparent that protective welfare legislation for women, youth, and the elderly has primarily resulted in a pattern of exclusion from equal participation in the work force. The type of paid work considered appropriate for women (part-time, low-entry, dead-end) has been increasingly questioned and deplored.

Other social movements, such as the civil rights movement, the counterculture of the '60s, and the grey panthers, have increased the attention given to upgrading part-time employment and to increasing alternate and flexible work options. At the same time, attitudes toward work, leisure, and education are changing (Long, 1977).

Experimentation and research on flexible working systems, permanent part-time employment, family work-sharing (Grønseth, 1970, 1972, 1975) and dual-career families (Rapoport and Rapoport, 1971a, 1971b, 1977) were well underway in Western Europe by the early 1970s, when American industry and business, prompted by changing demographic conditions, a nonexpanding economy, low morale, and reduced productivity, began to experiment with modified work patterns. Communes, cottage industries, and work collectives were popular during the 1960s and corresponded with the focus on alternative lifestyles. Today people demand increased individual options regarding work in order to achieve a personal balance between work, leisure, family, and education. This is particularly true among the professional and semiprofessional workers. In recognition of these changing demands, President Carter, in an address to the First Women's Action Agenda in November 1976, stated that he would

> Encourage—actively and aggressively—the adoption in the federal government and in the private business sector, of flexible working hours for men and women, and . . . take action to increase the availability of part-time jobs, with proper provision for fringe benefits and for job security [Long, 1977].

PART-TIME WORK MOVEMENT

Organized interest in part-time employment is directed at upgrading part-time work. Job restructuring is urged to change the status from temporary to permanent, to provide fringe benefits on a prorated basis, to enable job mobility, and to establish some means whereby privileges ordinarily available to full-time workers are available to those who work part-time. Organizations (such as Catalyst, Advocates for Women, New Ways to Work, National Council for Alternative Work Patterns), communications networks, conferences, publications, and legislation promote these changes. Currently, eight states—Alaska, California, Colorado, Connecticut, Maryland, New York, Oregon, and Wisconsin—have legislation pending or government programs experimenting with permanent part-time, and four of those states—California, Colorado, Oregon, and Wisconsin—are experimenting with job-sharing projects. The federal government has enacted legislation on flexible and compressed work schedules as well as the Part-time Career Opportunity Act for civil service positions, with the Hon. Patricia Schroeder acting as the primary force behind such change in the Post Office and Civil Service Subcommittee on Employment Ethics and Utilization.

Those who are represented by the part-time work movement include women who are reentering the workplace but do not wish to work full-time, dual-career couples who are faced with an increasingly difficult time finding two full-time jobs (that is, in the same university or even in the same town); persons with cardiac and other medical problems who are instructed to return to work but on a part-time basis; and persons ideologically committed to maximizing time for private, nonwork-related interests.

The economics of part-time work, no matter what the range of benefits, restrict it to professional, semiprofessional, and management-level workers who can adequately subsist on the reduced income without economic stress. While the expenses of working do not necessarily decrease with part-time income, part-time proponents value the perceived or real opportunity to manage their time and pursue additional experiences. Individuals who are presently drawn to the part-time worker movement have evaluated their personal, familial, and career priorities. Occupation, rather than being the primary source of personal fulfillment (Rapoport and Rapoport, 1977), is of lesser or equal importance to family and/or other sources of fulfillment.

These ideas and beliefs chalenge traditional, mandatory lifetime traps which relegate work to the middle years and force the young and the old to experience poverty in vocational and financial areas of life (Wirtz, 1977; Kreps, 1977). They have stimulated policy researchers to reexamine the old problems of youth unemployment, forced unemployment of retired persons, and underemployment of our nation's resources and potential. The personal rewards for various persons working part-time during certain periods in the life cycle suggest that flexibility in the youth/education/retirement cycle is likely to enhance rather than waste our nation's human resources. Because of this general reevaluation and/or redefinition of the work ethic and its traditional applications, job sharing, flexitime, permanent part-time, and job restructuring are being tried and studied.

It has been stated that

> Flexible working systems and part-time arrangements have many implications for family life. Because of the conflicting demands of work, home and other factors, it is generally acknowledged that there is now a great amount of stress on families [Long, 1977].

The close interplay between work and family life (Bernard, 1972; Rapoport and Rapoport, 1977, 1978; Grønseth, 1970, 1972; Arkin and Dobrofsky, 1978a, 1978b) has followed a course of changing role ideologies similar to work changes beginning in the 1950s. Bernard's analysis of role ideologies recognizes that considerations of effects on family life are absent from research and policy on work:

> The one-role ideology is based on traditional gender-role rigidity where the domestic role was the only one appropriate for women and the provider role belonged to men [1972:236].

The shift to "the two-role ideology" gained impetus from the basic recognition that modern industrialized society could no longer ignore women's essential contribution to the economy. The net effect of the new views of "family and work roles of both men and women has been the emergence of a shared role ideology to be implemented by some form of part-time work for both men and women" (Bernard, 1972).

Glazer (1978), writing on the family and the fallacy of alternatives, and Lopata (1978), commenting on work, arrive at the same basic conclusions regarding the obvious exclusion of family needs and variations from policy considerations. Lopata writes:

> The main point . . . is that society, and especially its business and otherwise employing community have not created policies making it easy for people to live multi-dimensional lives with flexibility over the life course.

JOB-SHARING COUPLES

Job-sharing couples are part of the part-time movement. They present a unique population for studying the integration of the family unit into the work domain; or the converse, the integration of the work ethic into family life. The family or "mom and pop" business and farming have provided similar situations which integrate work and family; however, working for wages adds a new dimension. Job sharing implies equal status for both working members with equal division of labor rather than the unequal division of labor which exists in most family enterprises.

Job-sharing couples are married or cohabitating individuals who are sharing less than two full-time equivalent positions. The couples focused on in this chapter are the result of two studies. The first consisted of couples in professional occupations: clergy, journalists, teachers, academicians, social workers, and administrators. The second study consisted only of academicians and their employers; 42 colleges and universities across the country, including prestigious public and private institutions as well as lesser known teaching institutions, were represented.

Most of the couples reported that their introduction into job sharing resulted from situational circumstances, either the unavailability of two positions or the unwillingness to become two-location families or commuting couples. Regardless of the circumstances and the initial desire for full-time dual careers, the couples generally chose to share a position rather than compete for one. As couples considering available alternatives, they are motivated toward a cooperative rather than a competitive venture and a shared-role ideology rather than a "his" and "her" orientation. Having experienced job sharing even with the relative difficulties, most of the couples stated they would not consider any other work arrangement today unless forced into it through economic or other personal difficulties.

The couples report a sense of liberation from the time constraints of work, with adequate nonwork time being available to pursue leisure and professional activities without experiencing the pressures of full-time work or domestic responsibilities. Nonwork time is defined as surplus time for self-management; this is contrasted to former feelings of being a "marionette" to externally imposed schedules. The academic couples, compared to the other job-sharing couples, regard this nonwork time *not* as free or leisure time, but as an opportunity to engage in professional activities such as research and writing.

Interpersonal relationships are affected by the job-sharing arrangement on various levels. Rigid gender-role divisions of labor are weakened, permitting cooperative processes to predominate. Varying degrees of movement *away from* gender-specific roles *toward* a shared-role ideology become gradually operationalized. Cooperative relationships are also influenced by flexibility, which appears to be a symbol of freedom to pursue professionalism, parenting, and/or other activities either individually or together.

Intimacy and spontaneity in the form of enhanced sexual relations is a frequent response of the couples (see also Catalyst, 1973). As a result of increased nonwork time and flexibility in scheduling and arranging priorities, intimate relations gain high priority; yet in a temporal sense, they are low in priority in that they usually give way first to work responsibilities and second to domestic duties and schedules.

Dual parenting is one of the more immediately recognized advantages for job-sharing couples. The opportunity for men to experience sole parenting responsibility while women are at work is new and provides for a sharing of parental responsibilities. Likewise, the economic role of breadwinner is shared by both working partners.

At this stage in the research, there appears to be one major drawback of job sharing for couples: reduced income. This can introduce unfamiliar economic hardships, particularly for those couples earning $15,000 or less per year. That full benefits accompany the single income may neutralize some of the economic stress. Furthermore, in partial recognition of the economic limitations, some employers are adjusting shared jobs/ positions to make one position equivalent to one and one-third or one and one-half.

Few of those in the lower annual-income range report moonlighting or free-lancing to supplement their income. This unexpectedly small amount reflects less the desire than the small-town situation in which many of these couples find themselves (for example, Oberlin, Ohio; Storm Lake, Iowa; St. Peter, Minnesota; Appleton, Wisconsin; Galesburg, Illinois). While reduced income is threatening to some couples, two considerations intervene in other situations: (1) there may be little or no change in family income *if* the woman was not working (for whatever reason) prior to the job sharing and/or if job sharing means that both persons could work (albeit part-time) in favor of one being able to work full-time and one not being able to work at all; and (2) reevaluating the meaning and priority of work, a feature of the movement toward alternative work patterns, includes a revised view of financial gains (less is more)—this is a major factor in making the decision to job share.

Not an obstacle, but an important hurdle of job sharing is confronting the competitive processes so dominant in our society and in our socialization. In achieving professionalism, the partners have already demonstrated a competitive spirit and drive. Operationalizing cooperation between equals may be extremely difficult, especially between woman and man who occupy unequal positions in our society. Adjusting the intimate relationship to reflect the structural equality of colleagues sharing a job may be difficult for some. The majority report that they are able to overcome hurdles stemming from competition by sharing activities whether work related (teaching classes, attending faculty meetings, attending professional conferences) or domestic related (child care, errands, meal preparation.)

Studies investigating the various advantages and problems have found the part-time work pattern, at least for women, to be correlated with high marital satisfaction. It is interesting to speculate that job sharing, while not traditional, keeps women in a nonthreatening work pattern and perhaps the greatest adjustments concern men and their nontraditional work status when job sharing. When we look at the different advantages for women and for men, this seems to be the case.

Spillover effects of the cooperative ideology are noted, primarily by teaching faculty. One couple explains the significance of the impact that job sharing has on others:

> The paucity of women professors is one reason; the virtual non-existence of wife-husband combinations is another. Both men and women students benefit more than we expected from the interaction of a team like ours. That they see something novel and important seems clear. What they see is behind their eye-balls, but we hope it is neither Tarzan-Jane nor Maggie-Jiggs. We hope it is the cooperation of equals. Such cooperation seems to be contagious [Carmody, 1975: p. 32].

The couples' children grow to know a working mother (part but not full-time), a working father (part but not full-time), and parents working together as an equal team. Colleagues who commonly function within the one- or two-role ideology are also exposed to alternate models of marriage and work.

EMPLOYERS

As employers, the colleges and universities included in our study of academia show substantial variation in their responses to job sharing as a work pattern and to job-sharing couples. The responses ranged from one institution demonstrating a commitment to job sharing, employing five couples, and developing formal procedures and policies to insure equity in the areas of fringe benefits, promotion, retention and tenure to another that stated "no jobs should be shared" and "We like our employees at all levels to be sufficiently dedicated to their jobs—to take *total* responsibility for the way it is performed."

Several reported no job sharers either in the past or present. These reports were particularly interesting, since only institutions which were known and confirmed to have job-sharing couples were contacted. Several conclusions can be drawn from the institutions not reporting job sharing. One is that the majority of the institutions currently employing job sharers use existing part-time policies and procedures for part-time employment; therefore, married couples may be identified only as part-time employees and the academic deans may not be aware of or identify them as a job-sharing couple. Another possible explanation is a split between departmental policy and institutional policy whereby departments will embark on job sharing using current part-time or reduced teaching load policies to hire a job-sharing couple to avoid confrontation with deans of faculty or senior administrations. Though this may be adequate and within the purview of the department chair, future questions regarding promotion, retention, and tenure are left in a vacuum. It should be noted, however, that the majority of the institutions where senior administrators stated no positions were shared were, in general, opposed to job sharing and permanent part-time employment, claiming that people who do not work full-time are not committed.

Since few of the schools had more than two known couples and none were systematically evaluating this work alternative, we had to conclude that the majority of the responses reflect ideological commitments and impressions rather than substantial experiential data.

In the majority of cases, employers included in the disadvantages increased fringe benefits and administrative detail, while only a few identified worker exploitation and less worker continuity as disadvantages. They also believe that advantages to the institution are primarily in the areas of increased resources and greater flexibility. Job sharers when compared to the average full-time worker, were rated as more productive, more satisfied with their work life, and less prone to absenteeism. In most situations, however, these advantages are attributed to the quality and uniqueness of particular job-sharing couples and are not perceived as characteristic of this work. The remaining institutions tended to report no difference between job sharers and full-time employees.

Generally, employers, employees, and peers all state that job-sharing couples put in up to 50 percent more time and are more productive than their counterparts occupying a single position. Although the institution does not require the additional labor, job-sharing couples feel it is necessary to preserve the work structure and prove their joint ability. They do admit that the additional work investment and time commitment produces less strain on them than on the full-time employee because of their cooperative orientation and schedule flexibility. One issue is whether or not employers would continue to hire them if they were not "over-achievers."

The reporting schools had employed job sharers for an average of three years, with three institutions reporting periods in excess of five years. The data from the employers was difficult to assess because of the fluid state of job sharing and the absence of policy in this area. With several exceptions, where firm policies do exist and a commitment to job sharing is evidenced, most agreements are worked out formally by letter, are realized in modifications to contracts, or are informal agreements between the university and the couple. In those institutions reporting four or more job-sharing couples, the process of implementing formal policies has begun.

There are no established patterns regarding promotion, tenure, and retention, and in several situations one member of the team has been promoted and/or tenured while the other has not. The slowness in developing procedures and formal structures to extend corporate and university employee rights and privileges to job sharing couples is typical of the absence of protection for *temporary* part-timers. For permanent, part-time employment, more rights are being granted. Historically, the underlying rationalization for denying part-time employees equal renumeration, benefits, and protection has been the belief that the employer is doing the employee a favor; that is, allowing mothers to parent, youth to go to school, and the elderly to supplement retirement incomes. To a degree, this attitude still seems to prevail, except in a very few cases.

At this point it is reasonable to conclude that job sharing is most likely to exist at an institution where policies allow for permanent, upgraded, part-time employment and, in the case of couples, do not observe nepotism rules. The pro and con positions on job sharing appear to reflect an ideological position on the nature of work and what constitutes a professional commitment, with those favoring job sharing recognizing that quality in the form of commitment and productivity is not determined by temporal status. Those who do not recognize job sharing or are reluctant to participate in this option tend to view those who desire and/or are forced to work part-time as not being serious about their profession or their work; the desire to have more time off whether for leisure, parenting, or to pursue other demands of their profession is viewed with suspicion.

The employing institutions, however, which oppose job sharing under work-ethic rhetoric of "a full day's work for a full day's pay" are likely to be those which hire part-time faculty and employees at minimum wages not prorated to the full-time equivalent position. They often hire part-time faculty at per-class wages of up to 50 percent less than full-time faculty equivalents. They also tend to have a disproportionate number of part-timers resulting from converting a single full-time position into part-time employment so that they can afford up to three part-timers at reduced salary rates for each full-time worker. Looking at the contradictions in responses and employment records, especially at universities, we think it is a vivid demonstration of how perceptions about work continue to operate to support institutional needs and not social goals. The employing institutions which do not view job sharing or permanent part-time with suspicion tend to believe that all university jobs—teaching, research, clerical, administrative, maintenance — could be shared *providing* the tasks can be identified and divided and the continuity of decision-making maintained.

With the exception of two, all institutions which recognize job sharing are taking a wait-and-see attitude toward expanding this option, responding favorably to the couples they have, but attributing their positive experience to the particular couple or individuals rather than to the work structure. As a result of the wait-and-see attitude, the tendency is to modify or circumvent existing policies and not to confront future issues. In regard to the upgrading of personnel policies, no pattern exists; personnel practices are generally dependent on the negotiating ability of job sharers within the existing policies and constraints of an institution. By not moving toward policies in this area, each job-sharing couple is an exception and objectivity in granting rights and benefits is difficult.

WOMEN

For women, the one-role ideology of homemaker emerges as a prime concern. Job sharing replaces the isolation of domesticity with the opportunity to work and to use professional training or experience. Working enables interaction with colleagues and part-time work allows the flexibility of participating equally in the domestic and work domain, involvements which at one time were perceived as mutually exclusive. The personal and professional self-esteem derived from being gainfully employed and interacting with others empowers women to grow professionally and personally.

Another advantage for women is the temporal escape from full-day domesticity. Work has been defined by some as stress-producing but necessary drudgery. In part, these definitions have served to keep women in the home while minimizing the importance and stress of domestic work and decision-making. While this definition may be true, also it must be recognized that work allows for temporary escape from the pressures of domesticity, as the domestic domain has provided an escape from the work world. Men traditionally have been able to utilize participation in the two worlds in order to preserve a healthy balance; each has the potential of providing breathing space from the other. Women working part-time or job sharing are quickly recognizing and reporting the advantages of temporary escape from domestic stress which previously was experienced as continuous and inescapable.

While job sharing reduces stress for the couple, it does pose a threat to some of their colleagues (Arkin and Dobrofsky, 1978a) due to beliefs that part-time work and professionalism are contradictory. The men who resist seem unwilling to share their jobs (and, by implication, domesticity) with their mates (Terrebonne and Terrebonne, 1976). Women, however, experience the greatest social pressure from colleagues and administrators as the traditionally low status of part-time work merges with assumptions of masculine preeminence. Colleagues will often seek out the male partner for consultation or important decision-making; rather than regarding a job-sharing couple as equally competent, interchangeable partners of a team, colleagues view the couple as a male-headed team. Even so, most women report an increase in professional self-esteem. They may have nonequal status in the eyes of their colleagues as women and as part-timers, but at least their professional membership is active.

Acceptance of the marginal professional membership is important to women because it is seen as a chance to demonstrate their individual competence and gain ultimate acceptance as an equal. Many do not realize that the part-time structure itself can be as constraining as gender in limiting professional acceptance and growth. They see work and productivity as objective criteria for status development.

For the women who are also mothers, job sharing enables major role identities to be more balanced; the professional works, the mother parents, and the wife shares the work and income load.

Finally, in a restricted job market like academia, it is entirely new to find women working, let alone sharing, a job with their mate. Their combined economic independence, societal contribution, and family involvement represent a major change in the way women's productivity is defined, and this has both objective (social) and subjective (personal) consequences.

MEN

For men, job sharing with their partner also makes the one-role ideology of breadwinner unnecessary. Grønseth's works (1970, 1972, 1975) point to the ways in which the Husband Economic Provider Role (HEPR) is dysfunctional to both industrialized societies and to the individual members of the family—father, mother, and child (1972:175). On a personal and interpersonal level, the provider role leads to repression of sexual, emotional, and supportive relations with partners as well as with children; traditional socialization expectations which men shoulder alienate rather than integrate them into intimate and family relationships. Because the economic burden is shared, men can cooperate in family life as well. Decreased participation in work allows for greater potential in managing both home- and work-produced stress.

At the same time and in contrast to the women, however, male job-sharing partners report a decrease in professional self-esteem, feeling the social disapproval of fellow colleagues for engaging in their profession only part-time. The decrease in the man's self-esteem is a better indicator of the social status of the job-sharing structure. Traditional values rate part-time employment as of lower status than the full-time career. The quantity of time one devotes to work remains as the more highly regarded criterion, not the quality of work or overall productivity.

Traditional gender-specific socialization appears to surface most strongly among the male partners, particularly when combined income was reported below $15,000. Tendencies toward more competitiveness was one characteristic of this cohort;

another was men's greater desire for full rather than part-time employment. Guilt arising from reduced family income to which male partners contribute less than the total is evidently at work on the men. Expectations of the traditional provider role seem to dominate under these conditions.

CONCLUSIONS

Job-sharing couples in general are able to achieve and maintain the critical balance between work and family while having sufficient opportunity for leisure and intimacy. The balance not only is achieved from having self-managed time, but from a cooperating, shared, or alternating role relationship. The data suggest that professional couples and individuals who are engaged in permanent, upgraded, part-time employment show increased patterns of intimacy, and marital and job satisfaction. The common variable is the opportunity for self-managed time. The degree of satisfaction appears to increase with individuals' ability to manage time for personal as well as work goals. Job-sharing couples functioning on a rigid schedule as opposed to a self-determined schedule experience more strains. Flexibility represents the optimum for satisfaction and productivity. This poses some difficulty in that some employers insist on scheduling each member of the couple rather than scheduling the couple as a unit. This detracts from the satisfactions of job sharing which derive from the flexibility in the arrangement.

Although the results of job sharing and other work variations are demonstrating the positive effects on family, parenting, and intimacy, one must be cautious and take a closer look at both family and work-related implications. In our society, where work involvements assume greater importance than family involvements, it is inadequate to emphasize only the advantages for interpersonal relationships and family from a work structure that runs contrary to a long tradition. Other work-related advantages must be demonstrated if the concept is to thrive. We know that flexitime, for example, originated not from workers' needs and desires, but because of overloaded urban transportation systems and traffic patterns. Low levels of worker morale, believed to be inhibiting maximum productivity, further stimulated interests in experimentation with new employment patterns.

In addition, attention to permanent, part-time employment or job is occurring at the same time that feminists are striving for equal job opportunities and participation in the workplace. Feminists view most part-time work for women with suspicion; it does not represent equality in the workplace and is potentially destructive in the long run to women's efforts for equal employment. As Long as stated:

> In Sweden, the Central Salaried Employees' Organization (TCO) has pointed to the danger that part-time work, while important for those who can not take up full-time employment, may counteract women's integration in the work force and their professional development besides offering women only a limited choice. . . . The unions emphasize that part-time work must not be regarded as the main means of resolving the conflict between women's participation in economic life on a footing of equality and the need of work in the home and child care [1977:56].

The degree to which these concerns apply to new forms of part-time employment like job sharing must be considered. Whether the personal advantages are short-term products requires ongoing research and monitoring, along with related questions of differential personal esteem and professional prestige. Family benefits will require the same long-term evaluation. Whether job sharing and permanent part-time are voluntary or involuntary means of employment is another major issue in the determination of policy. Another distinction must be made, that of the level of part-time work (such as low-level, professional, semi-professional) being considered. Clearly, different populations have different needs to be met from part-time work. The objective reality is that most part-time work is monotonous and low paid, without benefits, and relegated to workers who are older, younger, handicapped, or female.

REFERENCES

Arkin, W. and L.R. Dobrofsky. (1978a) "Job sharing." In R. Rapoport and R. Rapoport (eds.) Working couples. New York: Harper & Row/Routledge.

––– (1978b) "Shared labor and love: Job sharing couples in academia." Alternative Lifestyles: Changing Patterns in Marriage, Family & Intimacy 1 (November).

Bernard, J. (1972) "Changing family life styles: One role, two roles, shared roles." In L.K. Howe (ed.) The future of the family. New York: Simon and Schuster.

Carmody, D.L. (1975) "The home team." In A. Carr and N. Piediscalzi (eds.) The academic study of religion. Missoula, Montana: Scholars Press.

Catalyst. (1973) Resource notebook: A collection of papers. New York.

Glazer, N. (1978) "Alternative lifestyles: Societal crisis and personal solutions." Alternative Lifestyles: Changing Patterns in Marriage, Family & Intimacy 1 (November).

Grønseth, E. (1975) "Work-sharing families: Adaptations of pioneering families with husband and wife in part-time employment." Oslo, Norway: Instituttet for Sociologi.

–––. (1972) "The breadwinner trap." In L.K. Howe (ed.) The future of the family. New York: Simon & Schuster.

–––. (1970) "The dysfunctionality of the husband provider role in industrialized societies." Paper prepared for the 7th World Congress of Sociology, Family Research Session, Varina, Bulgaria.

International Labor Office. (1973) "Part-time employment: An international survey." In National conference on alternative work schedules resource packet. Washington, D.C.: National Council for Alternative Work Patterns, Inc.

Kreps, J. (1977) "Work, education and tomorrow." Address delivered at the Second General Session of the 32nd National Conference on Higher Education, Chicago, March.

Long, M. (1977) "Introduction." In National conference on alternative work schedules resource packet. Washington, D.C.: National Council for Alternative Work Patterns, Inc.

Lopata, H.Z. (1978) "Work and social policy." Alternative Lifestyles: Changing Patterns in Marriage, Family & Intimacy 1 (November).

Rapoport, R. and R. Rapoport. (1977) Dual-career families re-examined. New York: Harper & Row.

–––. (1971a) Dual-career families. England: Penguin Books.

–––. (1971b) Sex, career and family. Beverly Hills, California: Sage Publications.

Terrebonne, N. and R.A. Terrebonne. (1976) "On sharing an academic appointment." In L. Hoffman and G. DeSole (eds.) Careers & couples: An academic question. New York: Commission on the Status of Women in the Profession, Modern Languages Association of America.

Wirtz, W. (1977) "Education for what?" Address delivered at the Concurrent General Session 4 of the 32nd National Conference on Higher Education, Chicago, March.

8

DIRECTIONS FOR DAY CARE

KAREN WOLK FEINSTEIN

A book that examines the impact of female employment on family life would be incomplete without special consideration of the needs of children. In 1975, 44 percent of all children under the age of 18 and 36 percent of all children under six had working mothers. As a result, there are many children in this country who have no parent at home during the workday and no parent for whom the care of children and household affairs is a full-time responsibility. Feminists have argued that this is not, in itself, undesirable; children of any age do not require the full-time attendance by a mother to develop into happy, healthy adults. They cite the many advantages of jobs and careers for women and suggest that other societal institutions and new family arrangements can provide for the care of our nation's children (Safilios-Rothschild, 1973). National employment trends over the past decade indicate an increasing involvement of mothers in the labor force. As the chapters by Pifer, Walshok, and Mott suggest, women's motivations for employment are complex among all ages, races, and social classes; family economic considerations are wedded to desires for independence, occupational challenge, and adult companionship. Women of means work for economic independence as well as career satisfactions; poor and working-class women derive personal satisfaction as well as financial gain from employment.

Internationally, the increasing preference of women for paid employment and the reliance of families on external sources of child care is an almost universal phenomenon (Giele and Smock, 1977). Nations that have attempted to reverse the trend toward women's labor force participation, either to reduce unemployment or increase population growth, have found it difficult (Kahn and Kamerman, 1977). As Chafe states in reference to the experience of the United States:

> There appears to have been a simple cultural logic at work in the employment patterns of women since World War II. Those who first broke the barriers against married women's employment were middle aged. With no children in the home, they posed the least threat to traditional ideas of women's 'place' as homemakers and mothers. Later, a major increase in employment occurred among mothers with children six to seventeen years of age. By the late sixties, in turn, the major change took place among mothers of younger children. It was almost as though each step in the process was necessary to prepare the way for the next one, until by the mid-1970s there was consistent departure from the traditional norm of mothers staying at home full-time to care for children [1976:25].

Working mothers with young children need substitute care for infants, preschoolers, and primary school-aged children. In nations with institutionalized day care systems (state, locality, or employer-based), this procedure involves choosing among options: center-based care, family care, or in-home care. For instance, mothers in Sweden, Norway, Hungary, and the Soviet Union can participate in publicly sponsored or supervised full-day programs for infants and preschoolers in neighborhood creches, in licensed municipal family day care homes, in extended-day programs and sick-care services for school aged children, or they can make private arrangements with individuals and programs outside the national system. In nations where no day care system exists, where child care is a private, not public, responsibility and day care options vary considerably from city to city and neighborhood to neighborhood, families encounter more difficulties in providing for their children during work hours.

Extensive support systems have been legislated by governments in almost every European country to provide for the children of working mothers. These systems are often inadequate to care for all the children in need of service and to provide the high quality of care many parents prefer. Many parents will choose private, in-home arrangements even where an extensive national system of group care exists. However, what is important is that the governments of these countries *have assumed responsibility* for the welfare of children of working parents. In most of these nations, parents share similar concerns about day care. There are complaints about the quality and quantity of care, and real ambivalence about the value of group centers for children under three. Yet, the prevailing attitude is that such care is a national necessity; mothers of young children are entering the workforce and the national disposition is to minimize the harm such work preferences may have on women, children, and families.

In this chapter I will examine the national policy response to the day care needs of children with working mothers in America. Particular consideration will be given to the selective nature of this response. I will also identify the major providers of day care in America—both public and private, emphasizing the present potential for, or limitations to, growth in each sector. I use the term "day care" here to denote the custodial care of children (from birth to adolescence) while mothers work. Although a day care program may include special educational or social services, day care is primarily regarded as a "parent substitute" service and not as a cultural enrichment, preschool, or parent education vehicle. It may take place individually or in groups, in homes or in formal centers. Programs such as nursery schools which may, incidentally, provide day care for part of the day while addressing a major objective of preschool education, are not considered as day care providers *unless* they offer full-day care adjusted to the work schedules of employed mothers (e.g., 8:30 a.m.-5:30 p.m.).

In a final section, I suggest future directions for day care in America, which evolve from my exploration of the national day care terrain. These suggestions are predictive and descriptive rather than normative, and I offer no ideal model of a national day care system. However, I suspect that in spite of the unique economic and political factors which shape American day care policy and which have led us down a distinctive policy path, our final destination will be surprisingly similar to that of other industrialized nations. In communities throughout the world, authorities, service providers, and parents are searching for programs to provide care for children of working parents within the constraints of inadequate resources, inadequate consensus on child development principles, and limited models of group care.

In this chapter, I question whether our system will evolve "from the bottom up" or "from the top down"; will much of the day care programming occur at the local community level or emanate from national legislation? An important issue is who will pay for services and who will receive federal subsidies. Sometime in the future, will our "nonsystem" of care involve a far wider range of options for all families at the local community level, and by addressing universal child care needs, will it come to resemble the more deliberate and coherent day care systems already intact in other nations?

NATIONAL DAY CARE POLICY

Why do nations invest in social parenthood? I suggest that child welfare considerations are not sufficient motivation and that day care policy considerations are intimately linked with economic conditions. The more aggressive national response to day care needs in European countries, for instance, can be partially explained by the shortage of workers in economies that require more manpower. National day care efforts are directed at attracting new workers to the labor force as much as promoting family interests. In France, for instance, concern about underpopulation has resulted in the development of children's support services in an attempt to make childrearing more palatable and alter parental preferences for small families.

In the United States, there is no worker shortage at present; in fact, we are facing problems of unemployment. National policymakers are concerned about measures which might increase the existing pool of workers. Among the many Americans who have no children in need of day care, this costly service is not high priority.

Other authors have adequately chronicled the forces of resistance to a national day care program in the United States (Greenblatt, 1978; Kamerman and Kahn, 1976; and Steinfels, 1973). Primary among the forces working against any national system of care are:

- philosophical disputes over the purpose, sponsorship, program, and scope of such a system;
- financial resistance to subsidizing a costly service in the absence of a documented critical need;
- economic fears about stimulating maternal employment in an economy with high unemployment;
- political disagreements over who should administer such a program and control the day care dollar;
- organizational uncertainty over how to best administer and deliver a national day care system.

To overcome these obstacles, a concerted day care coalition must convince policy makers and their constituents that day care will address a critical national need. In the past, national leaders have been successful only in establishing a federal day care system during times of national emergency: the Great Depression and World War II. Extensive day care networks were set up to meet generally acknowledged national needs: jobs for the unemployed, social welfare services for children of the unemployed, and manpower for the war industries. In both instances, executive directive rather than legislative fiat created the day care programs, first under the Works Projects Administration in 1933, and then extended under the Community Facilities Act of 1941. Both acts were passed to meet critical manpower problems in depression- and later war-impacted areas, and were not aimed at establishing a new national social service. Housed within and administered by local school systems, these temporary day care programs did constitute a public day care system. Although extensive evaluations of the programs are not available, they were filled to capacity and seem to have provided adequate care. After the war, when such centers were believed to accentuate rather than relieve manpower problems by prolonging maternal employment, they were disbanded. No serious federal day care intitiatives were proposed until the 1960s.

During the 1960s, the federal government again became involved in preschool education and day care; the intent was not to provide relief for working mothers, but to (1) compensate for the emotional, physical, and intellectual deprivations of poverty, hence interrupting the "cycle of poverty," or to (2) enable and encourage mothers on welfare to enter the work force. Programs such as Head Start exemplify the first approach; day care funding through Titles IVa, IVb, and IVc and Title XX of the Social Security Act represent the second.

Both Head Start and Social Security policies addressed another national purpose of current concern: the need to reduce economic dependency and the welfare roll. They are targeted at small groups of children from low-income families. The popular Head Start program was instituted under the Economic Opportunity Act of 1964 to offer comprehensive child development services (educational experiences, medical and dental care, psychological counseling, nutritional support and social services) to children in poor families on a demonstration basis. It is essentially a compensatory educational program; except in those few centers operating for a full day, it is not a day care program. This program has received broad national acceptance. However, researchers have been unable to prove that it has long-term effects on school achievement. Furthermore, it has established a national standard for preschool care that is very costly. For these and other reasons, efforts to expand this project have been unsuccessful.

Most of the federal funds for day care in the 1960s were directed at welfare reform and came under the Social Security

Act of 1962. The objective was to enable and encourage welfare mothers to undertake employment or training. Other federal manpower and antipoverty initiatives also involved the establishment of day care centers, so that by 1970 there were more than 200 programs allocating funds for child care (Grubb, 1977:8). The Title XX amendments to the Social Security Act, effective in 1975, consolidated many of these funding sources by providing block grants in the form of matching funds to states for social services. Each state can decide which services to offer and can serve a broader range of clientele. Although federal guidelines permit individuals and families with incomes up to 115% of a state's median income to participate, funding limitations have tended to restrict eligibility to the poor (Grubb, 1977:10). It is uncertain whether the states will continue to allocate a high percentage of these monies to day care services. When the funding was categorical, day care services accounted for 30%-40% of the federal social service funds.

Other federal legislation, such as the Elementary and Secondary Education Act of 1965 (Titles I and III) and federal legislation for the handicapped (PL94-142), provided funding for preschool programs for children in deprived areas and with special needs. These are educational programs targeted at special populations and are not intended to meet the needs of working mothers. As I will discuss later, however, these acts are significant because they involve the federal government in financing preschool programs through the sponsorship of local school districts.

In 1971, a child development coalition of labor groups, day care proponents, liberal congressmen, and child welfare leaders did secure passage in both Houses of Congress of a comprehensive child development bill which would have established a national system of compensatory preschool education and day care for children in low-income families. The Nixon administration balked at issues of community control, the range of services proposed, and the number of children to be served. President Nixon vetoed the bill with the excuse that:

> For the Federal Government to plunge headlong financially into supporting child development would commit the vast moral author-

ity of the National Government to the side of communal approaches to child rearing over (and) against the family-centered approach [Steiner, 1976:113].

It is unlikely that Nixon and other prominent administration decision makers actually feared the "Sovietization" of American children through center-based day care. Sensing that support for the bill was not sufficient to damage him politically, Nixon had no reason to pass the measure other than to provide day care. No evidence has come forth to indicate that preschool programs are adequate to break the cycle of poverty. To accomplish a more important purpose—bringing welfare mothers into the labor force—a more direct, less comprehensive program would suffice (Steiner, 1976).

The government now provides general assistance for day care through its fiscal relief measures. The 1976 Tax Reform Act permits a tax credit for child care and household services for working parents. The Act extends to all taxpayers and allows a credit of up to $400 per year per child. Tax credits help pay for day care; they do not create programs. However, a provision of the Revenue Act of 1971, viable until 1982, permits businesses to deduct, at an accelerated capital-investment rate, the expenses of "acquiring, constructing, reconstructing or rehabilitating property" for use as child-care facilities (Canon, 1978:85). In addition, a 1973 ruling by the IRS (73-348) permits companies to take expense deductions under Section 162 of the Internal Revenue Code for the cost of child care for preschoolers if such expense (1) enables an employee to obtain proper care for children, or (2) reduces the company's costs of training, job replacement, and absenteeism. A bill (H.R. 3340) was submitted in 1977 to amend the Code to allow deductions for the incremental costs involved in using any portion of a dwelling unit to provide licensed day care services, even if not used exclusively for such service.

On paper, the government has tried a more aggressive approach to stimulating work organizations to establish day care. Executive Order 11478, the affirmative-action mandate to federal executive agencies, designates responsibility for enforcing the Equal Employment Opportunity Act among federal departments to the U.S. Civil Service Commission. In 1973, the Civil Service Commission issued Chapter 713 of the Federal Personnel Manual to comply with this responsibility. It called for agency programs to improve "employment opportunities and community conditions that affect employability;" and urged "cooperation with community groups in the establishment and support of child day care centers needed by employees or applicants" (Douglas, 1976:25). These national policies for equal employment and affirmative action also affect all private businesses and service contractors doing business with the federal government. The Office of Federal Contract Compliance in its Revised Order #4 of 1974 states that

> in order for government contractors to meet their affirmative action obligations to the Government regarding all employees—especially minorities and women, they are to encourage child care, housing, and transportation of employees and applicants with their firms [as quoted in Douglas, 1976:26].

The wording of these guidelines is vague and it is not surprising that compliance with this mandate, within government, industry, and higher educational institutions, has been weak and no organization has been penalized for noncompliance. There is no reason to anticipate more aggressive enforcement of these guidelines in the near future.

THE PUBLIC DAY CARE TERRAIN: STATES AND LOCALITIES

State governments serve primarily as conduits for federal day care funding, reimbursing public and private organizations for rendering care. As Kamerman and Kahn describe:

> Since most federal legislation offers options for states in relation to administrative arrangements and services, and since states and local governments in turn are organized in diverse ways and relate to different voluntary agency patterns, the resulting administrative and operational arrangements defy simple description. If the term system implies uniformity and coherence, there is no general child care system in the United States [1976:62].

Several state agencies, for example the welfare, education, and public health departments, may all share responsibility for day care programs.

Only one state, California, has subsidized what could be described as a statewide day care system. After World War II, California decided to maintain its Lanham Act day care centers through state subsidies to individual school districts on a matching funds basis. Today, many of California's school districts offer full-day preschool and school-age care for children of working mothers, often from infancy to 14 years of age. The introduction of federal funds in the 1960s which are earmarked for the disadvantaged, however, has limited participation to children of the poor.

In considering the role of localities in day care, primary attention will be paid to the local school systems—the most obvious source of child care services.

THE RESPONSE OF THE PUBLIC SCHOOLS

On the whole, the response of the public schools to new needs of children has been slow and tentative. Public school systems operate on limited budgets and, until recently, in limited space. Educators have been reluctant to undertake new responsibilities outside their areas of expertise. Efforts to propose new projects for the schools have met with resistance from parents of children who would not participate, faculty, taxpayers, and other providers of services to children.

Recently, however, some schools have expanded their services to include preschool education, extended-day care of school-age children, and even day care for infants and toddlers. James Levine, in his book *Day Care and the Public Schools* (1978), has described some representative programs. These include programs operated by a school district, programs operated through parent-sponsored independent corporations, a partnership between a school district and a large nonprofit day care agency. These programs were aimed at very different populations: one project was a school-affiliated, family day care program; another provided infant care for children of teen-aged parents as well as a laboratory for high school preparenthood education. All of these examples covered district-wide programs; many individual schools also offer day care services, such as full-day Head Start, outside of a school-system approach. Levine offers some reasons suggestive of greater public school involvement:

- Schools represent the major normalizing institution for children in our society; they are available to all families regardless of income, geographical location, race or religion.
- Passage of federal legislation for the handicapped in 1976 (PL 94-142) requires schools to provide preschool and other services for handicapped children. Public schools are becoming involved with preschool programming.
- With declining enrollments, public schools have the space and the staff to cover new projects.
- The political strength of the "school lobby" is very significant. It includes such groups as the American Federation of Teachers, the National School Boards Association, the National Congress of Parents and Teachers, the National Association of State Boards of Education. Its ability to secure program funds from Washington is not to be underestimated.

THE PRIVATE DAY-CARE TERRAIN

The vast majority of children in America, about 75 percent, are cared for by individuals (either relatives or nonrelatives) in their own or another home. These arrangements include individual and small-group care. Only 10-12 percent are cared for in center-based arrangements (Woolsey, 1977:131). Other than Head Start programs and public school day care, most day care centers are private facilities. Many are run by philanthropic organizations, (churches, settlement houses, social agencies), parent cooperatives, or nonprofit institutions (hospitals and universities). Most of these centers were developed to meet a specific need—substitute care for children of working mothers. However, the high cost of satisfactory center-based care restricts the use of licensed centers to the poor (who receive federal reimbursement) and the more affluent. Also, these centers are not evenly distributed around the country; some areas have very few nonprofit day care centers. These facilities do not, in any sense, constitute a national system of care and it is unlikely that the number of private nonprofit day care centers will expand significantly in the near future. Stringent federal licensing standards require costly programs to entitle operators to federal reimbursement. Few parents can afford to pay for such care on their own, particularly in single-parent families.

Proprietary day care centers operate to make a profit. During the 1950s, such centers represented the majority of day care providers (Greenblatt, 1978:105), but very little has been written about them. Some of these programs are simply nursery schools that offer full-day care or small programs in the homes of proprietors. Such centers are independent, widely scattered, and have a tendency to be financially unstable (Greenblatt, 1978). During the 1960s, in line with the current boom of other business franchises, much attention was paid to the potential of day-care franchises as a source of profit. When day care franchises proved unprofitable, many chains were discontinued, although several still remain on the scene. Susan Stein refutes criticisms about the inherent low quality of profit-making programs involving child care:

> The general bias against profit-making child care does not seem to be founded on a comparison of quality but rather on the idealogical notion that business doesn't belong in child care at all [1973:260].

Proprietary centers must struggle to balance competing priorities; that is, to make a profit, to keep costs low enough to attract participants, and to keep program quality sufficiently high to meet licensing standards and satisfy users; often the first two objectives supercede the last. Extensive expansion in the proprietary sector through public funding is not forecast, unless licensing standards are relaxed or federal subsidies increased.

DAY CARE IN INDUSTRY

Industrial day care, once widely available in European nations, has never been a factor on the American scene. During the heyday of welfare capitalism (1880-1930), a number of businesses offered day care to employees' children. During the

Civil War and the two world wars, some employers opened temporary day care centers to meet worker shortages. Greenblatt (1978) refers to industrial day care in the United States as a "miniature curiosity" because of its failure to become established. Federal day care initiatives during the 1940s and '50s bypassed the corporation almost completely.

Some of the reasons given for government's unwillingness to fund corporate efforts were: the noise and pollution of factory settings, the dangers of bombings, the inconvenience of bringing children to work, and parental preferences. Possibly, the government feared losing control over these centers after the war. The government's overall objective was to sponsor temporary services which would terminate at the end of the war, when all mothers would return to the home and the job vacancies would be filled by returning servicemen. If the industrial-based centers remained open, this goal might be impeded (Rothman, 1973:21).

After the war, a number of employers sponsored their own day care centers, particularly in work settings where large numbers of women were employed (textile plants, hospitals, and telephone companies). However, the vast majority of the 150-200 employer-sponsored centers were in health, university, or other nonprofit institutions. Relatively few private companies set up programs. A 1970 survey by the Women's Bureau discovered only eleven companies providing day care. Nevertheless, when the concept of day care gained great popularity in the early 1970s as many mothers of preschoolers entered the labor force, various persons heralded industrial day care as an answer to the critical shortage of services. A significant number of journal articles, pamphlets, and books were wirtten on industrial day care during the period 1971 to 1973, testifying to the growing interest in the issue. Actually, in spite of all the attention and enthusiasm over the potential of industrial day care, relatively few industrial projects were initiated. Most companies which did become involved with day care did not actually open centers themselves, but offered advice and start-up costs to independent sponsors. Of the handful of programs that were initiated during the late 1960s and early 1970s, many of the notable experiments (such as Whirlpool, Abt Associates, AT&T, Levi Strauss, KLH) have been terminated or transferred to different sponsors. Employers discovered that day care did not meet its intended goals: it did not reduce turnover, absenteeism, and tardiness; it did not seem to increase worker satisfaction; and many employees were either unwilling to pay the standard fee or preferred other arrangements (Levitan and Alderman, 1975:30-32). It is doubtful that industrial day care will ever become a significant factor in the American day care landscape.

CONCLUSION

In the previous pages, I have briefly mapped the national day care terrain, showing that we have no national system of care providing a spectrum of alternative day care arrangements available to persons of different incomes in all local communities. What we do have has been well summarized elsewhere.

> This city, in the meantime, typifies the situation—a pluralistic, decentralized, categorical system, varied in quality and philosophy, not adequately serving the very young and the school-age children of working mothers... and running the risk of pricing out of the market the working-class users above welfare eligibility scales [Kamerman and Kahn, 1976:117].

The day care picture in America consists of fragments of service scattered over the national landscape. Significant populations such as infants and school-age children go largely ignored by national programming and other institutional day care providers. At present, I forecast limited expansion for profit-making, philanthropic, and industrial centers unless significant new sources of funding for service reimbursement appear.

It is unlikely that a national system of care will be legislated in the near future. In the first place, we lack a national purpose for day care sufficiently compelling to overcome philosophical and economic resistance to a national day care program. As yet, there is no widespread evidence that large numbers of children are unable to obtain care or are receiving poor care. That does not mean that this is not, in fact, the situation, but that it has not been well documented to date. The lack of a coherent and effective political lobby also has hurt the "children's cause" in the last few years. As Gilbert Steiner concluded after the defeat of the comprehensive child development legislation of 1971:

> Both the appearance and the apparent disappearance of comprehensive child development from the congressional agenda came abruptly. Unlike national health insurance, medical care for the aged, federal aid to education, and other compelling social issues—in which determined congressional sponsors and interest group supporters assumed that success might ultimately take a decade and that interim failures were not final—child development had a quick fling and was gone. Its legislative success in 1971 resulted, in part, from the interaction of congressional initiative and HEW bungling. Comparable opportunities for the effective use of congressional initiative in child development are not readily foreseeable, one reason that future legislative success will be harder to accomplish [1976:91].

Disputes among child development professionals and advocates over what constitutes "adequate" day care programming, sponsorship, and parent involvement has served to further confuse and diffuse persons supportive of child welfare legislation in general. A refusal to eliminate compensatory education and comprehensive child development goals from day care programming has led some advocates to insist that day care homes and centers offer *more* than substitute parental care, thus making the service extremely costly and alienating potential supporters. Suzanne Woolsey (1977) suggests that parents are, at present, receiving the type of child care they prefer; that is, informal, in-home care by relatives and nonrelatives. This type of care is not easily addressed by federal day care policy, which thus deserves its position as a secondary political issue. Other writers (Grubb, 1977; Kamerman and Kahn, 1976; and Steinfels, 1973) acknowledge a serious need for more day care options, noting the imperfections of the private day care market and the selectivity of federal subsidies. They agree, however, that one national system of care is less desirable than federal support for a variety of public and private alternatives.

My prediciton is that incremental increases in federal financial subsidies (through Title XX, tax reform, and other special needs legislation) and local programming will result in substantially more formal day care options in communities throughout the United States. Many of these programs will be developed by local school districts and individual schools to serve children 3-12 years of age in response to parental demands for such services.

The public school is the one institution in our society equipped to coordinate a broad range of services to families of all incomes and in all parts of the country at the local level. There is reason to anticipate support for an expanded role for the schools from teachers and administrators, parents, and local communities who do not want to lose their schools or their jobs because of declining school enrollments. As extended day programs in existence have demonstrated, new services do not need to be a part of the standard school program. They will be contracted with other agencies; some will be parent-controlled and financed by a combination of user's fees and federal reimbursements for those with lower incomes. No national program of child care is necessary; different communities will initiate their own service package according to local need.

Depending on the vagaries of state welfare department purchase of service preferences, some expansion in the private voluntary and proprietary sector is also predicted. Ideally, agencies and schools will begin to address as yet unmet needs for (1) good infant care; (2) summer holiday and vacation care; and (3) care for sick children. In the meantime, these services will continue to be provided by private individuals through in-home and family day care, and by private summer camps.

An important issue is the future of day care under Title XX. Will the states continue to allocate a significant portion of their federal social services funds to day care? Will subsidies be extended to low and lower-middle income families so that these parents also have sufficient options of alternative service arrangements? In the long run, many parents will continue to prefer informal in-home arrangements, just as they do in countries with extensive national day care systems. However, more and more options will become available in our local communities as mothers with young children participate in the labor force in ever greater numbers, and eventually our nonsystem of care will resemble a system.

REFERENCES

Canon, B. (1978) "Child care where you work." Ms. magazine, April.

Chafe, W.H. (1976) "Looking backward in order to look forward." In J. Kreps (ed.), Women and the American economy. Englewood Cliffs, N.J.: Prentice Hall.

Douglas, J., (ed.). (1976) Dollars and sense: Employer-supported child care. Washington, D.C.: Office of Child Development.

Giele, J. and A. Smock. (1977) Women: Roles and status in eight countries. New York: John Wiley and Sons.

Greenblatt, B. (1978) Responsibility for child care. San Francisco: Jossey-Bass.

Grubb, W.N. (1977) Alternative futures for child care. Working Paper #11. Childhood and Government Project, Berkeley: University of California.

Kahn, A. and S. Kamerman. (1977) Social services in international perspective. New York: Columbia University Press.

Kamerman, S. and A. Kahn. (1976) Social services in the United States. Philadelphia: Temple University Press.

Levine, J. (1978) Day care and the public schools. Newton, Massachuetts: Educational Development Corporation.

Levitan, S.A. and K. Alderman. (1975) Child care and ABC's too. Baltimore: Johns Hopkins University Press.

Rothman, S. (1973) "Other people's children: The day care experience in America." The public interest, Winter.

Safilios-Rothschild, C. (1973) "Parents need for child care." In P. Roby (ed.), Child care: Who cares? New York: Basic Books.

Stein, S. (1973) "The company cares for children." In P. Roby (ed.), Child care: Who cares? New York: Basic Books.

Steinfels, M.O. (1973) Who's minding the children. New York: Simon and Schuster.

Steiner, G. (1976) The children's cause. Washington, D.C.: The Brookings Institute.

Woolsey, S. (1977) "Pied piper politics and the child care debate." In Daedalus, Spring.

9

NONTRADITIONAL WORK SCHEDULES
FOR WOMEN

DENISE F. POLIT

The extent to which women have participated in the American labor force has changed dramatically during the twentieth century, particularly during the years following the Second World War. By 1974, 46 percent of all women aged 16 years or older were in the labor force, compared with 38 percent in 1960, 34 percent in 1950, and 30 percent in 1940. Projections concerning the size of the labor force indicate that by 1990 there may be 43.7 million women working outside the home, a 22 percent increase over 1974 figures (U.S. Bureau of the Census, 1976). Even more impressive is the changing relationship between female labor-force participation and the female life cycle. There has been a decisive trend toward increased employment of young married women, including women with preschool children. Increasingly, employment is becoming an important and continuing part of women's lives, not just a temporary pastime before marriage and child rearing.

The growing involvement of women with work and careers outside the home reflects, for many, a desire to balance the benefits of family life with the rewards of personal growth, social activity, and monetary remuneration, which the restricted role of homemaker often fails to provide. Men in our society have long had the opportunity to participate in both working and familial spheres of activity. It is true that women have made unprecedented progress in the workplace during the last decade. Yet, despite increasing social support for women's entry into the labor market, the American economy continues to offer different status levels, rewards, and opportunities for men and women.

Sex discrimination in employment takes many forms, some obvious (such as unequal pay for the same work) and others more subtle. During the 1960s and 1970s, a number of federal laws prohibiting sex discrimination in employment were enacted, and existing legislation was modified to include sex discrimination. Most states have also enacted similar laws. Implementation and enforcement of anti-sex-discrimination legislation have been difficult, and deeply embedded attitudes of employers and employees (female as well as male), together with unprogressive and unresponsive organizational practices and structure, continue to be an obstacle in eliminating sex discrimination and sex segregation.

Numerous commentators concerned with the unique problems of working women (particularly those women with children) have noted that restricted and inflexible working hours are one means by which women are discriminated against (Agassi, 1975; Kreps and Leaper, 1976; Schonberger, 1971). Since women do not typically relinquish or even diminish their household and childcare responsibilities when they enter the work force, a traditional nine-to-five, five-day work schedule can pose excessive demands on a woman's ability to perform multiple roles comfortably. Thus, there is some concern that conventional "male" working arrangements not only discourage entry into the labor force for many women but also have a negative effect on the quality of life for those women who, by necessity or inclination, do have jobs.

The recent interest in and experimentation with rearranged work schedules by an increasingly large number of United States firms and organizations do not, for the most part, stem from management's concern over the working conditions of female employees, but benefits to women may indeed result. The discussion which follows examines some of the issues, evidence, and arguments relating to the effects of alternative working arrangements on the lives of women. The analysis will focus on the three major forms of nontraditional schedules: the shortened workweek, flexible working hours, and part-time employment.

THE SHORTENED WORKWEEK

The four-day workweek (or, in some cases, the three-day workweek) has attracted considerable publicity in the United States. A typical four-day arrangement reschedules work hours from five eight-hour days to four ten-hour days. Firms which began experimenting with compressed schedules in the late 1960s and early 1970s were mainly small, nonunion manufacturing, retail, and service companies, but more recently the innovation has spread to larger, more urban-centered organizations such as insurance companies, hospitals, and municipal agencies. Several thousand U.S. firms have adopted a form of shortened workweek schedule for at least some of their employees.

Research efforts to date have concentrated on the effects of the new workweek schedule on economic factors such as productivity, turnover, absenteeism, equipment utilization, as well as on employee morale and satisfaction with the schedule. Although the quality and depth of the existing data leave much to be desired, there is abundant support for the contention that employees themselves prefer the shortened workweek to conventional five-day schedules (Hodge and Tellier, 1975; Kenny, 1974; Mahoney, Newman and Frost, 1975; Nord and Costigan, 1973). For the most part firms have reported improvements on a number of corporate indices such as productivity, absenteeism, employee recruitment, and turnover, although some organizations have reported either no change or declines on these measures (Wheeler, Gurman, and Tarnowieski, 1972; Macut, 1974; Sverdloff, 1976; Calvasina and Boxx, 1975). Thus despite considerable variability in the reliability and validity of the data, the bulk of the available evidence suggests that compressed workweeks are reasonably successful from the point of view of both employers and employees.

When one attempts to discover the consequences of the four-day week on women, one finds that very little research has been done in this regard. Two "theories" concerning the reactions of women workers (especially working mothers) to the new schedule have been advanced. Some analysts predicted that working mothers would oppose the four-day week because the ten-hour day would result in difficulties in the performance of household and child care responsibilities, such as getting children off to school, preparing evening meals, and so forth. Others felt that the extra free day would be welcomed by working mothers who could use the day to manage household chores more efficiently. (Ironically, although the four-day workweek has been hailed as a "revolution in work and leisure" [Poor, 1970], few people have referred to the issue of leisure time when considering the pros and cons of the schedule for working wives and mothers.)

On the whole, despite the meagerness of existing data, it appears that women do favor the four-day week. Most of the research which has attempted to link employee characteristics with attitudes toward the shortened workweek have failed to reveal *any* significant relationships, and this includes such variables as sex, marital status, and number of children (Hodge and Tellier, 1975; Kenny, 1974; Mahoney et al., 1975). In other words, both women with and women without children seem to be as favorable toward the four-day week as other employees. Werther and Newstrom (1972), however, have made an interesting, though undocumented, point in reference to studies of the effects of a four-day work schedule, which merits further investigation:

> These studies only show that turnover is lower after installing a shorter workweek. They make no mention of the turnover which occurs immediately before the program is adopted. Some employees—most often women—resign once they realize that the longer hours will conflict with transportation, childcare arrangements, domestic responsibilities, or their personal dispositions [pp. 18-19].

Denise F. Polit 199

The majority of existing studies have unfortunately examined in a relatively superficial manner the effects of a four-day workweek on the lives of workers. We thus have little information concerning the aspects of the shortened work schedule which appeal the most to working women, the ways in which it has affected their family relationships, their opportunities for leisure and personal growth, the division of household labor, or the extent to which the entry of women into the work force has been affected. Most studies which have explored the reasons for employee endorsement of the four-day week have found that the most important advantage to workers is the additional free time for a variety of activities (Hedges, 1970; Hodge and Tellier, 1975; Steele and Poor, 1970). But we simply do not know whether this "free time" is contributing to a widening or diminishing of traditional sex-role differentiation and hence to patterns of behavior which perpetuate sex discrimination. If, for example, an extra free day is used predominantly by men to pursue leisure activities and by working women to complete household chores, it is obvious that sex inequality will be reinforced by compressed work schedules. However, it is possible that, in families where both husband and wife are working, the three-day weekend could result in increasing male participation in household tasks.

FLEXIBLE WORKING HOURS

In many European countries, the interest in rearranged work schedules has focused on flexible working hours, or flexitime. This innovation permits employees, within a designated band of time each day, to choose their starting and ending time at their own discretion. The practice of flexible working hours began in 1967 in the research and development plant of Messerschmitt-Bolkow-Blohm, a German aerospace company, when concern over traffic problems and subsequent tardiness prompted the management of that firm to change the conventional schedule. During the 1970s the concept spread rapidly throughout Europe; by 1975 about 6,000 European firms had adopted flexitime.

United States organizations have not kept pace with European firms in introducing flexible working hours to their employees. However, the situation appears to be rapidly changing. In a recent survey sponsored by the Business and Professional Women's Foundation, 59 out of 334 organizations responding to the survey reported having adopted a rearranged workday plan. For the most part, flexible working hours were most prevalent in office situations (banks, government offices, insurance companies), although manufacturing companies were also represented. These firms tended not to be unionized (Hartley, 1976).

A modification of the flexitime concept which is apparently more common in American firms is employee-chosen staggered hours. In this arrangement, employees work the same schedule every day, but they are able to choose their schedules from among a number of alternatives. Unlike the compressed workweek, both flexitime and flexible staggered hours directly affect the important issue of autonomous, worker-determined time allocation.

As was true in the case of the four-day week, the flexible hour concept has attracted considerable popular attention, and the literature contains numerous anecdotal reports about the advantages the system has to offer. While a few studies with adequate designs do exist, there is so little longitudinal data available that we can draw only very tentative conclusions about the long-term impact of flexitime and staggered hours.

For the most part, existing studies (which are mostly management-initiated) have revealed almost unanimously favorable employee reactions, whether those reactions are described as employee morale, liking for the innovation, job satisfaction, or sense of personal motivation (Elbing, Gadon and Gordon, 1975; Evans, 1973, 1975; Golembiewski, Hilles, and Kagno, 1974). Employers, too, have reported that corporate benefits, in addition to improved employee morale, accrue from the innovation. Once again, hard data are rare, so that we must be cautious in drawing conclusions, but the outlook is quite good: there have been reports of reduced turnover, fewer accidents, reduced absenteeism and elimination of tardiness, and improved work flow or task completion (Elbing et al., 1974; Golembiewski et al., 1974; Hartley, 1976; Partridge, 1973).

The effect of flexible working hours on women is again largely a matter of conjecture, although a number of commentators have hailed the innovation as particularly beneficial to working wives and mothers (Carmel, 1973; Simmons, Freedman, Dunkle and Blau, 1975). Economist Juanita Kreps has pointed out:

> If such arrangements came to be widespread, it would be possible for male workers to take on increased responsibility for nonmarket production which often involves irregular hours and sometimes conflicts with full-time market schedules [Kreps and Leaper, 1976:75].

The data that are available are too meager to gain any useful insights into the consequences of a widespread adoption of flexitime for women. Surprisingly few studies have even tried to analyze the relationship between employee attitudes toward flexitime and demographic variables such as sex, marital status and number and ages of children. The only exception is a British study, in which married women with children under 16 indicated as a group that they obtained more advantages from the flexitime plan than did any other group (Walker, Fletcher and McLeod, 1975). No study has analyzed in depth just what the nature of those advantages is. Although various employee benefits of flexitime have been cited (for example, the ability to adjust work schedules to individual needs, sense of personal freedom, increased sense of participation in working matters, greater ease in traveling, and so forth), there has been virtually no effort to link these benefits to different segments of the work force nor to probe beyond limited and superficial lists of advantages to a careful scrutiny of how these developments actually change workers' lives.

PART-TIME EMPLOYMENT

Permanent part-time work is not, of course, an innovation. Although variations of part-time schedules such as job sharing and job pairing have emerged relatively recently, regular, paid employment for fewer than 35 hours per week has virtually always been available to a small segment of the work force. Unlike flexitime and the shortened workweek, part-time schedules have rarely involved policy-level decisions in which employers systematically convert full-time jobs to multiple part-time openings, or systematically recruit part-timers for responsible or professional positions. There is, however, an increasing demand for firms to develop such policies.

Part-time employment is perhaps more obviously a women's issue than the other two forms of nontraditional schedules we have examined. The vast majority of all part-time employees (nearly 80 percent) are female (Simmons et al., 1975). In the past few decades, when overall employment of women was rapidly rising, part-time employment of women was growing at nearly twice the rate of full-time female employment (Greenwald, 1972). According to recent figures disclosed by the Department of Labor, 31.1 percent of the 20 million working wives in America in 1974 were employed part time (Hayghe, 1976).

In spite of these impressive figures, it would appear that the demand for part-time jobs is greater than the supply. In a 1968 Bureau of Labor Statistics survey, 27 percent of the women polled said they preferred part-time work, but over 60 percent of these women held full-time jobs. (U.S. Department of Labor, 1969). In another 1968 survey, nonworking mothers aged 18 to 49 were asked if they would accept the offer of a part-time job (not more than six hours per day) in their specialty. Twenty percent of these women said yes without qualification, and an additional 47 percent said yes with the stipulation that adequate public or employer-furnished childcare be provided (Schonberger, 1970). There is no evidence that the situation has dramatically changed in the 1970s.

Women face more obstacles than the mere availability of part-time schedules. "Good" part-time employment in higher level jobs is practically nonexistent. Most women working part-time in well-paying, challenging jobs appear to have obtained their positions by first demonstrating their competency as full-time employees. Few part-timers are ever promoted. Furthermore, part-time employees are often totally excluded from such benefit programs as sick pay, vacations, and holidays and health and pension plans. In an Area Wage Survey in four urban areas studied by the Bureau of Labor Statistics in 1972, only about half of the part-time workers were found to receive a prorated portion of the paid holidays and vacations received by full-time workers. Life or health insurance was generally not provided to part-time employees, and pension plans were available to less than one-fourth of the part-timers (Dsaki, 1974). In essence, part-time employees (mostly women) are often exploited in much the same way as other disadvantaged groups of workers, who are perhaps too grateful for the "opportunity" to find work which meets their personal needs to complain about discriminatory personnel policies.

Strong objections to permanent part-time work have been raised in several sectors. In particular, union leaders have expressed concern not only about the problem of inadequate compensation for part-timers but also about the more serious issue of eliminating full-time jobs to create part-time opportunities. John Zalusky at the AFL-CIO made the following comments at the 1977 National Conference on Alternative Work Schedules:

> the social purpose [of job sharing and part-time work] ostensibly is to create jobs for those who are not now interested in full-time employment. I find this particularly distasteful when we have approximately ten million people out of work looking for full-time positions. The only one that really seems to benefit from job sharing is the employer looking for workers as cheaply as he can get them regardless of the needs of the community. If we had a labor shortage, the use of job sharing would make a lot more sense. I know there are those that say that this allows women who are dissatisfied with staying at home an opportunity to work, but on the other hand there are over three million women who are actively seeking full-time employment who cannot afford to support their families on a part-time job [Zalusky, 1977].

Employers claim to be reluctant to expand part-time openings because "peripheral employees" are felt to be unreliable, low in ability, and uncommitted to work or the organization (Gannon, 1975). There is some evidence which not only refutes these myths but also suggests that employers can derive a number of benefits from part-time employees. For example, Catalyst, Inc., a nonprofit organization which works to expand part-time opportunities for college-educated women, convinced the Massachusetts Department of Welfare to hire 50 women with children as case workers on a part-time basis. A one-year follow-up study revealed that these part-time workers handled 89 percent of the case load of full-time workers and had a turnover rate one-third as great as their full-time counterparts (Greenwald and Liss, 1973). Felice Schwartz, President of Catalyst, has also pointed out such potential employer advantages of hiring part-time personnel as a larger recruitment pool, reduction in time lost from work to attend to personal matters, less "padding" to fill a full-time week, and a finer division of jobs by levels of skill required (Schwartz, 1974).

POLICY IMPLICATIONS AND RESEARCH NEEDS

Social scientists have been surprisingly slow in addressing important sociological and psychological issues which are implied by changing schedules of work. Although a change in work hours might seem a rather minor form of social change, innovative work schedules represent an alteration in the distribution of people's activities over time, which in turn can affect the general quality of life. Greater variety of work schedules and greater flexibility of working time will open the door to other complexities which can perhaps be anticipated by social scientists and analysts, who in turn can play an important role in the formulation of public policies. The discussion has focused on the special implications of rearranged work schedules for women, not because the effects on male workers will not be profound, but rather because women continue to be in special need of mechanisms to improve their status and role in the world of work in particular and society in general.

It is unlikely that the advantages offered by any work schedule would be equally appealing to all workers or potential workers. It is for this reason, among several others, that we need a richer perspective on what the various working time allocations *mean* to workers with different characteristics. It is understandable that existing research has had, for the most part, a distinctive managerial or administrative orientation. Managers seek data concerning the impact of innovations on productivity, costs, profits, and so forth, in order to facilitate the decision-making process relevant to their own organizations. It is thus not surprising that most research has been rather narrow in scope. This is not to minimize the value of management-based research. If firms are not convinced that they will experience benefits (or at least *not* experience disadvantages), they will be reluctant to make nontraditional schedules available to employees. However, it is conceivable and likely that rearranged work schedules may herald the introduction of important social change with regard to family life, life styles, quality-of-life perceptions, and the division of labor along traditional sex-role lines. It therefore seems appropriate for social scientists to increase their research involvement in this area. We are in serious need of more reliable information about women's reactions to nontraditional and traditional schedules as well as a careful analysis of the implications of making such working arrangements available. Which form of work schedule is most appealing and why? Do some schedules attract women in greater numbers than others? How do work schedules affect childcare arrangements? Do nontraditional schedules lead to increased leisure and educational or personal development opportunities for women? These and other important questions are all largely unanswered.

We can expect that nontraditional work schedules will come to be a growing concern to policy makers within the next few years.[1] Let us look at some examples of the way rearranged work schedules interface with existing policies. The availability of alternative work schedules could aid in the successful implementation of legislation aimed at eliminating sex discrimination. Revised Executive Order 4 requires companies with federal contracts over $50,000 to develop affirmative action programs for hiring more women in nontraditional fields and supervisory positions. Some firms have complained about these requirements, claiming that there are too few women with appropriate training in certain fields, such as engineering. The conversion of departments or whole organizations to flexible or four-day schedules, or the conversion of full-time openings to two part-time openings, could reveal a larger pool of applicants than would have hitherto been available and may thus lead to greater ease in compliance with anti-sex-discrimination legislation. At the same time, it must be recognized that the extensive use of part-time employment might promote rather than reduce discrimination against women if employers reserved full-time openings (which have more potential for advancement) largely for men.

Another manner in which the issue of sex discrimination relates to nontraditional schedules concerns training opportunities. The narrowness of women's occupational range has been well documented. For example, 1969 figures from the Bureau of the Census indicate that half of all working women were employed in 21 of the 250 occupations listed, compared with 65 different occupations for half of the working men (Hedges, 1970). Most women continue to work in "female" jobs. It is not the narrowness of job opportunities for women per se which is so problematic; rather, it is the concentration of women in the lowest paying, least prestigious jobs which figures so heavily into claims of sex discrimination. Women often lack the skills associated with higher paying jobs, however, and are therefore in exceptional need of training or retraining. Rigid, traditional schedules in jobs with a training or apprenticeship component may serve as a real obstacle to women with family responsibilities and may thus restrict or delay entry into nontraditional occupations.

Aside from the issue of discrimination, changing work schedules have other implications for women which are of relevance to policy and decision makers. Many economists agree that perhaps the most effective way to fight inflation and keep American goods competitive in the world market is to increase worker productivity. Despite the fact that U.S. productivity is growing, it has been growing at progressively lower rates in recent years. Job satisfaction has repeatedly been found to be a key element in a worker's productivity (Katzell and Yankelovich, 1975). While surveys have shown that job satisfaction is on the whole rather high in our country, certain categories of workers—including married women with children—consistently report levels of job satisfaction which are considerably below average (Gallup, 1974). It does not seem unreasonable to hypothesize that the relative dissatisfaction of this group stems in part from the conflicting demands of the worker/mother/wife roles. This conflict might be reduced if more flexible working arrangements were available to ease the burden of handling multiple roles. The implication is that rearranged work schedules have the potential for augmenting worker satisfaction and hence productivity.

There is an alternative way of linking schedules to productivity by discussing the problem of turnover. High turnover is associated with high employer costs and low productivity, and females are generally assumed to have higher turnover rates than males. Although total female rates of quitting are not substantially higher than those of males, women tend to quit more often than men because of household responsibilities, while men are more likely to quit for job-related reasons (Mattila, 1974). It is thus possible that providing women with scheduling options which enhance the "fit" between work and personal obligations would result in higher worker stability among females than males.

Employers, unions, and government alike are showing a growing concern for, and sensitivity to, what has been called the quality of life. The concept of work itself is moving increasingly from that of "earning a living" to that of "making a life." At the same time, leisure, continuing education, and other forms of personal growth are attracting expanded interest among workers. The quality of women's lives may depend to a much greater extent than that of men's on the kinds of opportunities which result from innovative work schedules. The government of the near future is likely to take steps that deal with the quality of working life of its citizens. Proposals have been advanced for government-initiated steps to monitor the quality of working life in private organizations and to offer incentives such as tax benefits to employers in compliance with established standards.

The reform of women's role in our society is still in its early stages. Despite the efforts of the federal government to impose legal restrictions on occupational sex discrimination, our society's commitment to sex equality is not complete, as the numerous unsuccessful attempts to enact child care legislation have shown us and as the Equal Rights Amendment still awaits ratification in many states. The opportunity for women (and men) to choose when to work and how many hours to work represents a change which could have a profound impact on our behavior, values, and goals. Individuals concerned with enhancing the quality of life of women (and men) should have an interest in promoting experimentation and research on nontraditional work schedules.

NOTE

1. Legislation has been submitted in both the U.S. House of Representatives and Senate to experiment with alternative work schedules in federal agencies (S. 517. H.R. 2732, H.R. 2930); to establish part-time work opportunities in executive agencies of the federal government (S. 518, H.R. 1627); and to stimulate permanent part-time employment in the private sector through a system of tax credits (H.R. 2402).

REFERENCES

Agassi, J.B. (1975) "The quality of women's working life." In Davis, L.C., and A.B. Cherns (eds.) The quality of working life. New York: The Free Press.

Calvasina, E.J. and W.R. Boxx. (1975) "Efficiency of workers on the four-day week." Academy of Management Journal 18.

Carmel, A.S. (1973) "Implications of the new workweek patterns for women in the work force." The Labor Gazette 73.

Dsaki, R.S. (1974) "Area wage survey test focuses on part-timers." Monthly Labor Review 97.

Elbing, A.O., H. Gadon, and J.R.M. Gordon. (1975) "Flexible working hours: The missing link." California Management Review 17.

Evans, M.G. (1975) "A longitudinal analysis of the impact of flexible working hours." Studies in Personnel Psychology 6.

Evans, M.G. (1973) "Notes on the impact of flexitime in a large insurance company." Occupational Psychology 47.

Gallup, G., Jr. (1974) "Are we living up to the promise of America?" Vocational Guidance Quarterly 21.

Gannon, M.J. (1975) "The management of peripheral employees." Personnel Journal 54.

Golembiewski, R.T., R. Hilles, and M.S. Kagno. (1974) "A longitudinal study of flexitime effects: Some consequences of an OD structural intervention." The Journal of Applied Behavioral Science 10.

Greenwald, C.S. (1972) "Working mothers: The need for more part-time jobs." New England Economic Review (September-October).

——— and J. Liss. (1973) "Part-time workers can bring higher productivity." Harvard Business Review 51.

Hartley, J. (1976) "Experiences with flexible hours of work." Monthly Labor Review 99 (May).

Hayghe, H. (1976) "Families and the rise of working wives—an overview." Monthly Labor Review 99.

Hedges, J.N. (1970) "Women workers and manpower demands in the 1970's." Monthly Labor Review 93.

Hodge, B.J. and R.D. Tellier. (1975) "Employee reactions to the four-day week." California Management Review 18.

Katzell, R.A. and D. Yankelovich. (1975) Work, productivity and job satisfaction. New York: The Psychological Corporation.

Kenny, M.T. (1974) "Public employee attitudes toward the four-day workweek." Public Personnel Management 3.

Kreps, J.M. and R.J. Leaper. (1976) "Home work, market work and the allocation of time." In Kreps, J.M. (ed.) Women and the American economy. Englewood Cliffs, N.J.: Prentice-Hall, Inc.

Macut, J.J. (1974) "Measuring productivity under a four-day week." Monthly Labor Review 97.

Mahoney, T.A., K.M. Newman, and P.J. Frost. (1975) "Workers' perceptions of the four-day week." California Management Review 18.

Mattila, J.P. (1974) "Labor turnover and sex discrimination." Working paper, Industrial Relations Center, Iowa State University of Science and Technology.

Nord, W.R. and R. Costigan. (1973) "Worker adjustment to the four-day week: A longitudinal study." Journal of Applied Psychology 58.

Partridge, B.E. (1973) "Notes on the impact of flexitime on a large insurance company: Reactions of supervisors and managers." Occupational Psychology 47.

Schonberger, R.J. (1971) "Inflexible working conditions keep women 'unliberated.'" Personnel Journal 50.

———. (1970) "Ten million U.S. housewives want to work." Labor Law Journal 21.

Schwartz, F.N. (1974) "New work patterns for better use of womanpower." Management Review 63.

Simmons, A., A. Freedman, M. Dunkle, and F. Blau. (1975) Exploitation from nine to five: Report of the Twentieth Century Fund task force on women and employment. Lexington, Massachusetts: D.C. Heath Company.

Steele, K.L. and R. Poor. (1970) "Work and leisure: The reactions of people at four-day firms." In Poor, R. (ed.) Four days, forty house reporting a revolution in work and leisure. Cambridge, Massachusetts: Bursk and Poor.

Sverdloff, S. (1976) The revised workweek. Washington: Bureau of Labor Statistics.

U.S. Bureau of the Census. (1976) "A statistical portrait of women in the United States." Current Population Reports 58, Series P-23.

U.S. Department of Labor, Women's Bureau. (1969) Handbook on woman workers. Washington: Government Printing Office.

Walker, J., C. Fletcher, and D. McLeod. (1975) "Flexible working hours in two British government offices." Public Personnel Management 4.

Werther, W.B., Jr. and J.W. Newstrom. (1972) "Administrative implications of the four-day week." Administrative Management 33.

Wheeler, K.E., R. Gurman, and K. Tarnowieski. (1972) The four-day week. American Management Association.

Zalusky, J.L. (March 21, 1977), Research Department of the American Federation of Labor and Congress of Industrial Organizations. Speech given before the National Conference on Alternative Work Schedules, Chicago.

10

HOURS RIGIDITY: EFFECTS ON THE
LABOR-MARKET STATUS OF WOMEN

RALPH E. SMITH

The issue of alternative work schedules—especially part-time jobs—has generated a debate among individuals concerned with improving the economic status of women. Would the existence of more part-time jobs really be good for women? Some proponents claim that part-time jobs should be encouraged because they permit women to work, while still meeting their home responsibilities. They assume that the traditional division of labor within the home is satisfactory or, at least, tolerable. Other advocates are not content with the traditional division of labor and see part-time jobs for women *and* men as a way of reallocating home responsibilities. This assumes that men will take part-time jobs. Opponents view part-time jobs as a means

AUTHOR'S NOTE: The opinions expressed do not necessarily reflect the views of the Urban Institute or its sponsors. I wish to thank Isabel Sawhill for her helpful comments on an earlier draft, Paul Flaim for providing unpublished tabulations from the Current Population Survey, and Kathi Newman and Sara Penn for research assistance. This article was originally presented at the National Conference on Alternative Work Schedules, March 20-23, 1977, Chicago, Illinois, and reprinted in *Hearing on Part-time Employment and Flexible Work Hours,* Subcommittee on Employee Ethics and Utilization, U.S. House Committee on Post Office and Civil Service, 1977, pp. 241-245.

of perpetuating the traditional division of labor outside and within the home. They argue that these jobs are bad for women because the jobs usually have low wages and little chance for advancement. To progress in the labor market women should be encouraged to take full-time jobs. They also contend that few men will take the part-time jobs.

The purpose of this article is to present some evidence relevant to this debate. The price that women who wish to work on a part-time schedule are now paying and the potential impact of broadening the range of occupations in which part-time schedules are available are estimated. As background for considering the effects of work schedules on women's labor market status, I will first discuss women's progress and failures in the labor market in recent years.[1]

WOMEN'S STATUS IN THE LABOR MARKET

Three patterns dominate: first, the sharp increase in the proportion of working-age women who have been seeking to participate in the paid labor market; second, the persistence of occupational segregation between men and women; and third, the persistance of lower wages received by women.[2]

The proportion of working-age females seeking to participate in the paid labor market has increased in nearly every year since World War II. In 1950, 34 percent of all women aged 16 and over were working or looking for work. In 1977, over 48 percent were engaged in the labor force. The reasons for this dramatic rise include increases in job opportunities and wage rates and changes in sex-role attitudes, marriage, and fertility patterns. Earlier retirements and longer schooling, meanwhile, have reduced the proportion of the male population participating in the work force. Consequently, six out of every 10 net additions to the work force since 1950 have been women. Most have found jobs.

However, a closer examination reveals a second pattern that is not very promising. The jobs that women have been able to find are often quite different from those held by men. There is a pervasive and persistent pattern of segregation in which some jobs are readily identifiable as "women's work" and others as men's. Examples of the former include prekindergarten, kindergarten, and elementary school teachers, cashiers, bookkeepers, waitresses, telephone operators, nurses, and secretaries. Women's jobs often have lower pay and status than men's jobs requiring an equivalent amount of education and training. Often the jobs are logical extensions of the homemaker role—with the boss being male. This pattern has improved only slightly in recent years.

The third pattern, closely related to the preceding one, is that women's average wages are much lower than those of men. This too has not changed much through the years. For the past two decades the typical female worker who worked at least 35 hours a week earned less than two-thirds of what the typical male earned. (U.S. Dept. of Labor, 1976)[3] A major reason for this differential is the pattern of occupational segregation. Women may sometimes be paid less than men for doing the same job, but the more important problem is that they perform in different jobs and the ones women are doing usually pay less. Both problems are particularly serious for women seeking part-time jobs, as will be discussed below.

THE PRICE WOMEN PAY

One-quarter of all women in the labor force are either voluntarily employed on a part-time basis (less than 35 hours per week) or looking for part-time jobs. This fraction has not changed much in recent years. (Employment and Training Report of the President, 1976, pp. 254-255) What price are women paying for their need or desire to work less than the standard week? What impact might more widespread use of nonstandard work schedules have on women's success in the labor market? In particular, would it help to break down the pattern of occupational segregation and would it help to narrow the gap in wage rates between men and women? The answers depend, of course, on the specific means by which alternative work schedules are introduced and the way employers, male employees and women, themselves, react to the changes.

Clearly, if an expansion in the number of part-time job opportunities merely means more of the same, the opponents have a strong case. Women *do* pay a price for their schedule preference. Existing part-time employment is heavily concentrated in low-wage occupations. For example, over one-third of all women with part-time schedules are employed in food service, retail sales, and private-household-service occupations. Furthermore, the wage rates of women part-timers are usually lower than those of women full-timers in the same occupations. For example, in May 1976 the median hourly wage rate of women on part-time schedules in food service was $2.28, $.13 below the median wage of women on full-time schedules (and $.86 below that of men on full-time schedules in this occupation). As a result of these differences in occupational distribution and wage rates within the same occupation, women with part-time schedules are paid about 25 percent less than women on full-time schedules. In May 1976 the average usual hourly earnings of female part-timers was $2.71, compared with $3.59 for females with full-time schedules.

Also, as the opponents point out, relatively few men take part-time jobs. In 1976, there were only 4.6 million males in the part-time labor force, compared with 9.3 million females; only three in 10 of the male part-timers were adults under age 55, compared with six in 10 of the female part-timers. (*Employment and Earnings*, Vol. 24 (January 1977), p. 144). Thus, under the existing conditions in the labor market and within the home, very few men choose to voluntarily work a part-time schedule after they have completed their education until nearing retirement.

The problems with part-time employment need not occur if such jobs could be made available across the entire occupational structure of the labor market. Suppose, for example, that women now working on part-time schedules were at least given the same occupational distribution as women with full-time jobs now have. A comparison of this hypothetical situation with the existing one provides information about the potential impact of *broadening* the range of part-time job opportunities, as distinct from *increasing* the number of part-time jobs.

To illustrate the potential *direct* effect on working women of schedule changes, I did some calculations using recent data on the usual hourly earnings of workers on part-time and full-time schedules in about 40 occupations. A description of these data and of my analysis is provided in a technical appendix.

As a standard for estimating the effects of hours rigidity on occupational segregation, I first computed an index of dissimilarity between the occupations in which men and women were employed in 1976. On a scale of zero to one, in which one equals complete segregation (all women are in one set of occupations and all men in another) and zero equals complete integration, the overall index was .581. This, incidentally, is only slightly lower than the degree of dissimilarity that existed in 1970.[4]

Next, I estimated the direct effect of redistributing the women who are presently on part-time schedules into the same occupations presently employing women on full-time schedules. This would bring the female workers, as a group, up to the level of segregation now experienced by female full-time workers. If women who were working on a part-time schedule had the same occupational distribution as women on full-time schedules, this would lower the degree of dissimilarity to .558. That is, redistributing the women currently on the part-time schedules would reduce segregation by about two percentage points. This is an improvement, but not a very dramatic one. It is about three-quarters of the integration that occurred between 1960 and 1970.

The direct effect is not very large because the jobs women with part-time schedules hold are not very different from those with full-time schedules. For the most part they are a subset of the traditional women's jobs. (The index of dissimilarity between the occupations of women working full-time versus part-time was only .281.) As previously noted, the retail sales and service sectors provide a large portion of part-time opportunities. These tend to be among the lowest paid of the traditional women's fields.

I used the same set of data to estimate the potential impact on women's wages of introducing widespread part-time job opportunities. In May 1976, the median usual hourly earnings of women with part-time schedules was $2.71, $.88 below the wage for female full-time workers. Part of this difference is due to lower pay within the same occupations; part is due to part-time workers being in occupations that have lower wages for everyone. If women with part-time schedules had the same occupational distribution as women with full-time schedules, the latter differential would be eliminated. I estimated this would raise the median wage rate of the part-timers by about $.35 per hour; that is, over one-third of the gap between the wage rates of part-time and full-time female wage earners is directly related to occupational dissimilarity. If the typical part-time worker worked 1,000 hours a year, this would increase her annual earnings by $350, a 13 percent increase. (Providing women currently in part-time jobs with the same wage rates as women in full-time jobs within the same occupations would have a similar impact.)

One major *caveat* to my estimates must be mentioned. I was not able to estimate the extent to which the different occupational distribution of part-timers and their lower wage rates are due to differences in the characteristics of the women themselves, such as their education and training. It would be useful to isolate the pure effect of being a part-time worker on one's job assignment and wage rate, but this would require additional data.

These estimates also ignore a more subtle way in which the distribution of part-time jobs contributes to segregation and lower earnings. They indicate only the impact of a minor redistribution of women who are already in the labor market. Undoubtedly some women currently employed in full-time jobs were influenced in their occupational choice by the availability of part-time employment. They may have started out as part-timers or may be planning to switch to a part-time schedule later. Thus, if part-time opportunities were more widespread, full-time workers would be affected as well. One reason that women take retail sales jobs, for example, is that it is relatively easy to switch back and forth between part-time and full-time schedules. The long-run impact of widespread availability of part-time and other alternative work schedules on the labor-market status of women would therefore be larger. As women began to make their education, training and first job decisions with less concern with how their future careers would fit in with their future home responsibilities, the global pattern of occupational dissimilarity would diminish.

Another important, but unknown, impact of a broader range of jobs with nonstandard schedules would be on the size of the female labor force. How many women not now in the labor force would enter if a broader range of such job opportunities were available? How many women who would have left the labor force would, instead, remain? This supply effect could diminish the potential short-run wage gains. In the longer run, however, the increased work experience that this would provide to working women would have a positive effect.[5]

CONCLUSION

Returning to the issue initially raised, I would conclude that considerable attention should be focused on the *kinds* of jobs that should be encouraged. Policies that do nothing more than encourage more part-time jobs in traditional part-time occupations may, as opponents fear, perpetuate a bad situation. My estimates indicate that the price of being a part-time worker is significant. On the other hand, if ways can be found to broaden the range of occupations in which part-time work is possible, this could lower that price.

Encouraging employers to offer alternative work schedules in job categories that have always been filled by people on fixed 40-hour schedules will not be easy. Policies intended to do so should be formulated with an understanding of the legitimate reasons for employer reluctance. There are real costs that firms would incur. (Sawhill and Smith, 1976) For example, there are substantial costs associated with recruiting and training a full-time worker in many of the better paying occupations. Hiring two part-time employees roughly doubles these costs. It is no coincidence that part-time employment opportunities are most common in occupations that require relatively little on-the-job-training.

Various proposals have been made for the federal government to encourage the growth of jobs with alternative work schedules. For example, in January 1977 Representative Conable reintroduced a bill to allow employers a tax credit for the expenses incurred in increasing the number of permanent part-time employees on their payrolls.[6] Such proposals should be examined very carefully to determine what effect they would have on the occupational distribution of part-time job opportunities. A fundamental goal of any policy or program to increase the number of jobs with alternative work schedules should be to broaden the range of such jobs.

TECHNICAL APPENDIX

In discussing the potential benefits of broadening the range of job opportunities with alternative work schedules, I presented some estimates of the direct effects on occupational segregation and wage differentials. These were based on hourly earnings statistics from the May 1976 Current Population Survey. This appendix provides a description of these data and of my calculations.

Data

The Current Population Survey (CPS) is a monthly survey of about 47,000 households conducted by the Census Bureau for the Bureau of Labor Statistics. It provides the major source of national data on employment and unemployment. Each May a special supplement to the CPS provides information on the "usual hourly earnings" of all wage and salary workers. This is based on the survey respondents' reported usual weekly earnings, divided by their usual weekly hours. Persons who report usually working less than 35 hours per week are classified as part-time workers. The data from this survey are subject to various kinds of errors due to reporting inaccuracies and small sample size. But they do provide a good indicator of basic patterns (Flaim, 1977).

Occupational Dissimilarity

Using data from the May 1976 CPS on the number of males and females working part-time and full-time in 40 occupations, several measures of occupational dissimilarity were calculated. The first (D_1) was an estimate of the overall degree of occupational dissimilarity between male and female workers. The second (D_2) was the dissimilarity between all male workers and female workers who usually work full-time. The third (D_3) was the dissimilarity between females who usually work full-time and females who usually work part-time.

Let E_1 be the number of people employed in the ith occupation, the subscripts M and F denote male or female, and the subscripts PT and FT denote whether their employment is part-time or full-time. For a mutually exclusive and exhaustive set of occupations we define three dissimilarity indices as:[7]

$$D_1 = \sum_i \left| \frac{E_{iM}}{E_M} - \frac{E_{iF}}{E_F} \right| \div 2,$$

$$D_2 = \sum_i \left| \frac{E_{iM}}{E_M} - \frac{E_{iF_{FT}}}{E_{F_{FT}}} \right| \div 2, \text{ and}$$

$$D_3 = \sum_i \left| \frac{E_{iF_{FT}}}{E_{F_{FT}}} - \frac{E_{iF_{PT}}}{E_{F_{PT}}} \right| \div 2,$$

where each would equal zero in the absence of segregation (for example, if the two groups of workers had identical occupational distributions) and unity with complete segregation (for example, if all of one group were in one set of occupations and the rest in another). I estimated that D_1 was .5808 in May 1976. To estimate the impact of redistributing female part-time workers such that they had the same occupational distribution as female full-time workers, I calculated the index of dissimilarity between male workers and female full-time workers (D_2). This was .5576, indicating that there would be about a .02 reduction in dissimilarity. The degree of dissimilarity between women on full-time schedules and women on part-time schedules (D_3) was only .2802. That is, women on full-time schedules held jobs that were much more similar to those held by women on part-time schedules than to those held by men.

Wages

The $.88 difference between the median hourly wage rate of female part-time workers and female full-time workers is generated both by part-time workers receiving lower wage rates than full-time workers within the same occupations and by part-time workers being disproportionately located in low-paying occupations. The former is estimated by comparing the actual median wage rate of part-time female workers with the hypothetical median wage of part-time females if each received the same wage rate as the average full-time female employee in her occupation. The latter is estimated by comparing the actual median wage with the hypothetical if part-timers had the same occupational distribution as full-timers (and still received the part-time wage rates).

Let $W_{iF_{PT}}$ be the median hourly wage rate of female part-time employees in the ith occupation, etc., and $W_{F_{PT}}$ be the median hourly wage rate of all female part-time employees. Then the impact of part-timers receiving lower wages rates within the same occupation is:

$$W_{F_{PT}} - \frac{\sum_{i} (E_{iF_{PT}} \cdot W_{iF_{FT}})}{E_{F_{PT}}} = \$ .33$$

and the impact of being in different occupations is:

$$W_{F_{PT}} - \frac{\sum_{i} (E_{iF_{FT}} \cdot W_{iF_{PT}})}{E_{F_{FT}}} = \$ .35.$$

Thus, \$.33 of the \$.88 difference in median wages between part-time female workers and full-time female workers is associated with part-timers being paid less than full-timers in the same occupations; \$.35 of the difference is associated with part-timers being in lower-paying occupations; and the rest is associated with an interaction between the two differences.

NOTES

1. For an analysis of the impact of the recent recession on women's employment and of women's prospects through the remainder of the decade, see Smith, 1977.

2. The consequences of anticipated continued growth in the female labor force through the next decade are examined in my forthcoming book, *The Subtle Revolution: Women at Work.*

3. In May, 1976, the median usual weekly earnings of female full-time workers was \$145, 62 percent of that of men; see Paul O. Flaim, 1977, p. 8.

4. In the *Economic Report of the President*, 1973, p. 155, it was estimated that the index was .598 in 1970 and .629 in 1960; these estimates were based on more detailed occupational categories, which tend to pick up more dissimilarity.

5. Morgenstern and Hamovitch (1976) analyzed differences in the supply behavior of full-time *vs.* part-time workers. One of their findings was that the availability of higher wage rates has a larger positive impact on women in part-time fields.

6. H.R. 2403, the Private Sector, Part-time Employment Act.

7. This type of index was used by the Council of Economic Advisers to measure occupational dissimilarity between men and women in 1960 and 1970 (*Economic Report of the President, 1973:155*). The value of the index can be interpreted as the minimum proportion of men or women who would be required to change occupa-

tions to produce complete integration. This assumes no replacement of the workers who departed. For a discussion of this and alternative measures of segregation, see Schnare, 1975.

REFERENCES

Flaim, P.O. (1977) "Weekly and hourly earnings data from the current population survey." U.S. Bureau of Labor Statistics Special Labor Force Report 195.

Morgenstern, R.D. and W. Hamovitch. (1976) "Labor supply of married women in part-time and full-time occupations." Industrial and Labor Relations Review 30.

Sawhill, I.V. and R.E. Smith. (1976) "Changing patterns of work in America." Hearings before the Subcommittee on Employment, Poverty, and Migratory Labor of the Senate Committee on Labor and Public Welfare, April 8. Washington, D.C.: U.S. Government Printing Office.

Schnare, A. (1975) "Residential segregation by race: Evidence from the past and prospects for the future." Washington, D.C.: The Urban Institute.

Smith, R.E. (1977) The impact of macroeconomic conditions on employment opportunities for women. Washington, D.C.: U.S. Government Printing Office.

———. [ed.] (forthcoming) The subtle revolution: Women at work. Washington, D.C.: The Urban Institute.

U.S. Department of Labor. (1976) Employment and training report of the president. Washington, D.C.: U.S. Government Printing Office.

———. (1976) The earnings gap between women and men. Washington, D.C.: The Women's Bureau.

11

EMPLOYMENT PROBLEMS OF WOMEN: FEDERAL GOVERNMENT EXAMPLES

NIJOLE V. BENOKRAITIS

The purpose of this chapter is threefold: to describe the position of women in the federal government, to explain why there has been little change in the characteristics of the federal female work force during the last decade, and to examine, briefly, the implementation and impact of affirmative action policies in the federal government. The following analysis has been limited to the period 1966-1976 for two reasons. The first is that although data on female employment have been gathered and published by the Civil Service Commission since 1959, collection methodologies and coverage have been most consistent only since the mid-1960s. Second, because the mid-'60s represented the beginning of the "affirmative action era," a presumed heyday of "quota" hiring, it is useful to concentrate on this time period.

AUTHOR'S NOTE: This paper seeks to update and extend some of the analyses presented in Nijole V. Benokraitis and Joe R. Feagin, *Affirmative Action and Equal Opportunity: Action, Inaction, Reaction* (Boulder, Colorado: Westview Press, 1978). I would like to thank Vitalius Benokraitis for helpful comments on an earlier draft of this paper.

GENERAL CHARACTERISTICS
OF THE FEDERAL FEMALE WORK FORCE

The federal government is the nation's largest employer, with nearly 2½ million civilian employees.[1] Almost 80 percent of these workers are in white-collar jobs.[2] Of these, women accounted for 710,596 (35.9 percent) of the federal white-collar workers in 1976.[3] Within the major pay plans, female employment traditionally has been highest in the General Schedule and equivalent pay plans. For example, in 1976 the distribution of women among major pay systems was as follows: General Schedule, 42.6 percent; wage pay systems, 8 percent; postal pay systems, 15.5 percent; and other pay systems, 21.1 percent (U.S. Civil Service Commission, 1976a: xii-xiii). Because women are predominantly employed in the white-collar (General Schedule) classifications, the analysis which follows concentrates on this group.

Between 1966 and 1976 both total federal employment and female federal employment fluctuated only slightly. As Table 1 indicates, female employment decreased from 1967 to 1972 and has been increasing slowly since 1973. Federal female employment has increased a total of only 2.3 percent from

TABLE 1: Women in Federal Employment 1966–1976

Year	Federal Employment[1]	Percent Women[2]
1966	2,303	33.6
1967	2,621	34.1
1969	2,601	33.4
1970	2,592	33.1
1971	2,573	a
1972	2,542	33.7
1973	2,385	34.0
1974	2,431	34.9
1975	2,419	35.3
1976	2,418	35.9

[1]In thousands; full-time employees, all pay systems.

[2]In full-time white-collar jobs.

a. 1971 data not shown due to differences in survey coverages.

Source: U.S. Civil Service Commission, 1969, 1973, 1975, 1976b.

1966 to 1976. This increase is especially modest since federal full-time civilian white-collar employment increased by almost 8 percent during this time period.[4] Moreover, most of the 2.3 percent increase in female employment has occurred since 1973. Although a causal relationship cannot be determined at present, it is interesting to note, nonetheless, that female employment increased slightly at about the time when passage of the Equal Employment Opportunity Act of 1972 (Public Law 92-261) brought federal employees under the Civil Rights Act of 1964 and reinforced the federal government's commitment to provide equal opportunity for all federal employees and applicants regardless of race, color, religion, sex, or national origin.

Table 2 shows the percentage of women employed in 19 major federal agencies during 1966 and 1976. Between 1966 and 1976 the percentage of women increased in eleven agencies and decreased in eight agencies. Except for the Veterans Administration, there were only three agencies in which slightly more than half of those employed were women in both 1966 and 1976—the Government Printing Office, the Department of Health, Education and Welfare, and the Civil Service Commission (CSC). In all of these agencies, however, women dominated the traditionally female and/or lower-paying occupations. For example, in the Department of Health, Education and Welfare and the Veterans Administration, the heaviest concentrations of women were in the predominantly female, medical-related occupations (U.S. Civil Service Commission, 1974:2). Also, almost 80 percent of the women in the Government Printing Office and more than 70 percent of those employed in the CSC were in the lower-salaried (GS 1-6) clerical positions (U.S. Civil Service Commission, 1976a:18, 44). In contrast, the National Aeronautics & Space Administration, where more than two-thirds of the positions are above GS-9, not only employed low percentages of women (19.8 percent in 1976), but was also characterized by a decrease in female employment between 1966 and 1976 (- 3.4 percent). Finally, the greatest declines in female employment between 1966 and 1976 occurred in three of the largest agencies—the Army, Navy, and Air Force (- 3.8 percent, - 4.6 percent and - 5.7 percent, respectively).

Since 1968 the number of women in the middle and higher pay categories has increased very modestly. As Table 3 indicates, between 1968 and 1976 the percentage of women employed in the lower levels (GS 1-6) decreased slightly—from 73.6 percent in 1968 to 72.7 percent in 1976—but has been increasing since 1972. The greatest increases, although low in

TABLE 2: Female Employment in White-Collar Positions, by Selected Agencies: 1966 and 1976

Agency[a]	Percent Women 1966	Percent Women 1976	Percent Change 1966–1976	Total Full-Time Employees 1976
General Accounting Office	27.0	28.0	1.0	5,086
Government Printing Office	53.3	51.7	-1.6	2,605
State	35.4	36.8	1.4	15,709
Treasury	42.5	47.5	5.0	110,073
Army	46.7	42.9	-3.8	225,464
Navy	43.6	39.0	-4.6	159,798
Air Force	49.8	44.1	-5.7	147,108
Justice	35.1	34.2	-0.9	49,938
Interior	29.7	32.2	2.5	56,693
Agriculture	25.4	24.3	-1.1	86,605
Commerce	31.7	35.3	3.6	29,141
Labor	46.7	45.1	-1.6	15,071
Health, Education and Welfare	57.7	61.7	4.0	139,602
Housing & Urban Development	40.7	44.4	3.7	16,325
General Services Administration	39.2	41.8	2.6	20,945
National Aeronautics & Space Administration	23.2	19.8	-3.4	23,028
U. S. Postal Service	12.3	16.2	3.9	498,106
Veterans Administration	49.6	56.8	7.2	157,532
Civil Service Commission	52.6	56.9	4.3	6,739
Total, All Agencies	33.6	35.9	2.3	1,981,163

[a]Represents world-wide agencies, all pay systems.

Source: U.S. Civil Service Commission, 1969:14-15; 1976b:22.

TABLE 3: Full-Time White-Collar Employment[a] by GS and Equivalent Grade Grouping 1968–1970, 1972–1976 (Excluding U.S. Postal Service Pay Plans)

Grade Grouping		1968	1969	1970	1972	1973	1974[b]	1975[c]	1976
1–6	Total	596,244	570,937	556,223	582,193	577,559	588,430	584,605	561,765
	Women	438,841	417,376	403,729	411,291	410,653	419,039	418,756	408,727
	%Women	73.6	73.1	72.6	70.6	71.1	71.2	71.6	72.7
7–12	Total	584,568	606,957	609,957	623,565	615,300	618,815	641,044	644,639
	Women	125,593	134,253	138,489	146,917	148,773	158,427	171,840	181,114
	%Women	21.5	22.1	22.7	23.6	24.2	25.6	26.8	28.0
13 and above	Total	168,578	181,068	187,555	197,481	198,962	197,337	202,832	205,054
	Women	6,357	7,012	7,469	8,336	9,014	9,317	10,368	11,158
	%Women	3.8	3.9	4.0	4.2	4.5	4.7	5.1	5.4
Total	Total	1,349,390	1,358,805	1,353,735	1,403,239	1,391,821	1,404,582	1,428,481	1,411,458
	Women	570,791	558,641	549,687	566,544	568,440	586,783	600,964	600,999
	%Women	42.3	41.1	40.6	40.4	40.8	41.8	42.1	42.6

[a]Data are as of October 31 of each year, except 1976 which is as of November 30. Data from 1971 are not shown due to differences in survey coverage.

[b]The 1974 data exclude 26,016 employees who are paid under white-collar pay plans that are not equivalent to the General Schedule.

[c]The 1975 data exclude 28,488 employees who are paid under white-collar pay plans that are not equivalent to the General Schedule.

Source: U.S. Civil Service Commission, 1975:xiii; 1976a:xiii.

absolute numbers, have been in the middle (GS 7-12) levels, where female employment has been increasing slowly—from 21.5 percent in 1968 to 28 percent in 1976. Female employment in the highest levels (GS-13 and above) has increased by a fraction of a percentage point each year, reaching only 5.4 percent in 1976. Thus, by 1976, almost three-quarters of all female white-collar federal employees were still found in the lowest-paying grade groupings, even though the total employment in this grade grouping has been decreasing for the last few years. By the same token, although total employment at the highest levels has increased by almost 22 percent since 1968, female employment has increased by only 1.6 percent.

As of October 1976, the average annual salary for male (white-collar) occupations was $18,249, and $12,154 for female. Across the same occupational categories, women's annual salaries were consistently lower than those of men. For example, in professional categories the average annual salary was $24,791 for men and $16,994 for women. Even in the traditionally female-dominated clerical categories, the salaries of men were higher than those of women ($13,905 and $10,552, respectively). Thus, within the same occupational categories, women consistently have lower salaries than men.

Women's overrepresentation in the lower-status categories is especially pronounced when we examine federal employment by both race and sex. Compared to men, both minority and nonminority women are disproportionately overrepresented in the lower-paying occupational categories. According to Figure 1, women are found predominantly in clerical occupations and rarely in professional occupations. There is some variation across sex groups. For example, Oriental women are more likely than both white and other minority women to be found in professional jobs. Compared to Oriental men, however, Oriental women still lag far behind in both professional and administrative categories, even though a higher percentage of women than men at grades 12-15 have had some graduate work (U.S. Civil Service Commission, 1974:28). Similarly, Spanish-surnamed women are overrepresented in clerical occupations even though, at grades 12-13, the percentage of Spanish-surnamed women

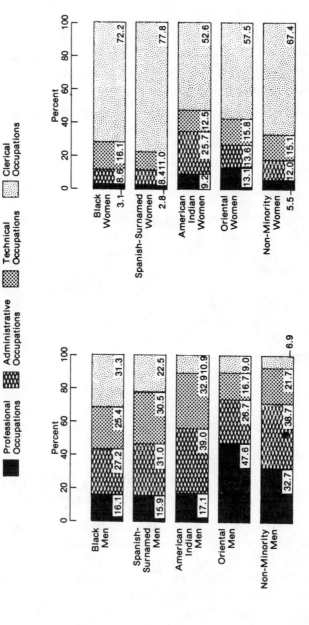

Figure 1: Percentage Distribution into Four Occupational Categories of General Schedule Employees of All Education Levels, by Minority Group and Sex, August 1974

college graduates is considerably higher than the figure for Spanish-surnamed men (74.1 percent and 56.8 percent, respectively). In examining the educational attainment of General Schedule employees by minority group and sex, one report concluded:

> In summary, then, for those women who achieve the upper grade levels—GS-12 through GS-18—their educational attainment is almost the equivalent of the men's. However, of all women college-graduate employees, relatively fewer women than men college graduates have as yet succeeded in reaching these upper levels [U.S. Civil Service Commission, 1974:29].

To summarize, during the last decade or so, the upgrading of female employment within the federal government has been less than dramatic. From 1966 to 1976, female employment increased by only 2.3 percent (Table 1). Some of this increase can probably be attributed to female hiring at some, but not all, governmental agencies (Table 2). Moreover, despite some overall increase, female employment is still, characteristically, in the low-paying federal government occupations (Table 3). Finally, compared to their male counterparts, minority and nonminority women are consistently found in the low-status employment categories—despite comparable educational levels (Figure 1 and related discussion). The next section discusses some of the reasons for women's inferior positions in federal government employment.

REASONS FOR WOMEN'S LOW STATUS
IN FEDERAL GOVERNMENT EMPLOYMENT

Because there is a paucity of research in this area and because the problems faced by women in federal employment are probably not dissimilar to those encountered by women in other sectors, the discussion which follows will present the findings of the federal government-related studies and some of the general literature regarding women in other employment settings (such as business, industry, and higher education). The latter studies should be helpful pending future research efforts which are directed at explaining the subordinate position of women in the federal government.

ATTITUDES

Both the attitudes *toward* women and *by* women have hindered female hiring and promotion in the federal government. For example, in a study of the Civil Service Commission's referral requests, Harrison (1964:80-81) found that, across all job categories, 29 percent of the requests specified men only, while 34 percent specified women only. When broken down by grade level, more than half of the requests to fill positions above the four lowest grades were for men only, while at the three higher grades (GS 13-15) 94 percent of the requests were restricted to men. Some of the reasons given for limiting certain appointments to women were that the positions involved monotonous, detailed, and repetitious duties or limited advancement opportunities; other reasons for precluding women workers were travel with men coworkers, exposure to weather, contact with the public, and working with teams of male employees.

Attitudinal employment barriers toward women in the federal government are based on assumptions that women are not interested in a career, have weak work motivations, do not like to accept responsibility, and contribute to high turnover rates. However, in a Civil Service Commission study of 30,000 employees at GS 5-15 grades, Harrison (1964:81-82) found quite the opposite. For instance, up to age 35, women averaged two and one-half more sick days than men, but at age 60 and above, men averaged a half-day more than women. In a national study of work absence, Hedges (1977:21-22) found that absence was higher for women workers as a group than for men, but that the differences by sex were related to marital status, age, and occupation (for example, single women have about the same absence rates as single men). Similarly, Harrison (1964) found that turnover in federal employment varied by age, occupation, and grade level, rather than sex—for example, women 40 years and over had a quit rate lower than men 30 years and under.

Another reason for not hiring women is the belief that women prefer male supervisors and do not get along with coworkers. Although such viewpoints may be representative of employers' attitudes (see, for example, Ginsberg and Yohalem, 1973; Schwartz, 1971; Loring and Wells, 1972), they do not reflect womens' own preferences. Harrison (1964) found that, across all federal grade levels, although almost 75 percent of the men preferred male supervisors, women had no preference for either sex as either coworkers or supervisors. In a study of female alumnae from the Harvard-Radcliffe Program in Business Administration, Goodman (1975:13) found that women encountered more discrimination in employers' attitudes than in coworkers' attitudes.

Besides the stereotypical attitudes of others, women's own attitudes hinder federal employment and promotion. Mac-Lennan (1973:9-12) suggests, for example, that "women conspire by their attitudes and behavior to perpetuate institutional sexism." That is, women fill out applications poorly, accept positions several grades below their rating, do not fight for salary and promotion increases, accept additional responsibilities without remuneration, are modest and nonaggressive about competing for awards and publicizing their achievements, are more critical of and less helpful to women than to men, and "are too unwilling to risk the security they have for a more respected position for women in the future."

The lack of competition is related, moreover, to women's low expectations about job mobility. For example, in a study of federal executive positions at grades GS 15-18, Lepper (1974:128-129) found that women do not compete for choice positions because of a deep-seated pessimistic belief that attempts to further their careers will prove futile. Thus, feeling that job prospects are limited because of sex, women have lower aspirations regarding job mobility.

QUALIFICATIONS

A common justification for the low participation of women in federal employment, as in other institutional employment areas, is that they lack the necessary "qualifications." Typically, it is argued that women do not have the experience, education, or skill to compete for jobs and promotions. Several studies indicate, however, that this is not the case. For example, after controlling for age, education, marital status, hours worked, and location, Long (1976) found that women earned considerably less than nonminority men in federal government employment. Also, Lepper (1974:117) found that 49 percent of the women executives, in contrast to 25 percent of the men, had a Ph.D. or equivalent professional degree. In examining federal white-collar work categories, Benokraitis and Feagin (1978) found that mean salary differentials existed for men and women in both professional ($21,267 versus $14,517) and nonprofessional ($13,835 versus $9,696) occupational categories. Harrison (1964) found, after controlling for GS level, that women were better educated than men: at GS-9 and higher, women had a higher rate of membership in professional societies, published more professional articles, and spent more time in job-related activities. In a study of 129,385 randomly-sampled, full-time GS employees in 22 major occupational groups, Taylor (1977) found (after controlling for education, number of degrees, years of service, age, supervisory status, location, veteran's preference, and government training) that substantial salary differences still existed between minority/sex groups and nonminority males. Taylor points out that "the net economic detriment" for not being a nonminority male is, on the average, $4,276 for minority females and $3,798 for nonminority females. Thus, despite having similar credentials on entering a job, women in federal employment fall behind men very early in their careers and the lack of mobility increases with job longevity: women typically enter at a lower grade level, get lower salaries (since salary is generally related to grade level) and take twice as long to advance to the same grade as men (Raloff, 1978:95).

Even when women have met objective standards (experience, high educational attainment, and professional activity), they are often judged "unqualified" in terms of more nebulous, subjective criteria. That is, women may be deemed "unqualified" because of other undesirable characteristics—whether real or imagined—related to personality traits (for example, not being "sociable" at office get-togethers), work motivations ("If she wasn't divorced she wouldn't be working"), educational pedigree (such as not having a degree from the "right" university), or quality of work ("Her research is irrelevant"). Such attributes have been used to disqualify women, but not men, in higher education (Hughes, 1973; Harris, 1970) and industry (Laws, 1976; Fogarty, Rapoport and Rapoport, 1967); it is quite likely that similar criteria, however invalid and unvalidated, are also used to disqualify women who are seeking entry or promotion in federal government employment.

SCREENING AND TESTING

Some of the strongest criticisms of the federal government which attempt to explain the low participation of women have been related to discriminatory screening and testing practices. First, few civil service exams have ever been validated for job-relatedness. For example, the CSC has been criticized for the lack of validation of tests to determine entry into managerial and professional jobs (Wallace, 1973:172-173).

Screening can be an important tool in employment disqualification in federal employment. Unless they are preselected and promoted through sponsorship, job applicants are routinely required to be interviewed for most federal jobs. Since job qualifications are very general, screening personnel and prospective employers have a great deal of power in accepting or rejecting an applicant on nonjob-related requirements. Moreover, if job requirements do not routinely specify evaluation criteria, interviewers may be left to their own devices in defining and setting standards of acceptability (Lopez, 1976:226-230).

Some qualification criteria which are based on stereotypes are especially detrimental to women. For example, employers may be warned to scrutinize older female applicants, since "Women are prone to lie about their age" or to evaluate a woman's marital status carefully because "Women who were recently divorced or separated sometimes make poor job risks"

(Ellman, 1967:35-36). Women's applications may be compromised not by an open denigration of their qualifications, but, more subtly, by a "not too enthusiastic" recommendation. For example, in a study of academic reference letters, male job-seekers were consistently and more strongly portrayed as "intellectually vigorous," "Professionally competent," and more "committed to careers" than female applicants (Guillemin et al., 1978). Since letters of recommendation are commonly required, especially in the professional occupations in the federal government, underendorsement of candidates may be important in limiting female entry into the higher job categories.

Also, women are screened out through restricted recruitment and arbitrary qualifications requirements. For example, the Merit Promotion Plan at NIMH has been "frequently and most skillfully . . . used to shut out applicants who are not wanted; thus, positions are not advertised until preselected candidates can qualify, or position descriptions are written in a way which specifies skills or experiences which women could not have obtained" (MacLennan, 1973:5).

HIRING AND PROMOTION

In a recent discrimination lawsuit (Chewning et. al. versus Seamans) against the Energy Research and Development Administration, the agency's attorneys conceded that the plaintiff had established a prima facie case of widespread discrimination throughout the "entire range" of scientific and other professional occupations. An analysis of the hiring and promotion data showed that the agency had hired 18 percent fewer women than were available with necessary qualifications, that "The longer women serve in government, the farther behind they fall relative to men with similar credentials," and that the salary differences increased with educational level, so that women in the higher categories had annual salaries which were $15,000 lower than those of men (Raloff, 1978:92).

Inequitable hiring practices derive from several factors. For example, a conscious cutback of federal employment is likely to affect the lowest salary levels which are occupied predominantly by women (Brimmer, 1972). The sex composition of employees at the executive appointment levels also may be affected by changes in administration. For example, the number of female Presidential appointees (GS 16-18) may fluctuate depending on the equal employment policies and commitment of the party in office. Also, isolation from sponsorship networks results in a loss of certain "fringe benefits." For example, women are not given the same traveling budgets and their scholarly accomplishments may be ignored while those of men are advertised in agency announcements (Raloff, 1978:93).

Women may be overlooked for promotion or not hired because they have been denied training opportunities. In a recent hearing alleging sex discrimination in the CSC's Bureau of Personnel Management Evaluation, for example, the examiner testified that the plaintiff, a woman, fit a "pattern" of job abuse:

> A disproportionate number of women reach the journeyman level of professional and technical employment and are not promoted into supervisory and managerial ranks. . . . Women come and go at GS-13, but seldom up to GS-14. . . . It is clear that women lost out in the promotion competition for lack of investigative training, supervisory training, management training, and on-site evaluation training" [cited in Badhwar, 1977a:6].

Also, the practice of preferential hiring and promotion of veterans (98 percent of whom are men) hurts women. Since about half of all federally employed men are veterans who qualify for preferential treatment throughout their careers, "it is against great odds that even the most forward-looking hiring policy could produce a [sexually] representative labor force" (Raloff, 1978:95).

Women are not promoted, furthermore, because they do not have qualifications which are important in the pre-selection process but are nonjob-related. For example, a supervisor might hire preselected men who have specialized computer experience or "wide field experience" even though such qualifications are not required by the job description (Badhwar, 1977a:6). Or, even if women happen to have these (and other) qualifications, their chances of promotion may be lessened considerably because they are not within the "old boy" sponsorship network and the "irregularities" in hiring and promotion which such networks produce in federal agencies and departments. Some of these "irregularities," which are "calculated to give favored candidates an advantage over those not picked for the job," include informally changing job requirements once job qualification standards have been posted and getting high supervisory ratings from nonsupervisors (Badhwar, 1977a:6).

It is not unlikely that the hiring and promotion practices which have kept women out of nonfederal jobs have also had an adverse impact on women in federal employment. For example, when the Equal Pay Act and Title VII were passed, it became illegal to have separate male and female salary rates. Some utility companies struck the words "male" and "female" from their guidelines but changed the grade structure so that women remained in only the lowest grades while men started at higher grades (Newman, 1976:267-269). In other cases women are promoted but still confined to what are considered "sex-appropriate functions." Laws (1976:159-160) found, for example, that at AT&T women managers at the lowest management levels supervised only women; if women were promoted to higher levels, they were placed in staff functions having advisory, rather than supervisory, responsibility.

Similar discriminatory hiring and promotion processes also characterize women's limited entry into and mobility within higher education. Women are disproportionately represented at community colleges and small colleges or in positions which are part-time, nontenured slots vulnerable to budget cuts (Robinson, 1973:212). Also, women may be hired for positions which preclude genuine career opportunities (such as peripheral administrative positions) or which reinforce traditional notions of women's nurturant roles (Mattfeld, 1974; Oltman, 1977). Like industry and higher education, the federal government is probably guilty of funneling women into powerless, nonsupervisory jobs.

MERIT

Early civil service reformers believed that merit systems, through open, rigorous, and competitive examinations, would both identify the most qualified applicants and eliminate the existing system of patronage and political favoritism (Subramanian, 1967:1011-1012). Recently, some argue that there is no "viable" alternative to the merit system in securing the most qualified employees in a fair and open manner (see McClung, 1973; Rosen, 1974). Others argue, however, that the merit system has resulted in a lack of equity in the civil service. Kranz (1974:436) maintains, for example, that about 21 percent of the federal, state, and local government employees have been selected through "authentic" merit systems; the rest have been selected on nonmerit factors which are determined outside the system (the military, professionals, political appointees and laborers who are governed by collective bargaining agreements).

According to Rosenbloom (1977:58), the introduction of the merit system had little impact on women because they had been formally excluded from most positions for many years. Formal exclusion has been replaced by more subtle and informal exclusionary practices. Promotions based on merit can be manipulated so that aspiring female applicants are never genuinely considered. A recent investigation of the CSC found widespread practices of illegal job referral and patronage activities at "the highest levels of the commission" (Badhwar, 1977b:1). Because women are typically outside of patronage networks,[6] they are passed by. For example, in a sex discrimination case, one CSC personnel management specialist stated that selection panel members were given insufficient materials to properly evaluate the female candidates and that the personnel officers made prejudicial remarks about female candidates seeking promotions (Badhwar, 1977a:6).

MARITAL STATUS

One of the most important barriers to female employment and promotion is marital status. If a woman is married, employers often assume that she will not move because of her husband's career. Prospective employers are more likely to interrogate women (but not men) regarding personal and domestic issues (Hughes, 1973.32). Many of the studies compare marital status and its effects on careers within rather than across sex groups, making it difficult to determine whether sex or marital status is more important in relation to occupational mobility.

The data which are available do not establish clearcut causality, but suggest certain hypotheses. For example, Ross: (1970) discovered that, after 20 years in an academic career, 90 percent of the men had reached a full professorship but only 53 percent of the single women and 41 percent of the married women had done so, suggesting that sex is a more important variable than marital status in explaining promotions. Ferber and Loeb (1973:996-997) found that, although there was no significant relationship between parental responsibility and either productivity or reward for women, men with children had higher salaries and higher ranks than men without children. Moreover, while there was no relationship between the amount of publications and marital status for women, professional honors, higher salary, and rank were slightly but significantly more likely to be awarded to single than married women. It appears, then, that professional success is least likely for married women with children and most likely for married men with children. If this situation also exists in federal employment, the least occupationally mobile women are those who are married and have children. Sexton (1977:15) has suggested that women's wage bargaining power with employers is reduced because married women are not free to migrate independent of their families.

JOB MOBILITY

Women's job instability is often cited as a reason for not hiring, not promoting, and otherwise not rewarding women. Job mobility rates, however, are very similar for both sexes. For example, in a study of scientists and engineers, Perrucci (1970:252-253) found that 80 percent of the women and 86 percent of the men reported having three or fewer employers after receiving their B.S. degrees. In psychology, "despite some significant differences between women and men . . . in training, type of employer, level of success achieved, and reasons for changing jobs, there was no significant difference in their job mobility" (Kimmel, 1974:538). According to Astin (1969:67), almost ten years after receiving their doctoral degrees, 45 percent of the women were with the same employer and an additional 30 percent had changed jobs only once.

There is little difference in job mobility by sex; why then is there a generally accepted myth regarding the extremely high mobility patterns of women? One reason, of course, is that such myths justify not hiring or promoting women who "are not going to stay anyway." Such myths may be especially damaging to women in nonclerical federal government positions—that is, if equally qualified male and female candidates are being considered for a job, the stereotypes surrounding women's lack of mobility can easily give the edge to the male applicant.

Mobility-related myths also might be used to justify paying women lower salaries than men for the same jobs. As discussed earlier, men have higher salaries than women within the same occupations in all federal government job categories. If employers can convince themselves that women have unpredictable mobility patterns, they can pay lower wages—even in clerical jobs—by arguing, for example, that job-training, which would increase salaries, is a risk (see Sexton, 1977:9-10).

The motivation for moving is usually financial for both males and females. Brown (1967:36-37) found, for example, that 69 percent of the moves in higher education resulted in higher incomes. Job mobility, however, can have different connotations for each sex. If a man moves, the general assumption is that he is upwardly mobile. If a woman moves, however, she is considered unstable and an employment "risk."

As this section has discussed, there are a number of unsubstantiated myths and stereotypes which continue to promote sexual inequality in federal and other employment areas. It might be expected that the federal government would be the most innovative and aggressive in promoting women's rights to equal employment opportunity practices. The last section examines the federal government's efforts in dismantling equal employment barriers for the female federal work force.

AFFIRMATIVE ACTION
AND WOMEN IN FEDERAL GOVERNMENT EMPLOYMENT

Little improvement in the participation and advancement of women in federal government employment has occurred during the last decade. This lack of improvement cannot be attributed wholly to the presence or absence of strong affirmative action efforts within the government itself. However, since women are still predominantly at the bottom of the occupational ladder in the federal government, it is reasonable to ask why the results of the presumably active affirmative action machinery have not been more striking. (That is, it might be argued that the little progress which has been made is due entirely to such factors as the larger number of women entering the labor force and their higher educational attainment.) The Civil Service Commission has the greatest power and responsibility for initiating and maintaining equal employment opportunity programs in the federal sector; therefore, the following discussion will focus largely on its affirmative action efforts.[7]

The Civil Service Commission is not highly committed to equal employment opportunity programs for women in the federal government. One indicator of the CSC's indifference has been its haphazard implementation of equal employment opportunity staffing regulations. In an investigation of the CSC and nine other federal agencies,[8] the Government Accounting Office (Comptroller General, 1977:14) noted, for example, that the agencies lacked systematic analyses to determine staffing needs, that equal employment opportunity personnel needed more training, and that the representation of minorities and women as complaint examiners and appeals staff should be improved.

According to one report (U.S. Commission on Civil Rights, 1975:26-40), the CSC has failed to comply with Title VII.[9] For example, CSC agencies have not been encouraged to recruit increased numbers of female applicants and have not conducted systematic reviews to determine what effect recruitment practices have on women. In employment selection, the CSC has failed to comply with the guidelines of the Equal Employment

Opportunity Commission by failing to determine whether examinations are valid and by encouraging the use of tests which are nonjob-related. In a study of equal employment opportunity in federal agencies, Short (1973:121-122) has pointed out that CSC officials are more committed to equal employment policies than actions.

CSC commitment even on the policy level, however, has been dubious. Rosenbloom (1977:110) argues that the Civil Service Commission has "accepted" the use of goals and timetables, but that it has "continued to deny the validity of the representational objective which the utilization of these devices was meant to achieve." Even though the CSC now "permits" usage of goals and timetables as a way of increasing female representation, its commitment to this issue has been unimpressive. According to Kranz (1974:437), the Civil Service Commission "has surrounded . . . [the permission of using goals and timetables] with rhetoric against 'quotas,' has hedged the definition of 'goals' with impossible requirements that minimize their utility, and has taken little action to ensure that agencies are progressing toward their goals on schedule."

Perhaps the strongest indicator of the federal government's noncommittal stance toward affirmative action has been its lack of enforcement. For example, of 27 federal departments and agencies ordered to submit plans for enforcing the law against discrimination in federally funded programs, only three had done so by March 1978 (U.S. Civil Service Commission, 1978). Recently, the CSC and nine other agencies were found lacking in a number of compliance and enforcement areas:

- Complainants were not always made aware of and afforded all of their rights.
- CSC guidance does not adequately protect the right of complainants to request reopening of their cases by CSC commissioners when new evidence becomes available.
- Agencies were not consistent in rejecting and canceling complaints.
- EEO officials named as alleged discriminatory officials can become involved in potential conflict-of-interest situations.
- Not all applicants for employment and employees were knowl-

edgeable about the complaint system [Comptroller General, 1977:31-32].

The CSC's weak enforcement efforts are especially striking in light of its budgetary allocation for civil rights enforcement. Although none of the agency outlays for enforcement are high, the CSC had the highest budget—$189 million in 1977.[10] Compared to the "poorer" agencies, then, it might be expected that the CSC should be somewhat effective in achieving equal employment opportunity. Instead, the CSC has failed in its responsibility to insure nondiscriminatory employment practices for women employed in the federal sector.

CONCLUSION

In examining the data and literature on female employment in the federal government, a prominent finding is the disappointing role of female employment in the federal government. Although a handful of descriptive and analytical studies are available which explain, in part, the inferior position of women in the federal work force, there is insufficient study of the external and internal processes and procedures which continue to operate in excluding women both from entry and mobility within the federal sector (for example, productivity, job specialization, availability of role models, effect of marital status, mobility, and so on). Even a cursory examination of the available data suggest that the employment prospects for women in the federal government are rather bleak. This chapter has shown that, despite widespread popularized rhetoric of "affirmative action" and "quotas," there has not been any evidence to indicate improvements in female employment—at least in federal government employment. To the contrary, overall female employment has increased minimally—especially in the higher-paying, higher-status jobs. The available studies suggest, moreover, that female federal employees continue to be victimized by their supposed defender—the federal government.

NOTES

1. The total civilian employment in the U.S. in May 1976 was 86.242 million (U.S. Department of Labor, 1976:81).

2. These white-collar occupations are in professional, administrative, technical, clerical, and "other" jobs, commonly referred to as PATCO.

3. As of November 1976, the number of women holding full-time federal jobs totaled 727,164, or 30.1 percent (U.S. Civil Service Commission, 1976a:xiii).

4. Full-time, federal, civilian white-collar employment was 1,837,062 in 1966 and 1,981,163 in 1976 (U.S. Civil Service Commission, 1976b:15).

5. The data in this paragraph are based on U.S. Civil Service Commission statistics (1976b:16-17).

6. For discussions of nonfederal government sponsorship, see, for example, Abramson (1975), Epstein (1970), and Dinerman (1971).

7. For a more thorough discussion of the affirmative action policies and problems in the federal government, see Benokraitis and Feagin (1978: ch. 3).

8. The other nine agencies and departments reviewed were the Departments of Agriculture, Commerce, HEW, Interior, Transportation, General Services Administration, Air Force, Postal Service, and the Veterans Administration.

9. Under Title VII, the Civil Service Commission is responsible for ensuring that federal employment practices are nondiscriminatory, for reviewing affirmative action plans annually, and for enforcing Executive Orders since 1965. The CSC governs all phases of the employment process, including retirement, hiring, placement, transfers, promotions, and conditions of employment.

10. For the same year, the enforcement budgets of other departments were the following: HEW, $26.5 million; Justice, $22.5 million; Labor, $12.9 million; Commission on Civil Rights, $8.9 million; Equal Employment Opportunity Commission, $68 million; and Defense $58.4 million (*Special Analyses,* 1976).

REFERENCES

Abramson, J. (1975) The invisible woman: Discrimination in the academic profession. San Francisco: Jossey-Bass.

Astin, H.S. (1969) The woman doctorate in America. New York: Russell Sage Foundation.

Badhwar, I. (1977a) "Cole's CSC unit guilty of sex discrimination." Federal Times. December 12.

———. (1977b) "FBI investigating key CSC officials." Federal Times. December 12.

Benokraitis, N.V. and J.R. Feagin. (1978) Affirmative action and equal opportunity: Action, inaction, reaction. Boulder, Colorado: Westview Press.

Brimmer, A. (1972) "Economic situation of blacks in the United States." The Review of Black Political Economy 2.

Brown, D.G. (1967) The mobile professors. Washington, D.C.: American Council on Education.

Comptroller General of the United States. (1977) System for processing individual equal employment opportunity discrimination complaints: Improvements needed. Washington, D.C.

Dinerman, B. (1971) "Sex differences in academia." Journal of Higher Education 42.

Ellman, E.S. (1967) Managing women in business. Waterford, Connecticut: Prentice-Hall.

Epstein, C.F. (1970) "Encountering the male establishment: Sex-status limits women's careers in the professions." American Journal of Sociology 75.

Ferber, M.A. and J.W. Loeb (1973) "Performance, rewards, and perceptions of sex discrimination among male and female faculty." American Journal of Sociology 78.

Fogarty, M., R. Rapoport and R. Rapoport (1967) Women and top jobs. London: Political and Economic Planning.

Ginsberg, E. and A.M. Yohalem [eds.]. (1973) Corporate lib: Women's challenge to management. Baltimore, Maryland: Johns Hopkins University Press.

Goodman, N.C. (1975) Women and management. Cambridge, Massachusetts: Radcliffe College.

Guillemin, J., L.L. Holmstrom, and M. Garvin. (1978) "The portrayal of male vs female job applicants in academic letters of recommendation." Unpublished manuscript.

Harris, A.S. (1970) "The second sex in academe." AAUP Bulletin 56.

Harrison, E. (1964) "The working woman: Barriers in employment." Public Administration Review 24.

Hedges, J.N. (1977) "Absence from work measuring the hours lost, May 1973-76." U.S. Department of Labor, Bureau of Labor Statistics.

Hughes, H.M. (1973) The status of women in sociology, 1968-1972. Washington, D.C.: American Sociological Association.

Kimmel, E. (1974) "Women as job changers." American Psychologist 29.

Kranz, H. (1974) "Are merit and equity compatible?" Public Administration Review (October).

Laws, J.L. (1976) "The Bell Telephone system: A case study." In P.A. Wallace (ed.) Equal employment opportunity and the AT&T case. Cambridge, Massachusetts: M.I.T. Press.

Lepper, M.M. (1974) "A study of career structures of federal executives: A focus on women." In J.S. Jaquette (ed.) Women in politics. New York: John Wiley.

Long, J.E. (1976) "Employment discrimination in the federal sector." The Journal of Human Resources 11.

Lopez, F.E. (1976) "The Bell System's non-management personnel selection strategy." In P.A. Wallace (ed.) Equal employment opportunity and the AT&T case. Cambridge, Massachusetts: M.I.T. Press.

Loring, R. and T. Wells (1972) Breakthrough: Women into management. New York: Van Nostrand Reinhold.

McClung, G.G. (1973) " 'Qualified' vs. 'most qualified': A review of the issues of competitive merit selection." Public Personnel Management (September-October).

MacLennan, B.W. (1973) "Women's part in institutional sexism." Speech given at the New York Academy of Sciences, January 10.

Mattfeld, J.A. (1974) "Many are called, but few are chosen." In W.T. Furniss and P.A. Graham (eds.), Women in higher education. Washington, D.C.: American Council on Education.

Newman, S. (1976) "The policy issues: Presentation III." In M. Blaxall and B.

Reagan (eds.) Women and the workplace: The implications of occupational segregation. Chicago: The University of Chicago Press.

Oltman, R. (1977) "Women in academic governance." In J. Pottker and A. Fishel (eds.) Sex bias in the schools: The research evidence. Rutherford, N.J.: Associated University Presses.

Perrucci, C.C. (1970) "Minority status and the pursuit of professional careers: Women in science and engineering." Social Forces 49.

Raloff, J. (1978) "The unequal scientists." Science News 114.

Robinson, L.H. (1973) "Institutional variation in the status of academic women." In A.S. Rossi and A. Calderwood (eds.) Academic women on the move. New York: Russell Sage Foundation.

Rosen, B. (1974) "Affirmative action produces equal employment opportunity for all." Public Administration Review 34.

Rosenbloom, D.H. (1977) Federal equal employment opportunity: Politics and public personnel administration. New York: Praeger.

Rossi, A.S. (1970) "Status of women in graduate departments of sociology, 1968-1969." American Sociologist 5.

Schwartz, E.B. (1971) The sex barrier in business. Atlanta, Georgia: Georgia State University School of Business Administration.

Sexton, P.C. (1977) Women and work. U.S. Department of Labor, Employment and Training Administration, R & D Monograph 46.

Short, L.E. (1973) "Equal employment opportunity as perceived by government officials." Public Personnel Management 2.

Special Analyses (1976) Budget of the United States Government.

Subramanian, V. (1967) "Representative bureaucracy: a reassessment." American Political Science Review 61.

Taylor, P.A. (1977) "Equal employment opportunity in the federal government: An examination of the available evidence." Paper presented at the 72nd annual meeting of the American Sociological Association, Chicago, September 5.

U.S. Civil Service Commission, Bureau of Manpower Information Systems. (1975) Federal civilian manpower statistics: Employment of women. Washington, D.C.: Government Printing Office.

———. (1974) Federal civilian personnel statistics: Educational attainment of general schedule employees by minority group and sex. Washington, D.C.: Government Printing Office.

———. (1973) Study of employment of women in the federal government. Washington, D.C.: Government Printing Office.

———. (1969) Study of employment of women in the federal government. Washington, D.C.: Government Printing Office.

U.S. Civil Service Commission, Bureau of Personnel Management Information System. (1976a) Federal civilian work force statistics: Equal employment opportunity statistics. Washington, D.C.: Government Printing Office.

———. (1976b) Federal civilian workforce statistics: Occupations of federal white-collar workers. Washington, D.C.: Government Printing Office.

U.S. Commission on Civil Rights. (1978) Civil rights update, March.

———. (1975) The federal civil rights enforcement effort–1974, Volume V, to eliminate employment discrimination. Washington, D.C.

U.S. Department of Labor. (1976) Monthly Labor Review, June.

Wallace, P.A. (1973) "Employment discrimination: Some policy considerations." In O. Ashenfelter and A. Rees (eds.) Discrimination in labor markets. Princeton, N.J.: Princeton University Press.

12

WOMEN'S RETIREMENT INCOME

WILLIAM D. SPECTOR

A cursory examination of retirement income statistics reveals the following: elderly women are more likely to be poor than elderly men. In 1973, 19 percent of women 65 years or older as compared to 12.4 percent of men aged 65 or older were in poverty (U.S. Bureau of the Census, 1975). One might be tempted to dismiss the difference as merely a reflection of the past labor force participation and level of earnings differences between women and men. Although it is indeed true that retirement income is a function of the work pattern and level of preretirement earnings, one must examine the role of social policies in distributing income between older women and older men to fully understand the causes of the income gap in retirement.

The Social Security Act of 1935, as amended, the Internal Revenue Code, as amended, and the Employee Retirement Income Security Act of 1974 (ERISA) are the major pieces of legislation that regulate the distribution of retirement income. Old Age Survivor Insurance (OASI), commonly known as Social

AUTHOR'S NOTE: The author is indebted to the following people: James H. Schulz for encouraging this research; Thomas Leavitt, Sandra Kretz and Regina O'Grady for substantive criticisms; Susan Forbes, Phyllis Glick and Kent Boynton for helpful editorial comments; and Marianne Muscato who expertly typed the final draft.

Security, is the major source of retirement income. It provides at least half of the annual income for 70 percent of individuals who are retired and for 50 percent of elderly couples (U.S. Senate, Special Committee on Aging, 1978:79). Second pensions, both public and private, are another important source of retirement income. In 1975, 35.7 percent of elderly couples and 22.9 percent of individuals were receiving second pensions (Harris, 1978:56).

The pension system has recently become a concern of social policy analysts. To a large extent, the concern surfaced in the 1960s as the media sensitized the public to the private "Pension Crisis." After thousands of workers were deprived of their pensions when the Packard and Studebaker Companies merged, newspaper editorials, Congressional debate, and general public awareness focused on the unkept promises of the pension system. As a result, the Employee Retirment Income Security Act (ERISA) was passed in 1974. More recently, the "Social Security Crisis" has caused new attention to be given to the pension system. Adequacy and equity questions involving the total retirement income system are being raised. What factors determine who retires in comfort and who retires in poverty? What are the rules of the game? These questions are particularly important in understanding the circumstances of women in retirement. Before discussing the particular issues facing elderly women, it is helpful to briefly review the key events that have shaped the pension system.

HISTORY OF PRIVATE PENSIONS

In 1875, the American Express Company instituted the first employer-sponsored private pension plan. Since that time, the pension system has undergone significant change and growth. Early plans were typically unfunded[1] and the employee had few rights. Not until 1926 were pensions regulated by the government. At that time, federal tax exemption status was extended to pension plans. If a plan was "qualified," employer contributions were deductible, investment income was not taxed, and employees were not taxed on contributions when made. Pension income was taxed when received in retirement.

The 1942 Revenue Act amendments prohibited qualified plans from discriminating in favor of higher-paid employees. Regulations were introduced in 1943 specifying the precise meaning of "discrimination." However, the regulations, in fact, allowed plans to provide better wage replacement for higher-paid employees if the plan was integrated with Social Security.[2] Therefore, a plan could in effect discriminate if the wage replacement from both private pension and Social Security was approximately the same for employees at all earning levels.

The tax exempt status and the "discrimination" amendments provided an impetus for the growth of the pension system; however, its growth did not accelerate until after World War II. This can be attributed to:

(a) the wage freezes during World War II and the Korean War which encouraged the growth of fringe benefits in lieu of wages;

(b) the National Labor Relation Board and Supreme Court rulings in 1947 that pensions were subject to collective bargaining under the Taft-Hartley Act; and

(c) the growing recognition by unions of the inadequacy of Social Security benefits and the need for supplementation.

The expansion of the pension system included an increase in the number of workers covered, liberalization of vesting requirements[3] and improvement in the size of the pension benefit (Skolnik, 1976). Even though the system was expanding, however, certain workers never received a pension benefit. ERISA established federal standards for funding, vesting, and established termination insurance to increase the likelihood that covered workers would receive a pension benefit. The law also attempted to discourage abuse of the tax regulations. Nevertheless, major inequalities still remain within the pension system.

WOMEN AND PENSIONS

Women are covered by pensions as survivors of covered male workers and/or as covered workers in their own right. It is important to examine the impact of pensions in both circumstances. Almost one-half (48.1 percent) of all adult women in 1977 participate in the work force and are, therefore, potential recipients of pensions as workers (U.S. Department of Labor, 1978b:24). On the other hand, many other women still remain, either totally or at some time in their life, in the traditional roles of child carer and housekeeper. In 1978, for example, of the over 38 million women who did not want a job, 29,687,000 explained that they were "keeping house." Moreover, of another 3.7 million women who were too discouraged to look for a job, 1,195,000 explained that "home responsibilities" prevented them from seeking work (U.S. Department of Labor, 1978a:57). Because of these responsibilities, women are more likely than men to have an intermittent labor force attachment.

The unequal distribution of pension provisions, the intermittent labor force experience of women, and the long life expectancy of women have all contributed directly or indirectly to the inadequacy of the income of elderly women. The long life expectancy of women affects both nonemployed women as well as employed women. Nonemployed women are likely to outlive their husbands and must rely on the survivor provisions of pension plans and Social Security survivor provisions, while the retirement income of employed women is directly affected by the long life expectancy when sex-differentiated mortality tables are used to determine the size of the pension annuity that accumulated pension savings can purchase.

Pension plan provisions vary considerably, and the quality of these provisions varies across occupations and industries. In addition, many provisions specify stringent requirements for eligibility, which are often related to the length of service. Most pension benefit formulas used to calculate the retirement benefits are related to length of service and level of earnings. Women, on the average, have lower levels of service and earnings than men; also, they tend to be employed in occupations and industries in which either pension coverage is not available or pension benefits are inadequate. Employed women, as a result, are less likely than men to be covered by a private pension in their own right; even when covered, they are less likely to actually receive a pension benefit and even when receiving a benefit, they get approximately one-half the median benefit of men.

This chapter will focus on three issues:

(1) a review of survivor's benefits and their importance for women as recipients and providers of such funds;
(2) an analysis of the factors that determine the pension income of employed women; and
(3) the impact of the Employee Retirement Income Security Act (ERISA) on the pension income of women.

SURVIVOR BENEFITS AND THEIR IMPACT ON WOMEN AS PROVIDERS AND RECIPIENTS

Survivor provisions in pension plans have become a common method of supplementing the traditional means of protecting family income on the death of an income provider. Both the public and private sectors have been traditional sources of survivor funds. For instance, employers have provided group life insurance and profit-sharing plans and, since 1939, the Social Security system has offered survivor provisions.[4] Also, many people have purchased individual life insurance to augment their personal savings.

Survivor benefits are important to women for two very different reasons. First, because many women spend much of their worklife out of the labor force and are much less likely than men to receive adequate pension income on their own, they are dependent on the earnings and pensions of men to maintain their standard of living. The death of a husband who has not provided a survivor benefit could cause a catastrophic decrease in a widow's income. This is compounded by the fact that women are likely to live six to eight years longer than men (National Center for Health Statistics, Feb. 11, 1977). Second, many employed women are contributing a significant portion of the total family income. In 1970 the median contribution to family income by a full-time employed married woman was 39 percent (Bell, 1976:241). Therefore, survivors of a female worker must be concerned with the potential loss of family income on her death.

Survivor provisions can be categorized as either preretirement or postretirement, and as either employer- or employee-financed. Pension plans are more likely to contain preretirement *employer*-financed survivor provisions and postretirement *employee*-financed survivor provisions.

PRERETIREMENT PROVISIONS

There has been significant growth in the number of plans offering survivor provisions. Before 1960 preretirement provisions were uncommon. By 1965 only 28 percent of plans offered employer-paid preretirement provisions (Bankers Trust,[5] 1970:21). By 1975, 63 percent of plans covering about 75 percent of pension-covered workers offered employer-paid, preretirement provisions (Bankers Trust, 1975:20).

Preretirement, employer-paid survivor provisions are normally limited to workers who could qualify for early retirement benefits but who choose to continue working until the normal retirement age. Either 10 or 15 years of service have been required for early retirement. The majority of preretirement, employer-paid benefits were based on the employee's full accrued benefit or on the early retirement benefit.[6] About 59 percent of plans with provisions and 55 percent of workers in these plans were covered by a 50 percent survivor's pension (Schulz, 1978:15).

Originally, survivor provisions in many plans were designed for women survivors only. For example, in 1970, 14 percent of conventional plans[7] limited beneficiaries to "widows only" (Bankers Trust, 1970:23). By 1975, however, only two percent of plans specified "widows only" (Bankers Trust, 1975:21). In 1970, only 22 percent of plans allowed "any beneficiary," and this figure actually fell to 16 percent in 1975. Typically, single parents and single and divorced workers are not eligible. Clearly, preretirement benefits were designed for the two-parent family and discriminate against single and divorced women and men.

About seven percent of plans offer only preretirement joint and survivor options. Joint and survivor options allow the employee to receive an actuarily reduced normal benefit in exchange for the protection of a survivor during the preretirement period. Normally the early-retirement qualifications must be met.

ERISA mandated that as of 1976 all plans had to offer at least a 50 percent joint and survivor option if a preretirement benefit was available, with an age requirement equal to the early retirement age or an age equal to 10 years less than the normal retirement age, whichever is later. If the employee qualifies but does not opt for the provision, which reduces the normal pension, the entire pension is lost on death. By 1976 approximately 51 percent of conventional plans offered only preretirement joint and survivor benefits and the remaining offered employer-paid benefits (Bankers Trust, 1976:5). To understand the importance of ERISA, however, data need to be collected to determine the frequency that workers opt for the joint and survivor coverage.

POSTRETIREMENT PROVISIONS

Postretirement, employer-paid survivor provisions are less common than preretirement provisions. By 1970 only 22 percent of plans offered these provisions (Bankers Trust, 1970:23). By 1975, 34 percent of plans covering 53 percent of pension-covered workers had these provisions (Schulz, 1978:16). Collectively bargained plans were more likely to offer these provisions than conventional plans (Bankers Trust, 1970:24).

There are a variety of postretirement provisions. The majority of plans provided either a lump-sum payment, a fixed period annuity, or a lifetime annuity. Lump-sum benefits originated in union plans in the 1920s and were designed to cover funeral expenses (Blostin, 1977:61-63); consequently, they are typically inadequate (the majority of plans in the Bankers Trust sample offered a lump-sum benefit between $750 and $3000). American Telephone and Telegraph, which employs over 840,000 workers, provided a lump-sum benefit greater than $3,000. Lump-sum plans cover survivors of about 30 percent of workers with postretirement, employer-paid survivor benefits. Survivors of an additional 20 percent of these workers receive fixed-period annuities. Normally, fixed-period annuities pay a fixed monthly benefit for five or 10 years. Survivors of the remaining 50 percent are covered by lifetime annuity equal to a period of the worker's accumulated benefits.

By 1975 many plans offered a variety of employee-paid options, including a joint and survivor option and a greater-than-actuarily-reduced joint and survivor option. In the latter option, the cost is shared by both the employee and the employer (Schulz, 1978:13-16).

ERISA mandates that as of 1976 all plans must offer a postretirement, 50 percent joint and survivor option which the employee must opt *out* of to receive the unreduced normal retirement benefit. Presumably, if the worker has to opt out instead of opting for the benefit, more spouses will be protected. Unfortunately, as with the preretirement regulations, no data have been collected to determine if workers are in fact opting out of this provision.

ERISA also allows plans to require that a spouse be married to an employee/participant both on the starting date of the annuity and for one year before the participant's death to qualify for survivor benefits. Therefore, survivor coverage may be nullified by divorce.

ADEQUACY OF SURVIVOR PROVISIONS

To determine the adequacy of survivor pension provisions, a comprehensive study is necessary of the entire survivor benefit package, including all forms of life insurance, profit-sharing plans, survivor provisions in Social Security, and survivor provisions in pension plans. However, a crude calculation can be made to assess the adequacy of the survivor provisions in pensions.

For this example, let us assume the survivor is covered by a 50 percent normal retirement benefit. If the retired worker dies, the survivor is eligible for 100 percent of the Social Security benefit plus the survivor pension benefit. Assume, also that this family is a single-earner household and the earner dies in retirement after having earned $14,000 on the average in the final years in the labor force. Prior to his death, he had been receiving an annual pension of $3,750 and a Social Security benefit of $3,750 for himself and a spouse benefit of $1,875, totaling $9,375. In this example, the worker is replacing 66.9 percent of the preretirement earnings. On his death, the survivor receives 100 percent of the $3,750 from Social Security and 50 percent of the pension ($1,875), totaling $5,625. This is a replacement of only 37.5 percent of the $14,000 preretirement earnings. If the worker did not have a pension or survivor pension coverage, the survivor would receive only $3,750 (from Social Security) on his death. This is a replacement of only 26.7 percent of the couple's preretirement income.

In the second example, assume that a retired full-time employed woman dies who had contributed approximately $6,000 to an annual family income of $14,000. Her pension was $900 and her Social Security benefit was $2,400. Also, assume her husband receives a $1,600 pension and a $2,800 Social Security benefit. They are receiving a total of $7,700 in retirement or 55 percent of the preretirement family income. On her death, the worker's husband is only eligible for 50 percent of the pension, or $450. Because his Social Security benefit is larger than her benefit, he is not eligible for a survivor's benefit from Social Security. His total income is now $4,850. The $450 is only 7.5 percent of her annual contribution of $6,000; in addition, it is only 13.6 percent of her retirement income before her death, and only 34.6 percent of the family's preretirement $14,000 earnings. If the female worker did not have pension or survivor pension coverage, her husband would receive no survivor income on her death. His $4,400 income, earned on his own right, replaces only 31.4 percent of the couple's preretirement income.

To evaluate the adequacy of the survivor provisions, it is necessary to determine the replacement rate (percent of the couple's preretirement earnings) needed to maintain the widow's or widower's preretirement standard of living. A rough calculation is possible. First, an estimate of the replacement rate that maintains the couple's preretirement standard of living is made; and second, this figure is reduced to determine the replacement rate for a single aged adult.

Although this replacement rate is a function of a person's income, James H. Schulz suggests that the preretirement standard of living is maintained with a replacement rate of 65 and 80 percent (Schulz, et al. 1974:231). Using 1966 data, Mollie

Orshansky estimated that a single aged person needs approximately 70 percent of the income of an aged two-person household to have the same standard of living (Pechman, Aaron, and Taussig, 1968:83). On the basis of these two estimates, a widow or widower needs between 45.5 and 56 percent of the couple's preretirement income to maintain the standard of living. Comparing the results of the above two examples (replacement rates of 37.5 and 34.6 percent) with this estimate indicates that survivors of workers with both Social Security and survivor pension coverage do not have adequate protection.

In conclusion, both widows and widowers are presently faced with a reduced standard of living on the death of a spouse who had participated significantly in the labor force. There are three major reasons for this circumstance:

(1) the inadequacy of Social Security survivor provisions;
(2) the inadequacy of survivor benefits in private pension plans even when combined with Social Security benefits; and
(3) the fact that many workers have no pension coverage for themselves and/or their survivors.

THE PRIVATE PENSION INCOME OF EMPLOYED WOMEN

To a large extent, the private pension system has penalized women for their labor force experiences. According to the Survey of Newly Entitled Workers (SNEB),[8] a cross-sectional study of workers who had recently received Social Security retired worker benefit payments in 1969, one-fifth of women and less than one-half of men were covered by a private or public pension plan on their longest job.[9] To understand these figures, it must be noted that workers in public plans were more likely to be covered. Only about one-third of workers in private industry were covered, whereas three-quarters of government workers were covered. According to Gayle Thompson (1978) using the sample from the Retirement History Study (RHS), a longitudinal sample of a cohort of workers aged 58-63 in 1969, 21 percent of women and 49 percent of men private wage and salary workers in 1972 were covered by a pension on their longest job.

There are many reasons why employers adopt pension plans.

Pension plans were valued by some employers as a means of inducing long service and employee identification with the employer. . . . The expected reduction of costly employee turnover is of great importance [Bernstein, 1964:10-11].

Turnover costs become prohibitive in occupations where on-the-job training is significant. Employers of workers in such occupations are likely to adopt a pension plan. On the other hand, employers of workers in occupations demanding limited job training may actually encourage turnover to permit low wages; they are not likely to adopt a pension plan.

In the early seventies, many working women who were covered by a pension did not receive a pension benefit at retirement.

Seventy-two percent of the men but only 55 percent of the women private wage and salary workers who were covered by a pension on their longest job and who earned no money in 1972 received benefits from a private or union pension in that year [Thompson, 1978:8-10].

Of women aged 61 or 62 who were nonearners in 1972 and wage and salary workers on their longest job, 88 percent retired with only Social Security as compared to 58 percent of men.

Although the size of the pension benefit had increased over time in real terms (see Spector and Schulz, 1978), the median benefit of women remained approximately one-half of the median benefit of men. In the SNEB study, the 1969 female median private pension benefit was only $970 as compared to $2,080 for men (Kolodrubetz, 1976:171). In the RHS study, the 1972 female median private pension benefit was $1,200 as compared to $2,230 for men (Thompson, 1978).

Another important measure of the pension benefit is the replacement rate, which measures the percentage of preretirement earnings that are replaced by the private pension.[10] In 1969, the median replacement rate for the longest job of newly retired women was 20 percent, compared to 27 percent for men. These data demonstrate the apparent inequities between women and men in the private pension system.

It is not clear at first, however, whether the apparent unequal treatment of women and men stems from overt discrimination within the pension system or a benign transference by the pension system of the labor force inequities into retirement. The pension system exacerbates and perpetuates the covert sex discrimination that exists in the labor force. Women are employed in low-wage, unstable occupations and industries, and these occupations and industries characteristically have inadequate pensions. In addition, pension plans discriminate against women workers by using sex-differentiated mortality tables.

On April 25, 1978 on a writ of certiorari, the Supreme Court affirmed the Court of Appeals decision in the City of Los Angeles versus Manhart case. The City of Los Angeles' Department of Water and Power had required women employees to make larger contributions to the pension fund than male employees.

The employer argued that since women as a class have a lower mortality rate than men, the cost of a given pension benefit for the average female retiree is greater than an average male retiree. Since the 1972 EEOC guidelines, which state that pension plans that give differential normal retirement benefits based only on sex violate the Civil Rights Act, noncontributory plans had to absorb the extra cost. However, many contributory plans compensated by requring women to contribute more than men.

The court presented two main arguments. First, it ruled that the 1964 Civil Rights Act was violated. The Act, which is concerned with fairness to classes of individuals, makes it unlawful to discriminate against employees on the basis of sex. It is true that women as a class live longer than men; however, many individual women do not live longer than many men. The Civil Rights Act, said the court, precludes discriminating against a woman because she is a member of a class (women) who live longer than another class (men).

Second, "The Equal Pay Act requires employers to pay members of both sexes the same wages for equivalent work, except when the differential [is] . . . based on any factor other than sex" (Justice Stevens, 1978:4349). The court argued that only the employee's sex was taken into account when determining the required contributions. This results in women receiving less take-home pay than men. Therefore, it was held that the Equal Pay Act had been violated.

The narrowness of the ruling is very important. To quote Justice Stevens,

> Nothing in our holding implies that it would be unlawful for an employer to set aside equal retirement contributions for each employee and let each retiree purchase the largest benefit which his or her accumulated contributions could command in the open market.

Employees and third parties are not governed by the Civil Rights Act or the Equal Pay Act. Presumably, when women purchase a retirement annuity, the insurance company can legally sell her a smaller annuity than a man for the same price (Justice Stevens, 1978:4351).

To the extent that employers begin using unisex mortality tables and absorb the higher cost of a pension for an average female employee, this ruling will be beneficial to women workers in contributory plans. However, the ruling still reaffirms the legitimate use of sex-differentiated mortality tables by insurance companies in selling retirement annuities. To the extent that employers convert to "money purchase" pension plans, which do not specify a pension benefit and require employees to purchase an annuity at retirement with their accumulated pension account, this ruling will produce minimal benefits.

COVERAGE

In 1969, 41.7 percent of the wage and salary labor force were covered by a private pension or a profit-sharing plan (Skolnik, 1976:4). In 1975, 46.2 percent were covered (Yohalem, 1977:21).

Both the SNEB and RHS studies concluded that coverage as well as receipt of benefit and size of benefit are a function of length of service and earnings. As will be discussed below, since plans have vesting requirements based on service and benefits based on service and/or earnings, it is obvious that receipt of

benefit and size of benefit are a function of length of service
and earnings. The manner in which service and earnings relate to
coverage, however, is more complicated.

In looking at pension coverage by occupation and by industry, it becomes apparent that women are less likely than men to
be covered across *all* categories and, to some extent, have the
least coverage in categories in which women predominate. The
private pension coverage of women varies by nonfarm occupation from only five percent for service workers to 38 percent
for both clerical workers and professional and technical workers
(see Table 1). In contrast, coverage of men by occupation varies
from 35 percent for laborers to 73 percent for managers and
technical workers. Coverage is not, however, low for all female
occupations. A woman is much more likely to be covered in a
clerical occupation than in services. Services, an occupational
category which is 55 percent women and in which 15 percent of
all employed women work, covers only five percent of its

TABLE 1:   1972 Pension Coverage of Women and Men by
           Occupation (Private Wage and Salary Workers)

	(Percent)	
	Women	Men
Total	21	49
Professional and technical	38	73
Managers and officials	32	49
Clerical	38	63
Sales	10	39
Craftsmen and foremen	32[a]	52
Operatives	24	50
Service	5	38
Laborers	15[a]	35
Farm, all types	--	2

a. No percents were calculated in 1972 for women in these occupations.
The data reported are from the 1969 SNEB study.

Sources: Gayle Thompson, "Pension coverage and benefits, 1972: Find-
           ings from the retirement history study," *Social Security Bulletin,*
           Vol. 41, No. 2, February 1978, p. 5; Walter Kolodrubetz, "Char-
           acteristics of workers with pension converage on the longest
           job," in *Reaching retirement age,* Research Report No. 47,
           Washington, D.C.: U.S. Government Printing Office.

TABLE 2:   1972 Pension Coverage of Women and Men by
Industry (Private Wage and Salary Workers)

| | *(Percent)* | |
	Women	*Men*
Total	21	49
Forestry, fisheries and agriculture	1[a]	4
Mining	21[a]	48
Construction	a	33
Manufacturing	31	63
Transportation, communications and public utilities	52	51
Trade	15	29
Finance, insurance and real estate	46	54
Professional services	20	58
Other services	3	23

a. See Table 1. The SNEB study combines mining and construction.

Sources: See Table 1.

employees. In contrast, clerical work, in which 74 percent of workers are women and 33 percent of all employed women work, covers 38 percent of its employees.

The private pension coverage of women also varies by non-farm industry from three percent in "other services" to 52 percent in transportation, communications and public utilities (see Table 2). In contrast, the coverage of men by industry varies from 23 percent in "other services" to 63 percent in manufacturing. The high coverage for women in transportation, communications, and public utilities and finance, insurance and real estate is of minimal importance because only 10 percent of employed women are working in these industries. However the low coverage in "other services" and trade is important because 31 percent of employed women are working in these industries.

The low coverage for women in general can be partially explained by the following:

(a) women are more likely than men to be in part-time employment. In 1974, 3.8 percent of women were employed part-time (less than 35 hours a week) because of economic conditions, compared to 2.1 percent of employed men, and 24.5 percent were voluntary part-time, compared to only 7.8 percent of employed men (Women's Bureau, 1975:57). Pre-ERISA part-time workers typically did not qualify for pension credits. In the RHS study only five percent of part-time women and 20 percent of part-time men were covered on the longest job, as compared to 24 percent for full-time workers.

(b) In the late 1960s and early 1970s participation requirements were still very common in pension plans. About 22 percent of workers who were in companies with pension plans had to meet certain conditions before they became participants in a pension plan. These participation requirements were very popular in single employer plans involving about one-half of these plans, but were almost totally missing from collectively bargained plans. The requirements were usually based on age and/or service. The most common requirements were age 25 and one year of service, and age 30 with one, three, and five years of service. In plans with just service requirements, the most common were one and five years (Davis and Strasser, 1970:48).

Coverage does not necessarily guarantee the actual receipt of pension benefit. Workers who have changed jobs often throughout their work history or who have moved in and out of the labor force may lose pension credits before retirement. Therefore, it is important to look at the factors that affect the receipt of a pension benefit.

RECEIPT OF A PENSION

The likelihood of receiving a pension benefit depends on two factors: the abilities of a covered worker to qualify for a vested benefit, and the likelihood that the pension plan will not terminate before the worker retires. Vesting refers to the employee's right to receive a nonforfeitable retirement benefit on attainment of the retirement eligibility age, whether or not the worker is employed with the firm at that time. In the early 1970s there was no legal requirement to provide for vesting of employer-financed benefits prior to retirement, except when an employer terminated the pension plan.[11] If a plan did not have vesting, a worker terminating for any reason before the normal retirement age lost all his accrued benefits. For example, in 1974, 12 percent of covered workers were in plans with no vesting provisions (Spector and Schulz, 1978).

The most commonly used vesting provisions are deferred full vesting and deferred graded vesting. Deferred full vesting entitles the employee to 100 percent of the accrued benefit on meeting the vesting requirements. Deferred graded vesting entitles the employee to a percentage of the accrued benefit after completing a specific number of years of service. The percentage rises as the number of years increases, until the right to 100 percent of the accrued benefit is achieved. In 1974, 78.1 percent of workers in plans with vesting were under a deferred full vesting provision and 13.6 percent were under a deferred graded vesting provision (Spector and Schulz, 1978).

Typically, there are age and service vesting requirements which vary significantly among plans. For example, in 1974 almost half of covered workers had no age requirement.[12] However, it is not uncommon for a plan to have an age 40 requirement. An analysis of the 1974 data shows that 12 percent of the plans had an age 40 requirement. A few plans have a requirement as high as age 60. Moreover, most plans have a service requirement of 10 or 15 years. Spector and Schulz calculated the probability that a worker age 60 years or over with less than 10 years of service would be vested was only .03 in 1974. However, if a worker age 60 years or over had 10 years of service, the probability jumped to .43, and if he had 20 years of service it was .86.

Since the 1950s there has been a liberalization of age and service vesting requirements. However, the benefits of this liberalization have been confined to workers with 10 or more years of service. For example, in 1952, the probability of a worker age 60 and over with less than 10 years of service receiving a vested benefit was .04. In 1974 it was only .02—there had been no increase. In contrast, the probability of a worker age 60 and over with 10 years of service receiving a vested benefit is .09 in 1952. It increases to .36 by 1969 and .43 by 1974. The probability for 20 years of service increases from .14 in 1952 to .76 in 1969 to .86 in 1974. Clearly, for workers with 10 or more years of service at retirement the likelihood of receiving a vested benefit has increased significantly.

Women workers are less likely than men to achieve the years of service on the longest job that are necessary to qualify them for a vested benefit. According to the SNEB study, 31 percent of female workers receiving retired worker benefits in 1969 had less than 10 years of service on the longest job (Kolodrubetz, 1976:157). Moreover, 52 percent had less than 15 years on the longest job and 68 percent had less than 20 years on the longest job. In comparison, 10 percent of private wage and salaried male workers had less than 10 years of service on the longest job. Only 22 percent had less than 15 years, and 37 percent had less than 20 years on the longest job.

There are no adequate studies that calculate the percent of male and female workers with different tenure achievement who received a pension.[13] However, Gayle Thompson (1978) in the RHS study calculated the percent of male and female workers who received a benefit by the number of years on the longest job. Although this calculation is not totally comparable with the Spector and Schulz calculation, the results are consistent.

The distribution of covered workers who received a benefit by the number of years on the longest job is similar for men and women. Three percent of covered women with a pension benefit and four percent of covered men had less than 10 years of service on the longest job. In contrast, 76 percent of covered men and 70 percent of covered women with a pension benefit had 21 or more years of service. It can be concluded, therefore, that women are less likely than men to achieve the requisite years of service for vesting, and therefore have a smaller likelihood of receiving a benefit. However, among the covered women who do receive a benefit, there is little difference in the number of years of service between men and women. This implies that women and men are generally in plans with similar vesting requirements.

Pension plans terminate in both viable and failing businesses. In 1976, 86 percent of terminating plans were in viable businesses. During downturns in economic activity, the financial strength of a firm may be weakened. Since pension plans are essentially voluntary, they become expendable during cutbacks. Normally, small businesses are more sensitive to the business cycle than large businesses. In 1976, half the terminations were in plans with less than eight participants. The impact of the business cycle varies among occupations and industries. For example, in 1976, 39 percent of the plans that terminated were in retail and wholesale trade. Another 27 percent were in manufacturing (Pension Benefit Guaranty Corporation, 1977).

If a pension plan terminates, all rights under the plan become vested. However, as a business cuts back, it is common for many workers to be separated without vested rights before the plan terminates. In the 1960s and '70s many workers in this situation lost all rights to their pension benefits. As will be discussed below, the termination insurance in ERISA was designed to protect workers from the loss of benefits when a plan terminates.

There is no evidence that women are more likely than men to be in plans that terminate. However, it has been argued above that because women are in and out of jobs and therefore on the average have lower tenure than men, they are less likely to receive a pension benefit. The practice of requiring 10 years or more to become fully vested has almost totally eliminated from eligibility the large number of women with less than 10 years of service on their longest job.

Plans use service requirements as an incentive to encourage long tenure and also to decrease the cost of the pension plan. A policy that reduces the vesting requirements to five years may significantly increase the number of women who receive a pension benefit. The dilemma is that it may also increase the number of terminations in plans that cannot absorb the increased costs.

SIZE OF THE PENSION BENEFIT

Pension plans can be classified as either defined contribution or defined benefit plans. A defined contribution plan specifies the contribution rate but does not define a method for explicitly calculating a benefit. A defined benefit plan (the vast majority) determines benefits by a formula explicitly stated in the plan. The majority of workers are covered under formulae that are based on years of service only or on earnings and years of service. In 1974, 38.9 percent of workers were covered by "service only" formulae and 21.2 percent of workers were covered by "earnings times service" formulae. Many plans include more than one formula, and in these plans, workers are paid the benefit from the formula which produces the highest amount. Plans that had both "service only" and "earnings times service" formulae covered 18.5 percent of workers (Spector and Schulz, 1978). Therefore, to a large extent, the low benefit levels for women can be explained by the few years of service and low earnings levels typical of women workers. In 1969, the median annual pension benefit was approximately $43 per year of service for women and $71 per year of service for men (Kolodrubetz, 1976:176). Little insight can be derived from an analysis of benefit levels by industry and occupation because of the large variation in their earnings levels (see Table 3).

TABLE 3: Median Replacement Rates for Recipients Who Receive
           a Pension, 1969

| | \multicolumn{6}{c}{*Percent*} | | | | | |
| | \multicolumn{2}{c}{*Social Security*} | \multicolumn{2}{c}{*Private Pension*} | \multicolumn{2}{c}{*Combined*} |
	Women	*Men*	*Women*	*Men*	*Women*	*Men*
Average Taxable (High 3 of last 10)	34	29	20	29	54	58
Average Total (High 3 of last 10)	32	24	20	25	52	49
Longest Job (Final Earnings)	32	23	20	27	52	49

Sources: Alan Fox, "Alternative measures of earnings replacement for social security beneficiaries" and Walter Kolodrubetz, "Earnings replacement for private pension and social security," in *Reaching retirement age,* Research Report No. 47, 1976, Washington, D.C.: U.S. Government Printing Office.

REPLACEMENT RATES

The replacement rate is a ratio of a measure of retirement benefits and a measure of preretirement earnings. However, it is necessary to clarify the means of arriving at the appropriate measures of both the numerator and denominator of the replacement rate. There are many replacement rates that can be calculated. First, the benefit and earnings measured may be based on individual benefits and earnings or on family benefits and earnings. Second, there are many possible measures of earnings—for example, final earnings on the longest job, career average earnings, and the average of the three highest years of earnings. Third, the benefit calculation may be made for Social Security income only, private pension income only, or private pension income combined with Social Security income.

Because there is no "best" manner to calculate a replacement rate, the discussion that follows will report alternative replacement rates which utilize different earnings measures. In addition, replacement rates for recipients who receive a private pension will be reported and discussed.

Using the SNEB data, Kolodrubetz and Fox calculated replacement rates for workers with pension income. Kolodrubetz defined earnings as the final earnings on the longest job. Fox defined earnings as the average of the high three of the last ten years of taxable earnings and of estimated total earnings. Since the Social Security Administration data only report earnings up to the Social Security taxable ceiling, total earnings were estimated.

Male replacement rates were more sensitive to the earnings measure than female replacement rates because men are more likely than women to have earnings above the Social Security taxable ceiling. In general, there was little difference between the "total earnings" measure and the "last job" measure.

The median female replacement rate from Social Security is larger than the median male replacement rate. This results directly from the use of a weighted benefit formula which replaces a higher percent of preretirement earnings for low-income workers. As discussed above, women on the average earn less than men. Women replace 32 percent of preretirement earnings as compared to 24 percent for men.

In contrast, the median female replacement rate from a private pension was smaller than the median male replacement rate. According to Kolodrubetz, the lower replacement rates for women resulted from fewer years of service; in fact, the median replacement rate was proportionate to years of service. The replacement rates for earnings on the longest job were approximately .8 per year of service for both women and men workers. This relationship was almost constant across all years of service and earnings. For women, the lower replacement rate from a private pension is apparent across all occupations and industries, although there is not a strong indication that replacement rates are lower in female occupations and industries (Kolodrubetz, 1976:184).

The combined median replacement rates for women and men do not vary significantly. In fact, women have a slightly higher replacement rate, 52 percent, as compared to 49 percent for men who received a private pension (see Table 3).

It may be slightly misleading to look at median replacement rates for men and women when, in fact, there is a large variation within these groups. For example, the median combined replacement rate for men was 49 percent and for women it was 52 percent, whereas 24 percent of men and 28 percent of women had replacement rates greater than 60 percent, and seven percent of men and 19 percent of women had replacement rates of 30 percent or less.

Very few employed women, however, received both a private pension and Social Security benefits in retirement. In 1972, among all nonearners aged 61 and 62 who were wage and salary workers in their longest job, 88 percent of women retired with only Social Security, as compared to 58 percent of men. The replacement rates of persons receiving only Social Security are significantly lower than the combined replacement rates of persons with pensions. The female replacement rate was 40 percent as compared to a male replacement rate of only 33 percent (Fox, 1976:208).

In 1974, the median income of a year-round full-time woman worker aged 55 to 64 was $7,374 (U.S. Bureau of the Census, 1977). A replacement rate of 40 percent produces a retirement income of about $3,000. The poverty threshold for one person 65 years and over in 1975 was $2,608 (U.S. Bureau of the Census, 1977).[14] Clearly, for many employed women who face retirement alone and whose earnings are below the median income, the prospect of poverty or near-poverty is very real.

Since 1969 there has been a small increase in the combined replacement rate, with the largest increase coming from the Social Security system. Spector and Schulz estimated the average replacement rate from a private pension did not increase from 1969 to 1974 (Spector and Schulz, 1978). The replacement rate from Social Security, however, increased by about six percent—for women this means an increase of from 32 to 38 percent (Schulz, 1976:94).

It has been suggested that the goal of the retirement system should be a target replacement rate which maintains the pretirement standard of living. This has been estimated at between 65 and 80 percent (Schulz et al., 1974:231). The analysis of replacement rates has shown that most workers do not receive a replacement rate from the retirement system as high as 65 percent and, therefore, unless they can supplement their retirement income with savings, will retire to a standard of living lower than they experienced in their working years. In summary, it is apparent that employed women are less likely to be covered by a private pension than men and, if covered, are less likely to receive a pension benefit of any substance. As a result, large numbers of women retire with only a Social Security benefit. This section has argued that three factors contribute to this result:

(a) women have lower earnings and lower tenure on the longest job;
(b) they are employed in occupations and industries with low coverage; and
(c) they are disproportionately excluded from benefit eligibility by the vesting requirements of many plans.

THE IMPACT OF ERISA ON EMPLOYED WOMEN

Because most of the available data precede ERISA, the discussion above has not included the impact of ERISA on the pension system. The next section of this chapter will briefly review key provisions in the legislation and will then analyze the impact of ERISA on the retirement income of women.

ERISA was legislated to protect the anticipated retirement benefits of employees and their beneficiaries. The preamble of ERISA states "that despite the enormous growth [in private pension plans] . . . many employees with long years of employment are losing anticipated retirement benefits owing to the lack of vesting provisions in such plans" (P.L. 93-406, Title 1, 1974:Sect. A-2). Standards were established for vesting, funding, and termination insurance, among others.

ERISA set minimum vesting and participation standards: after completing one year of employment and reaching age 25, an employee must be allowed to participate in the pension plan. In addition, ERISA defined a "year of service": if an employee works 1,000 hours during the first 12 months on the job, he/she must be eligible for coverage in the pension plan. Three vesting options are permitted. However, according to a 1976 Bankers Trust study, 10 years deferred full vesting has been the most popular choice of plans. This option gives the employee 100 percent full vesting after 10 years of service (Bankers Trust Company, 1976).

With respect to funding, ERISA increased the Internal Revenue standards by requiring past service costs to be amortized over a period of 40 years for existing single employer plans and 30 years for new plans (P.L. 93-406, 1974:Sec. 302).

With respect to termination insurance, the Pension Benefit Guaranty Corporation (PBGC), a self-financed, nonprofit corporation, was established and housed within the Department of Labor to insure against the loss of vested benefits resulting from the termination of a defined benefit private pension plan (P.L. 93-406, 1974:Sec. 4002). Termination insurance was necessary because at any point in time a plan did not have to be fully funded for its total liability.

ERISA will have an impact on the pension income of women by improving the likelihood of coverage and receipt of benefit. Two groups of women have had little or no pension coverage: (a) women who work for employers with pension plans, but who are not themselves eligible; and (b) women who work for employers who do not have a pension plan.

ERISA, by liberalizing participation standards, "break-in-services" regulations, and by redefining "year of service," will increase the number of full-time, part-time, and part-year women workers who will be eligible for coverage. Prior to ERISA, some plans had participation requirements of as much as five years. The one-year standard established by ERISA will increase the number of workers who will be eligible for coverage. Prior to ERISA, a "break-in-service" could result in the total loss of pension credits even if the break was for only a short duration. Under ERISA, a one-year break is defined as a year in which the worker is employed for less than 501 hours. No credits can be lost from an interruption of service shorter than one year. All *vested* benefits earned prior to a break are no longer lost. However, in a defined benefit plan, if the employee is not vested, *unvested* credits can be lost if the number of years of the break equals or is greater than the number of years of the prebreak credited service. In a defined contribution plan, the rules are less liberal. Although limited, the break-in-service regulations will help women workers who leave the labor force for short periods of time. Prior to ERISA, workers in tax-qualified plans were eligible for pension coverage if they worked 20 hours a week or five months a year. ERISA's new definition of "year of service" pertains to all plans and will increase the number of part-time and part-year workers who are eligible for coverage.

For workers who are not employed in companies with a pension plan, ERISA will have little positive impact on coverage. In fact, it has been argued that ERISA, by increasing the costs of pension plans, has encouraged plan terminations and discouraged new plan formation. In 1976, 35 percent of employers terminating plans mentioned ERISA as a reason (PBGC, 1977). Moreover, the annual ratio of new plans to terminated plans has fallen from 14.4 pre-ERISA to 1.6 in 1976

(Schmitt 1977). However, this phenomenon is expected to be temporary.

To the extent that the new funding standards reduce termina-tions in the future and termination insurance reduces pension losses, ERISA will increase the likelihood that covered workers will receive a benefit at retirement. Vesting requirements, how-ever, will continue to exclude many covered workers from pension receipt. Before ERISA many plans had 15 and 20 year vesting requirements; after 1974, ERISA established a 10-year standard. Spector and Schulz (1978) calculated that the proba-bility of a worker aged 60 or over with 10 years of service receiving a vested benefit in 1974 was only .43. If a plan conforms to the ERISA 10 year standard, the probability will increase to 1.0. They conclude that "this represents a significant increase in the likelihood of receiving a benefit and should make a major difference in the number of workers who will actually receive benefits" (Spector and Schulz, 1978). For many women, however, the 10-year standard will not be enough. As stated above, in 1970, 31 percent of employed women worked less than 10 years on their longest job, and these women with low tenure will still remain without pension income at retire-ment.

POLICY IMPLICATIONS AND
FUTURE RESEARCH RECOMMENDATIONS

This study indicates that the large discrepancy in retirement income between men and women results from lower level of coverage and pension receipt by women. Any workers who receive only Social Security benefits will retire at a lower standard of living than they experienced during their working years. For some this means a poverty or near-poverty existence. We have seen that women are more likely than men to be in this category.

The retirement system in the United States has been based on two premises: first, private pensions are voluntary, and second, the right to income is based on a previous labor force attach-ment. Therefore, the income inequities of elderly men and women reflect the inequitable treatment and participation of men and women in the labor force. The income discrepancy between elderly men and women will not be totally eliminated if sex-based wage discrimination and the sexual division of labor are perpetuated. However, some of the inequities can be eliminated by reforming the private pension system.

Based on the available information, this study has concluded that:

(a) survivor benefits in pension plans are inadequate;
(b) the vesting standards in pension plans disproportionately exclude women from benefit eligibility; and
(c) although ERISA has improved the pension prospects of many workers, many women will still not be eligible for a private pension in retirement.

Social research on the private pension of women is almost nonexistent. Before responsible social policies in this area can be developed and collective decisions made, more scholarly work needs to be done. The following are examples of needed research:

(a) a comprehensive study of the entire survivor's benefit package, including individual and group insurance, private pension survivor benefits, and Social Security survivor's provisions; and
(b) a feasibility study to determine the impact on pension receipt of decreasing the vesting requirements to five years or less, including an estimate of the increased cost of such provisions to pension plans.

NOTES

1. In an unfunded plan, the participants must rely on the abilities of the employer to honor their claims. In a funded plan, assets are equal to a percent of the accrued liabilities at any point in time. The higher the ratio of assets to liabilities, the more secure the pension promise. The contributions placed into the funds are based on actuarial assumptions of plan continuity and continued earnings and contributions. Normally, if a plan terminates, assets cannot cover all the liabilities.

2. Integrated plans explicitly or implicitly reduce the pension benefit by a percentage of the Social Security benefit. The offset method and the step-rate method are the most popular. An offset formula reduces an earnings-type pension

benefit by a percent of the Social Security benefit. For example, the pension benefit may be calculated as two percent of average earnings, in the highest five years of the last 10, times years of service, minus 50 percent of the Social Security benefit. The step-rate formula applies two different percentages to earnings below and above an integration level to calculate the benefit. The integration level may be a specified dollar value or a variable amount that adjusts with changes in the Social Security tax base. For example, the benefit may be calculated as one percent of the first $7,800 of career average earnings and 1.5 percent of the remaining earnings, times years of service.

3. Vesting refers to the employee's right to receive a non-forfeitable retirement benefit upon attainment of the retirement eligibility age, whether or not the worker is employed with the firm at that time.

4. *The widows or widowers benefit* provides 100 percent of the employee's primary Social Security amount. Payments may begin at 60 but they are reduced 19/40 of one percent for each month before age 65. *The child's benefit* provides 75 percent of the primary amount until each child is 18 or marries. If the child is a student he/she is eligible to age 22. *The mother's or father's benefit* provides 75 percent of the primary amount as long as there is a child who qualifies for the Child's Benefit.

5. The Bankers Trust surveys are not representative of the private pension universe. Their sample includes a higher percent of the largest and best plans. Therefore, a discussion that uses the Bankers Trust data will give an unrealistically favorable view of the pension system.

6. The early retirement benefit is a percent of the normal retirement benefit. It is reduced because of the loss of interest which the reserves would have accumulated, the loss in contributions which wouuld have been credited because other workers terminated before their benefits had been vested (the benefit of survivorship), the extended period over which the payments must be made, and, finally, the loss due to the number of years of service that are calculated in the benefit formulas.

7. The Bankers Trust study makes a distinction between conventional and pattern plans. In this chapter I have used the term collectively-bargained plans instead of pattern plan. In these plans the benefit calculation does not include earnings. Conventional plans are plans that use earnings-type formulas.

8. There has been a dearth of research in this area. The SNEB and RHS are the major studies of retirees, but both precede ERISA. The SNEB study includes all marital status categories; however, the RHS study only includes women who had no husband in the household in 1969. Both studies analyze workers on the "longest job."

The remaining studies are based on pension plan characteristics. Any benefit calculations from this data assume hypothetical wage histories and traditionally have assumed a continuous work pattern (see the 1975 Bankers Trust study for an example).

9. The "longest job" is appropriate for a study of pensions because it is most likely that vested pension benefits will come from the longest job. However, use of the "longest job" underestimates coverage and overestimates the likelihood of receiving a benefit and the size of the median benefit. Moreover, replacement rates for the longest job are not ideal because they do not necessarily reflect a replacement of earnings for the same reference period for all workers.

10. See below for a more detailed explanation of replacement rates.

11. To assure that the pension plan was a bona fide plan for the exclusive benefit of employees in general, the Internal Revenue Code stipulated that all accrued benefits become fully vested and all unallocated assets in the plan be applied to meet the claims.

12. This estimate is based on tabulations by the author of data provided by the Bureau of Labor Statistics (derived from the D-1 and D-2 reports) for a representative sample of 1,467 defined benefit plans with at least 100 covered workers. These plans represented 23.5 million workers.

13. The SNEB study made estimates; however, the estimates were biased upward for the following reasons:

(a) the question only asked if a pension would be received—it did not ask if a vested benefit would be received. Many workers could have included employee contributions returned at retirement as a pension benefit, although they did not receive an employer-contributed vested pension benefit.

(b) A worker may have had low tenure on the longest job, but been covered under a multiemployer plan which allows the worker to transfer pension credits among companies covered by the plan.

(c) If the longest job had been terminated in the past, many workers may not have reported coverage when in fact they were covered.

14. Data on the median earnings of women are not available. Since earnings provide most of the income for most earners, median income is a close approximation. The median earnings are less than median income; therefore, the estimate of the Social Security benefit is high.

REFERENCES

Bankers Trust Company. (1976) ERISA Related Change in Corporate Pension Plans. New York: Bankers Trust Company.

———. (1975) 1975 Study of Corporate Pension Plans. New York: Bankers Trust Company.

———. (1970) Study of Industrial Retirement Plans. New York: Bankers Trust Company.

Bell, C.S. (1976) "Working wives and family income." In J.R. Chapman (ed.) Economic independence for women. Beverly Hills, California: Sage Publications.

Bernstein, M.C. (1964) The future of private pensions. New York: Free Press.

Blostin, A.P. (1977) "Noninsured death benefits under union and company programs." Monthly Labor Review 100.

Davis, H.E. and A. Strasser. (1970) "Private pension plans, 1960 to 1969—an overview." Monthly Labor Review 93.

Fox, A. (1976) "Alternative measures of earnings replacement for social security beneficiaries." In U.S. Department of Health, Education and Welfare, Social Security Administration. Reaching retirement age: Findings from a survey of newly entitled workers 1968-70. Research Report No. 47, Washington, D.C.: U.S. Government Printing Office.

Harris, C.S. (1978) Factbook on aging: A profile of America's older population. Washington, D.C.: National Council on the Aging.

Kolodrubetz, W.W. (1976) "Earnings replacement from private pensions." In U.S. Department of Health, Education and Welfare, Social Security Administration. Reaching retirement age: Findings from a survey of newly entitled workers 1968-70. Research Report No. 47. Washington, D.C.: U.S. Government Printing Office.

National Center for Health Statistics. (1977) Monthly labor statistics report, advance report, final mortality statistics 1975. Health Resources Administration 77-1120, 25 (11) Supplement. February 11.

PBGC. (1977) Analysis of single employer defined benefit plan terminations, 1976. Publication No. PBGC 505. Washington, D.C.: Pension Benefit Guaranty Corporation.

Pechman, J.A., H.J. Aaron, and M.K. Taussig. (1968) Social Security: Perspectives for reform. Washington, D.C.: The Brookings Institution.

Schmitt, R. (1977) "Congressional research service report on pension plan terminations." In BNA Pension Reporter, No. 129 (March). Washington, D.C.: Bureau of National Affairs.

Schulz, J.H. (1978) "Private pensions and women." In U.S. House of Representatives Select Committee on Aging. American women in middlelife: Preparing for security in later years. Washington, D.C.: U.S. Government Printing Office.

–––. (1976) The economics of aging. Belmont, California: Wadsworth Publishing.

––– et al. (1974) Providing adequate retirement income–pension reform in the United States and abroad. Hanover, New Hampshire: New England Press for Brandeis University Press.

Skolnik, A.E. (1976) "Private pension plans, 1950-74." Monthly Labor Review 99.

Spector, W.D. and J.H. Schulz. (1978) "Trends in vesting and benefit levels, 1952-1974." Work and Aging.

Justice Stevens. (1978) "City of Los Angeles, Department of Water and Power, et al. v. Marie Manhart, et al. In United States Law Week 46 (41). Washington, D.C.: Bureau of National Affairs.

Thompson, G.B. (1978) "Pension coverage and benefits, 1972: Findings from the retirement history study." Social Security Bulletin 41.

U.S. Bureau of the Census. (1977) Money income in 1975 of families and persons in the United States. Current Population Reports, Series P-60, No. 105. Washington, D.C.: U.S. Government Printing Office.

–––. (1975) Characteristics of the low-income population: 1973. Current Population Reports, Series P-60, No. 98. Washington, D.C.: U.S. Government Printing Office.

U.S. Department of Labor. (1978a) Employment and earnings 25.

–––. (1978b) Employment and training report of the President. Washington, D.C.: U.S. Government Printing Office.

U.S. Special Committee on Aging. (1978) Part 1 Developments in aging: 1977. U.S. Senate 95th Congress 2nd Session Report No. 95-771. Washington, D.C.: U.S. Government Printing Office.

Women's Bureau. (1975) U.S. Department of Labor 1975 Handbook on women workers. Washington, D.C.: U.S. Government Printing Office.

Yohalem, M.R. (1977) "Employee-benefit plans, 1975." Social Security Bulletin 40.

13

CONCLUSION

FAMILY WHOLENESS:
NEW CONCEPTIONS OF FAMILY ROLES

ELISE BOULDING

The last decade has been distinguished by many demands for social change: the liberation of women, an end to mandatory retirement, improved quality of work life, and a return to more basic lifestyles. In a sense, all these demands are related. They are attempts to free adults from "programmed" existences, to permit the utmost flexibility in decisions regarding where and when to work outside the home and inside the home or to pursue other interests. Women with children need not be confined to the home, men to the workplace, or older persons to retirement villages for large portions of the day. Work and leisure need not be two ends of a spectrum: one representing the ultimate sacrifice, the other self-indulgence. Persons are seeking ways of life that include a variety of experiences all drawing on a large number of capacities and permitting a satisfying balance of purposive action, reflection, and enjoyment. Even within the lifespan of the "ideal-typical" family, there is opportunity for much role flexibility in making work/leisure choices for all members. When job and household responsibilities are chosen (not preordained) and regarded as temporary (not lifetime) commitments, family members are likely to experience both work and leisure choices as more productive and satisfying. The family womb need not be a barrier constraining the life choices of family members.

THE FAMILY IN LIFESPAN PERSPECTIVE

An examination of the family lifespan presents the structure within which family members presently function. Figure 1 presents the family life span for an "ideal-typical" family in which, for simplicity, it is assumed a woman and man marry at age 20, have two children by age 25, and live to be 85 and 75, respectively. Their children leave home around the age of 20, marry at 25, and each have two children in turn. The shape of the "family womb" over time reflects the expansion and contraction of the family life space over the 65 years of family duration, marked off in five-year periods on the center family lifeline. In the first five years of family life the space is relatively narrow—private to the married pair. As the children are born and a whole new array of family-community linkages are developed to express the couple's concern for their children and their community, the family space widens. By the time the children have reached puberty, they are beginning to bounce in and out of the family space, bringing in friends with them.

By age 20, roughly, the children have left home. At this time the parents are 45 years of age and the family is 25 years old. During this 25 year space the husband has been in the labor force without interruption. The wife, (who had probably participated in the labor-force during the first five years of marriage, has been engaged in part-time or full-time employment several times over the 20 years of childrearing. Now, at age 45, she is very likely to return to full labor-force participation until the age of 65, when she retires together with her husband and they both enter a new life phase. The "empty nest" trauma, as it is often called, is a precursor to another severe trauma, one much less noticed by sociologists; the trauma caused by death of the spouse's parents. In terms of personal growth challenges, the combination of death-of-parents and children-leaving-home provide middle-years adults with a significant opportunity for developing richer social identities as they enter the last third of their lifespan. The family-life space is still fairly large in the

Figure 1: Family Life Span for Woman and Man at 20, with Two Children Who Each Marry at 25 and Have Two Children

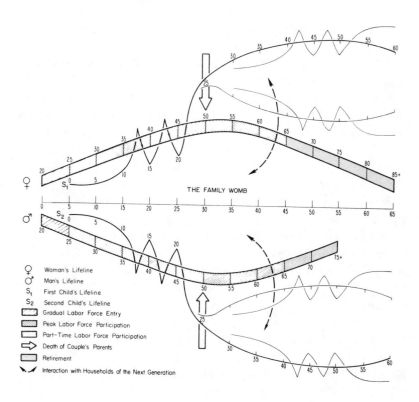

years from 45 to 65, because so much of the community is present in it. The married children return home with spouses and grandchildren. After age 65 the family space begins to contract, physically and psychologically, as activity patterns change and a lifetime of experience is consolidated to prepare for new kinds of reflection and growth and different community roles. From this time on, the couple is more apt to enter the family space of the children as visitors than receive the children back into the home nest. Although physical quarters may change—from house to apartment to nursing home—and in the last years one spouse will predecease the other, the family womb as a psychosocial entity continues to nurture the remaining partner until death.

Marital dissolutions and recombinations are not included in the diagram. The overall forecast for a single-parent or recombined family is very similar. In a single-parent family, the children and the remaining parent regroup to make the family space whole again. In a recombined family, regrouping also takes place. The family space becomes more complex as more persons are brought into it with other family memories and other emotional ties to persons and groups outside the immediate family. Childbearing years also may be stretched out further in time. But from the perspective of either spouse in a recombined family, there is still a family lifespan that reaches back to the day of the first marriage, and that will end only with death.

One fact that emerges with particular force from this lifespan overview is how brief are the childrearing years. This period accounts for roughly 20 years out of 60 or more years of marriage—one-third of the family lifespan at most. Another revelation is the breadth of the family womb. Even if a wife/ mother were home full-time for 20 years, she would account for only a small part of the total family dynamic. Most of the common behavior patterns of family members are a result of social convention, not of constraints inherent in the family womb.

CHANGING CONCEPTIONS OF
WOMEN'S ROLE IN THE FAMILY

The process of industrialization separated living space from space for economic productivity. Men left the home during the day for the office or factory, and women and children, for the most part, were left behind. For men, home was the refuge from toil, the setting for leisure interests, rest, and play. Women were assigned the responsibility of maintaining the home and preparing the family living space to sustain and entertain other family members. For husbands and children, the home served as leisure space; for women, it was workplace and resort, and work and leisure became inextricably mixed. Thus, the real labor involved and the considerable energy invested in work in the home was demeaned for many women. The role of mother as keeper of the home, family leisure, and culture gained a romanticized legitimacy as the "true and appropriate" purpose of woman. This romanticization of the homemaker's role has been hardest of all for women who are single—never married, widowed, separated, or divorced. The closure of child care facilities after World War II signalled a national consensus—women's place is in the home. Yet women have, since this time, been entering the work force in larger and larger numbers, indicating a societywide decision to renegotiate the unwritten terms of industrial-era marriage contracts which confine wives to child and housekeeping responsibilities. Whether the move is out of suburban home to a job in town or to a rural acreage with demanding home production activities, women are making statements about lifestyle preferences by their actions. Although it is irrefutable that the homemaker is very truly a "working woman" and contributes substantial but unrecorded amounts of the GNP by her activity, the pattern of full-time urban homemaking does not absorb a large percentage of women's energies, particularly when children are no longer small. Many women are demanding new options for career and household responsibilities. They do not feel that their daily activities are preordained by the family "womb." Care of children can be accomplished inside or outside the home by qualified care givers. Household responsibilities can be shared with husbands and children, to the benefit of all family members.

WORK, LEISURE, AND THE EMPLOYMENT OF WOMEN

As more choices exist for women in terms of daily employment and long-term work commitments, including options for work inside or outside the home (or a combination of both), the divisions between work and leisure are likely to break down. Women will find both work and leisure more satisfying when neither are enforced or precluded by societal conventions. Studies have indicated that, although employed women do have somewhat less opportunity for leisure, they tend to use that time well. Also, the differences between employed women and homebased women in terms of hours spent on "leisure" pursuits are not as significant as anticipated. Three studies illustrate these points: a UNESCO twelve-country time-budget study of 1965-1966 (Ferge, 1972), a French time-budget study of 1971 (Rianday, 1976), and my own 1976 research on Colorado families (Boulding, 1977a).

Figure 2: Percent of Women Who Rise Before 6 A.M. According to the Age of the Mother

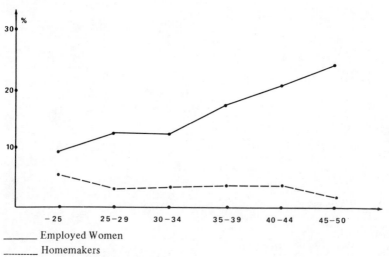

_____ Employed Women

_____ Homemakers

Source: Rianday, 1976, p. 50

The first thing to be noted about women working outside the home is that they stretch their available time by getting up earlier in the morning. Figure 2 shows the percentage of employed and homemaking French mothers getting up before 6:00 a.m. The 1,820 mothers included in this study all had from one to five children. Note that employed women not only rise earlier than home-based women, but the older they get, the more of them rise early. The experience of a new excess of energy in the mid-thirties, when there are no longer toddlers around, is felt by many women, and further excesses of energy seem to come in the forties and also in the fifties. Home-based women in contrast, rise later as they get older. Table 1 compares the average daily time budget of employed and home-based mothers. By sleeping an hour less, spending one-third less time on housework, a little more than half as much time on meals, and streamlining personal care activities and "odds and ends," the employed mother manages her double load. She also has less leisure and less time with the children, but the amazing thing is how much time she can squeeze out of a working day. Her weekday leisure activities range from reading to visiting with friends to taking walks (an important end-of-day activity in French urban families with young children). Employed women watch less TV than home-based women, both on weekdays and Sundays. Sunday time budgets are different, of course; employed women sleep a little longer, but still less than their home-based counterparts. They spend a little more time on housework than on weekdays, and for the rest have a wider range of activities than their nonemployed sisters. They go on more excursions, and engage in organizational activity and study that their sisters do not record. At the same time, they engage in the same range of social activities as do their sisters. Home-based women spend more of Sunday in front of the TV. Activities with children are not well recorded, so unfortunately no comparisons can be made on that score.

The impression of a greater diversity of activities during nonworking hours for employed women is further confirmed in the UNESCO study. A detailed analysis of total mobility during the day for employed and home-based women carried out in

TABLE 1: Averaged Daily Time Budget for Employed and
          Home-Based Women

	Homemaker	Employed Woman
Work	0.0	8.0
Travel	0.7	1.0
Home maintenance	6.2	2.4
Child care	1.8	0.7
Leisure	2.8	1.4
Sleep	8.5	7.6
Meals	2.0	1.4
Personal care	0.8	0.6
Miscellaneous	1.2	0.9
Total	24.0	24.0

Source: Rianday, 1976, p. 62.

Osnabruck (Rosenbladt, 1972) leads the researcher to conclude
that "employed women, in spite of the fact that they undergo
higher strain than housewives, are prepared to cover longer
distances and to leave the town oftener. This result holds for all
categories of activities" (Rosenbladt, 1972:343). Table 2 presents the relevant data.[1] Susan Ferge, in her analysis of leisure
activity choices in the same UNESCO study, identifies the
search for variety as a key component of creative leisure. In
addition, a high degree of awareness of choice, another component of creative leisure is displayed by these employed
women.

The finding of greater ranges of leisure activity among
employed mothers compared to home-based mothers is partly
tautological because employed mothers are already more
mobile, and further mobility does not involve the same degree
of psychological effort that a similar mobility level would
involve for a woman who stays at home to care for her children.
The latter may have fewer transportation facilities at her disposal as well, and her children may be younger. The employed
women may have less time at her disposal, but it is more clearly
demarcated into segments. The home-based mother rarely
knows when her free time is coming, and it may be harder to
make good use of unpredictable free time.

TABLE 2: Distance Travelled in Kilometers by Employed Women and Homemakers for Eight Categories of Activity

	Shopping	Services	Leisure	Walking	Visits	Discretionary Activities	Work	Other
Employed women	.87	1.11	1.34	1.23	1.54	.99	2.01	.60
Homemakers	.77	.87	1.29	1.09	1.44	.87	–	1.16

Source: Rosenbladt in Szalai, 1972, p. 343.

The data given above does not actually tell us what kinds of things employed and home-based mothers are doing in their leisure time, particularly that part of their leisure time spent at home. A recent time-budget project undertaken in Colorado, in which employed and home-based mothers (as well as fathers and children) kept records by fifteen-minute intervals each day for seven days of their activities while in the home, gives some insight into quality of leisure time spent at home. I have chosen four activity categories from a much longer list developed to cover what was reported by the families. The categories chosen reflect creative use of free time in the home: conversation "for fun" (as contrasted to counseling, problem-solving, and the like); creative activities (artistic, handicraft, other); sports and games; reflective activities (including reading, writing, meditating, revery). Social life with nonfamily members and TV-watching are not included here. It will be seen from Table 3 that while the home-based mothers were able to spend more minutes on these free-time activities, the employed mothers also spent quite a lot of free time. From notes made about mealtime preparation by each mother, we discovered that home-based mothers were using more fast foods, and employed mothers spending more time preparing food "from scratch"—a reversal of stereotyped expectations. The single-parent employed mothers had the least time to spend, but even they put in over two hours per day on creative family leisure.

Fun conversation, not an activity normally recorded, is important in these households and particularly important to the quality of adult-child relations. Most of these conversations included the children. Most of the handicraft activities also involved mothers with their children. (All activities were coded by with what family member they were done, but tabulation of this information in the time budget schema proved difficult.) The significance of shared conversation and shared handicraft activity in families is taken for granted, but not studied. TV has made sharp inroads on this kind of interaction in many families, but not in those of our study. Another little-understood phenomenon, well reported here, is the practice of quiet times, alone or together, and the significance of reading, alone or together, for family life. Family well-being is equally measured by what is done together and what is done in solitude in the home, and these time budgets reflect a balance in together leisure and separate leisure which we would do well to analyze further.

Table 3 represents a fairer comparison of employed and home-based mothers than the data from Europe, because it does not consider activities outside the home which may be physically harder for home-based mothers to manage. What the Colorado data suggest is that both employed and home-based mothers may make creative use of free time alone and in interaction with other family members within time and space constraints.

TABLE 3: Use of Free Time in the Family by Employed and Home-Based Mothers in Eight Households with Two or More Children, Recorded in minutes.[a]

	Employed Mothers (Two-Parent Household)		Employed Mothers (One-Parent Household)			Home-Based Mothers (Two-Parent Household)			
	#1	#2	#3	#4	#5	#6	#7	#8	#9[b]
"Fun" Conversation	57	62	45	34	58	93	62	96	45
Creative Activities	45	16	34	11	38	41	46	6	60
Sports	2	4	–	–	8	–	–	17	–
Reflective Activities	58	85	62	86	39	79	96	63	105
Total Minutes	162	167	141	131	143	213	204	172	210

a. Daily average based on a one-week record

b. Family #9 not part of the original study, but added later

Source: Boulding, 1977a.

CHANGING CONCEPTIONS OF HUSBANDS' ROLES

Missing in this discussion is consideration of new roles for men and improvements in the overall quality of husbands' lives. Husbands need not be relegated to full-time labor-force participation from age 20 to retirement. Housework shared by husbands and wives would clearly provide more opportunities for overall family interaction while both partners work and "play" in the home. Working wives relieve husbands of the sole responsibility of providing for the family unit economically. Job and career change, part-time work, and time out for child care are new options.

Men are now beginning to discover the joys of homemaking and child care. A policy of childbirth leave which permits either parent to take time at home for the first year of a newborn's life, as now exists in Sweden, and increasing opportunities for part-time and flexitime work schedules, will help to crumble the dehumanizing aspects of a rigidly gender-based social division of labor. The dehumanization has operated equally on men and women, for both are caught in practices that do violence to their individuality. As society's expectations become more flexible, marriages will become more comfortable, and couples can realize how many years they have to experiment with various ways of working and being at home, various ways of being with the spouse, and various ways of being with offspring well beyond the empty-nest stage. Double households spanning considerable geographic distance are part of the new flexibility. It is important to recognize that different stages can invite different patterns without threatening the integrity of the family life space. New roles and new lifestyles can continue to develop in a healthily functioning family space up to the end of the lifespan.

CHANGING TRENDS IN FAMILY LIFESTYLES

A new trend is developing in the United States which is small but meaningful in terms of new demands for a wholeness of life—a satisfying fusion of work and leisure. The rural-to-urban migration trend, ongoing throughout United States history, has now reversed itself. The net back flow to rural areas in the South and parts of the West is small, but probably significant, in light of recent survey data indicating widespread preferences for rural over urban life. A recent Stanford Research Institute survey (Elgin and Mitchell, 1977) of voluntary simplicity preferences estimates that possibly as high as 50 percent of the population will prefer a simpler, less consumption-oriented lifestyle 50 years from now. This projection fits the scenario described by Burns of a return to a household economy with home-based production by men (suggesting that women are entering the labor force just at the wrong time), because the market economy cannot supply a satisfying lifestyle (Burns, 1975).

More labor-intensive lifestyles lead to different kinds of interdependencies and different kinds of autonomies in family life. When these interdependencies and autonomies are by choice, life satisfactions increase. Most of the world's homemakers do not have choices; they live on farms or in villages, with kitchen gardens to care for and a variety of home production tasks, leaving them with less time to "devote" to the children than the urban employed women. The U.S. farm woman shares with her third world sisters the long working hours. Recent interviews with Oklahoma and Colorado farm women have given ample evidence of the very long working hours of rural women compared to urban homemakers. The average farm family in the U.S. harnesses its labor to far better equipment than third world families possess, but the pride in the family enterprise may not be that different. Interviews with American women also brought out very clearly the extent to which children become coworkers with their parents on the farm at a very early age, and how much pleasure these hardworking families, who have little time to "do for" one another, take in family companionship at work.

CONCLUSION

The main conclusion I would draw about the quality of life in families is that it is dependent on the options available to all family members for satisfying work and leisure; this depends on a maximum of choice and also a sharing of necessary work. On the one hand, there are many decades in which to alternate working and nonworking patterns if one wishes; on the other hand, a lifetime commitment to working or to homemaking can also be viable for men and women. At the moment a rigid attitude toward gender-based division of labor prevents an easy alternation of styles, but once men are more fully liberated to enjoy homemaking, both women and men will have richer lives. The mini-trend noted earlier, toward a lifestyle of more home-based production outside the market economy, adds one more possibility for future lifestyle choices. The children's movement will also contribute to the future diversity of family lifestyles, as adults come to understand that children need more than the simple protections that law and custom now require. Productive work and shared involvement in household labor are valuable for all family members. We are moving toward a time when women and men no longer will be branded at birth as future homemakers or workers, but welcomed as persons who in their time will create new households, new communities, and new futures for humankind.

NOTE

1. Employed women with and without children unfortunately are not distinguished in this analysis.

REFERENCES

Boulding, E. (1978) Children's rights and the wheel of life. New Brunswick: Transaction Press.
———. (1977a) "The human services components of nonmarket productivity in ten Colorado households." Paper presented at the Roundtable on the Economy and Sociology of the Family, Royaumont, France, January.
———. (1977b) Women in the twentieth century world. New York: Halsted Press.
———. (1976) Underside of history. Boulder, Colorado: Westview Press.
Boulding, E. and P. Bolton (Trainer). (1977) "Quality of Life, USA: Costs and Benefits of Urbanization and Industrialization, 1900-1970." Conference Proceedings, Second Annual Session, Institute of Environmental Sciences, Environmental Awareness, San Diego, California, April 27.
Burns, S. (1975) Home, inc.: The hidden wealth and power of the American household. Garden City, New York: Doubleday.
Elgin, D. and A. Mitchell. (1977) "Voluntary simplicity (3)." The CoEvolution Quarterly 14.

Ferge, S. (1972) "Social differentiation in leisure activity choices: An unfinished experiment." In A. Szalai, The use of time: Daily activities of urban and suburban populations in twelve countries. The Hague: Mouton.

Rianday, B. (1976) "Besoins et aspirations des familles et des jeunes." Analyses complementaires, Tome III, Le budget-temps des meres de famille. Paris: Caisse Nationale des Allocations Familiales.

Rosenbladt, B. von. (1972) "The outdoor activity system in an urban environment." In A. Szalai, The use of time: Daily activities of urban and suburban populations in twelve countries. The Hague: Mouton.

Stone, L.J., H.T. Smith, and L.B. Murphy. (1973) The competent infant: Research and commentary. New York: Basic Books.

THE CONTRIBUTORS

WILLIAM ARKIN is currently teaching in the Departments of Sociology and Administration of Justice at San Jose State University. His ongoing research is in social deviance as a mechanism of social control. As a result of these interests, his recent research and articles have been in the area of work and the military as agents of social control. He and Lynne R. Dobrofsky have most recently collaborated in research on job sharing.

NIJOLE V. BENOKRAITIS is Assistant Professor of Sociology at the University of Baltimore. She has recently coauthored a book on affirmative action and equal employment opportunity. Her current research is in the areas of sex and racial inequality and gerontology.

SARAH FENSTERMAKER BERK is Assistant Professor of Sociology at the University of California, Santa Barbara. Since 1975, she has been engaged in a national survey of household labor, funded by the National Institute of Mental Health. Her special focus has been on the division of household labor. Her work has appeared in *Pacific Sociological Review, The Sociology of Work and Occupations* and *Sociological Methods and Research.* She is currently completing a book (with R.A. Berk) on the content and organization of household labor activities.

ELISE BOULDING is Professor of Sociology and Project Director at the Institute of Behavioral Science at the University of Colorado at Boulder. Dr. Boulding's publications focus on international conflict resolution, family life, and women's studies. She is author of *The Underside of History: A View of Women Through Time, Handbook of International Data on Women, Women in the Twentieth Century World,* and *From a Monastery*

Kitchen. A book written especially for the International Year of the Child, to be entitled *Children's Rights and the Wheel of Life*, will be published in September. A textbook for introductory social science courses, *The Social System of the Planet Earth*, will be published in 1979 (coauthored with Kenneth Boulding and Guy Burgess).

LYNNE R. DOBROFSKY is currently teaching in the Departments of Sociology and Women's Studies at Mills College. Over the last several years, she has been engaged in research on gender roles and the family, and changing patterns of work and family, with a special interest in alternative work structures and women in nontraditional occupations.

KAREN WOLK FEINSTEIN is Managing Editor of *The Urban & Social Change Review*, a publication of Boston College, which focuses on a wide range of social problems. Her particular research interests are women in the labor force and the needs of children of working mothers. She is presently affiliated with Brandeis University where, under a grant from the National Institute of Mental Health, she is studying the impact of public policy on the family.

SHARLENE HESSE is Assistant Professor in the Department of Sociology, Boston College and is currently teaching a course on Women at Work. She has written several articles on the linguistic sex-role bias of social science research methods. Dr. Hesse is the national coordinator of the Job Market Newsletter for Sociologists for Women in Society.

FRANK L. MOTT is Associate Project Director for the National Longitudinal Surveys in the Center for Human Resource Research, as well as an adjunct associate professor in the Faculty of Labor and Human Resources at The Ohio State University. He has written extensively on issues related to women in the labor force, concentrating on the relevance of demographic phenomena for interpreting changing social and economic trends in this area.

DIANA PEARCE is currently Assistant Professor of Sociology at the University of Illinois at Chicago Circle. Her current research interests are in understanding the mechanisms that perpetuate occupational segregation, especially among working-class women workers. She has also done extensive research on the racial practices of real estate brokers, and also has worked on the distribution of welfare services in the metropolis. During the summer of 1978, Ms. Pearce was Honorary Fellow at the Institute for Research on Poverty at the University of Wisconsin in Madison.

ALAN J. PIFER is President of The Carnegie Foundation for the Advancement of Teaching. He has served on the President's Commission on White House Fellowships, the Commission on Private Philanthropy and Public Needs, the National Assembly for Social Policy and Development, the U.S. Advisory Committee on Higher Education and is a Fellow of the American Academy of Arts and Sciences.

DENISE F. POLIT is currently a research scientist at the American Institutes for Research in Cambridge, Massachusetts. One of her principal research interests concerns alternatives for working women. In addition to her examination of rearranged work schedules and their effects on women, Dr. Polit has studied the utilization of women in nontraditional blue-collar jobs and attitudes toward women in nontraditional military assignments.

RALPH E. SMITH is Senior Research Associate at the Urban Institute, Washington, D.C. An economist, Smith has published numerous analyses of the U.S. labor market. His recent research has focused on the determinants and consequences of the women's movement into the labor force. He is author of *The Impact of Macroeconomic Conditions on Employment Opportunities for Women* (1977), published by the Joint Economic

Committee of Congress, and is editor of a forthcoming Urban Institute book, *The Subtle Revolution: Women at Work.*

WILLIAM D. SPECTOR is Assistant Professor of Economics at Salem State College, Salem, Massachusetts. At the Florence Heller School, Brandeis University, he has been studying the factors which determine retirement income, focusing on the private pension system and the special problems of women. His most recent publications have been "The Dilemma of ERISA: A Closer Look at Pension Plans and Benefits" (*The Urban & Social Change Review,* 10(2), 1977) and, with James H. Schulz, "Trends in Vesting and Benefit Levels, 1952-1974," (forthcoming in *Work and Aging*).

MARY LINDENSTEIN WALSHOK is a sociologist at the University of California, San Diego campus where she is the Associate Dean for Academic Affairs for University Extension. Dr. Walshok taught at California State University, Fullerton before going to the University of California. She has numerous papers and publications on women and is in the process of completing a book on her three year NIMH-funded study of women in skilled and semi-skilled jobs.